The

Sun	☉	The
Moon	☽	The subconscious self, habits
Mercury	☿	Communication, the intellect
Venus	♀	Emotional expression, love, appreciation, artistry
Mars	♂	Physical drive, assertiveness, anger
Jupiter	♃	Philosophy, ethics, generosity
Saturn	♄	Discipline, focus, responsibility
Uranus	♅	Individuality, rebelliousness
Neptune	♆	Imagination, sensitivity, compassion
Pluto	♇	Transformation, healing, regeneration

instincts—are the products of the Moon. Modes of expression that you feel truly reflect your deepest self belong to the Moon: art, letters, creative work of any kind; sometimes love; sometimes business. Whatever you feel to be most deeply yourself is the product of your Moon and of the sign your Moon occupies at birth.

Mercury

Mercury is the sensory antenna of your horoscope. Its position by sign indicates your reactions to sights, sounds, odors, tastes, and touch impressions, affording a key to the attitude you have toward the physical world around you. Mercury is the messenger through which your physical body and brain (ruled by the Sun) and your inner nature (ruled by the Moon) are kept in contact with the outer world, which will appear to you according to the index of Mercury's position by sign in the horoscope. Mercury rules your rational mind.

Venus

Venus is the emotional antenna of your horoscope. Through Venus, impressions come to you from the outer world. The position of Venus by sign at the time of your birth determines your attitude toward these experiences. As Mercury is the messenger linking sense impressions (sight, smell, etc.) to the basic nature of your Sun and Moon, so Venus is the messenger linking emotional impressions. If Venus is found in the same sign as the Sun, emotions gain importance in your life and have a direct bearing on your actions. If Venus is in the same sign as the Moon, emotions bear directly on your inner nature, add self-confidence, make you sensitive to emotional impressions, and frequently indicate that you have more love in your heart than you are able to express. If Venus is in the same sign as Mercury, emotional impressions and sense impressions work together; you tend to idealize the world of the senses and sensualize the world of the emotions to interpret what you see and hear.

Mars

Mars is the energy principle in the horoscope. Its position indicates the channels into which energy will most easily be directed. It is the planet through which the activities of the Sun and the desires of the Moon express themselves in action. In the same sign as the Sun, Mars gives abundant energy, sometimes misdirected in temper, temperament, and quarrels. In the same sign as the Moon, it gives a great capacity to make use of the innermost aims, and to make the inner desires articulate and practical. In the same sign as Venus, it quickens emotional reactions and causes you to act on them, makes for ardor and passion in love, and fosters an earthly awareness of emotional realities.

Jupiter

Jupiter is the feeler for opportunity that you have out in the world. It passes along chances of a lifetime for consideration according to the basic nature of your Sun and Moon. Jupiter's sign position indicates the places you will look for opportunity, the uses to which you wish to put it, and the capacity you have to react and profit by it. Jupiter is ordinarily and erroneously called the planet of luck. It is "luck" insofar as it is the index of opportunity, but your luck depends less on what comes to you than on what you do with what comes to you. In the same sign as the Sun or Moon, Jupiter gives a direct and generally effective response to opportunity and is likely to show forth at its "luckiest." If Jupiter is in the same sign as Mercury, sense impressions are interpreted opportunistically. If Jupiter is in the same sign as Venus, you interpret emotions in such a way as to turn them to your advantage; your feelings work harmoniously with the chances for progress that the world has to offer. If Jupiter is in the same sign as Mars,

2014
SUN SIGN
BOOK

Forecasts by
Kim Rogers-Gallagher

Cover Design by Kevin R. Brown
Editing by Andrea Neff
Background with Sunflower: iStockphoto.com/ulimi
Sunflower: iStockphoto.com/nick73
Interior Zodiac Icons: iStockphoto.com/Trillingstudio

Copyright 2013 Llewellyn Publications
ISBN: 978-0-7387-2155-2
A Division of Llewellyn Worldwide Ltd., www.llewellyn.com
Llewellyn is a registered trademark of Llewellyn Worldwide Ltd.
2143 Wooddale Drive, Woodbury, MN 55125
Printed in the USA

Contents

2013

SEPTEMBER
S	M	T	W	T	F	S
1	2	3	4	5	6	7
8	9	10	11	12	13	14
15	16	17	18	19	20	21
22	23	24	25	26	27	28
29	30					

OCTOBER
S	M	T	W	T	F	S
		1	2	3	4	5
6	7	8	9	10	11	12
13	14	15	16	17	18	19
20	21	22	23	24	25	26
27	28	29	30	31		

NOVEMBER
S	M	T	W	T	F	S
					1	2
3	4	5	6	7	8	9
10	11	12	13	14	15	16
17	18	19	20	21	22	23
24	25	26	27	28	29	30

DECEMBER
S	M	T	W	T	F	S
1	2	3	4	5	6	7
8	9	10	11	12	13	14
15	16	17	18	19	20	21
22	23	24	25	26	27	28
29	30	31				

2014

JANUARY
S	M	T	W	T	F	S
			1	2	3	4
5	6	7	8	9	10	11
12	13	14	15	16	17	18
19	20	21	22	23	24	25
26	27	28	29	30	31	

FEBRUARY
S	M	T	W	T	F	S
						1
2	3	4	5	6	7	8
9	10	11	12	13	14	15
16	17	18	19	20	21	22
23	24	25	26	27	28	

MARCH
S	M	T	W	T	F	S
						1
2	3	4	5	6	7	8
9	10	11	12	13	14	15
16	17	18	19	20	21	22
23	24	25	26	27	28	29
30	31					

APRIL
S	M	T	W	T	F	S
		1	2	3	4	5
6	7	8	9	10	11	12
13	14	15	16	17	18	19
20	21	22	23	24	25	26
27	28	29	30			

MAY
S	M	T	W	T	F	S
				1	2	3
4	5	6	7	8	9	10
11	12	13	14	15	16	17
18	19	20	21	22	23	24
25	26	27	28	29	30	31

JUNE
S	M	T	W	T	F	S
1	2	3	4	5	6	7
8	9	10	11	12	13	14
15	16	17	18	19	20	21
22	23	24	25	26	27	28
29	30					

JULY
S	M	T	W	T	F	S
		1	2	3	4	5
6	7	8	9	10	11	12
13	14	15	16	17	18	19
20	21	22	23	24	25	26
27	28	29	30	31		

AUGUST
S	M	T	W	T	F	S
					1	2
3	4	5	6	7	8	9
10	11	12	13	14	15	16
17	18	19	20	21	22	23
24	25	26	27	28	29	30
31						

SEPTEMBER
S	M	T	W	T	F	S
	1	2	3	4	5	6
7	8	9	10	11	12	13
14	15	16	17	18	19	20
21	22	23	24	25	26	27
28	29	30				

OCTOBER
S	M	T	W	T	F	S
			1	2	3	4
5	6	7	8	9	10	11
12	13	14	15	16	17	18
19	20	21	22	23	24	25
26	27	28	29	30	31	

NOVEMBER
S	M	T	W	T	F	S
						1
2	3	4	5	6	7	8
9	10	11	12	13	14	15
16	17	18	19	20	21	22
23	24	25	26	27	28	29
30						

DECEMBER
S	M	T	W	T	F	S
	1	2	3	4	5	6
7	8	9	10	11	12	13
14	15	16	17	18	19	20
21	22	23	24	25	26	27
28	29	30	31			

2015

JANUARY
S	M	T	W	T	F	S
				1	2	3
4	5	6	7	8	9	10
11	12	13	14	15	16	17
18	19	20	21	22	23	24
25	26	27	28	29	30	31

FEBRUARY
S	M	T	W	T	F	S
1	2	3	4	5	6	7
8	9	10	11	12	13	14
15	16	17	18	19	20	21
22	23	24	25	26	27	28

MARCH
S	M	T	W	T	F	S
1	2	3	4	5	6	7
8	9	10	11	12	13	14
15	16	17	18	19	20	21
22	23	24	25	26	27	28
29	30	31				

APRIL
S	M	T	W	T	F	S
			1	2	3	4
5	6	7	8	9	10	11
12	13	14	15	16	17	18
19	20	21	22	23	24	25
26	27	28	29	30		

MAY
S	M	T	W	T	F	S
					1	2
3	4	5	6	7	8	9
10	11	12	13	14	15	16
17	18	19	20	21	22	23
24	25	26	27	28	29	30
31						

JUNE
S	M	T	W	T	F	S
	1	2	3	4	5	6
7	8	9	10	11	12	13
14	15	16	17	18	19	20
21	22	23	24	25	26	27
28	29	30				

JULY
S	M	T	W	T	F	S
			1	2	3	4
5	6	7	8	9	10	11
12	13	14	15	16	17	18
19	20	21	22	23	24	25
26	27	28	29	30	31	

AUGUST
S	M	T	W	T	F	S
						1
2	3	4	5	6	7	8
9	10	11	12	13	14	15
16	17	18	19	20	21	22
23	24	25	26	27	28	29
30	31					

Meet Kim Rogers-Gallagher

Kim fell in love with astrology in grade school and began her formal education close to thirty years ago. She's written hundreds of articles and columns for magazines and online publications, contributed to several astrological anthologies, and has two books of her own to her credit, *Astrology for the Light Side of the Brain* and *Astrology for the Light Side of the Future*, both available from ACS/Starcrafts Publishing. Kim is the author of daily e-mail horoscopes for astrology.com, and her work appears in the introductory sections of *Llewellyn's Astrology Calendar*, *Llewellyn's Witches' Datebook*, and *Llewellyn's Witches' Calendar*.

At the moment, Kim is having great fun on her Facebook page, facebook.com/KRGFenix, where she turns daily transits into fun celestial adventures. She's a well-known speaker who's been part of the UAC (United Astrology Conference) faculty since 1996 and has lectured at many other international conferences.

An avid animal lover, Kim occasionally receives permission from her seriously spoiled fur-kids (and her computer) to leave home for a while and indulge her ninth-house Sagg Sun by traveling for "work"— that is, talking to groups about astrology (which really isn't work at all). In typical Sagg style, Kim loves to laugh, but she also loves to chat, which comes in handy when she does private phone consultations.

She is a twenty-year "citizen" of Pennsic, an annual medieval event, where she gets to dress up in funny clothes, live in a tent, and pretend she's back in the 1300s for two weeks every year—which, oddly enough, is her idea of a good time.

Kim can be contacted at KRGPhoenix313@yahoo.com for fees regarding readings, classes, and lectures.

New Concepts for Zodiac Signs

The signs of the zodiac represent characteristics and traits that indicate how energy operates within our lives. The signs tell the story of human evolution and development, and all are necessary to form the continuum of whole-life experience. In fact, all twelve signs are represented within your astrological chart.

Although the traditional metaphors for the twelve signs (such as Aries, the Ram) are always functional, these alternative concepts for each of the twelve signs also describe the gradual unfolding of the human spirit.

Aries: The Initiator is the first sign of the zodiac and encompasses the primary concept of getting things started. This fiery ignition and bright beginning can prove to be the thrust necessary for new life, but the Initiator also can appear before a situation is ready for change and create disruption.

Taurus: The Maintainer sustains what Aries has begun and brings stability and focus into the picture, yet there also can be a tendency to try to maintain something in its current state without allowing for new growth.

Gemini: The Questioner seeks to determine whether alternatives are possible and offers diversity to the processes Taurus has brought into stability. Yet questioning can also lead to distraction, subsequently scattering energy and diffusing focus.

Cancer: The Nurturer provides the qualities necessary for growth and security, and encourages a deepening awareness of emotional needs. Yet this same nurturing can stifle individuation if it becomes too smothering.

Leo: The Loyalist directs and centralizes the experiences Cancer feeds. This quality is powerfully targeted toward self-awareness, but can be shortsighted. Hence, the Loyalist can hold steadfastly to viewpoints or feelings that inhibit new experiences.

Virgo: The Modifier analyzes the situations Leo brings to light and determines possibilities for change. Even though this change may be in the name of improvement, it can lead to dissatisfaction with the self if not directed in harmony with higher needs.

Libra: The Judge is constantly comparing everything to be sure that a certain level of rightness and perfection is presented. However, the Judge can also present possibilities that are harsh and seem to be cold or without feeling.

Scorpio: The Catalyst steps into the play of life to provide the quality of alchemical transformation. The Catalyst can stir the brew just enough to create a healing potion, or may get things going to such a powerful extent that they boil out of control.

Sagittarius: The Adventurer moves away from Scorpio's dimension to seek what lies beyond the horizon. The Adventurer continually looks for possibilities that answer the ultimate questions, but may forget the pathway back home.

Capricorn: The Pragmatist attempts to put everything into its rightful place and find ways to make life work out right. The Pragmatist can teach lessons of practicality and determination, but can become highly self-righteous when shortsighted.

Aquarius: The Reformer looks for ways to take what Capricorn has built and bring it up to date. Yet there is also a tendency to scrap the original in favor of a new plan that may not have the stable foundation necessary to operate effectively.

Pisces: The Visionary brings mysticism and imagination, and challenges the soul to move beyond the physical plane, into the realm of what might be. The Visionary can pierce the veil, returning enlightened to the physical world. The challenge is to avoid getting lost within the illusion of an alternate reality.

Astrology Basics

Astrology is an ancient and continually evolving system used to clarify your identity and your needs. An astrological chart—which is calculated using the date, time, and place of birth—contains many factors that symbolically represent the needs, expressions, and experiences that make up the whole person. A professional astrologer interprets this symbolic picture, offering you an accurate portrait of your personality.

The chart itself—the horoscope—is a portrait of an individual. Generally, a natal (or birth) horoscope is drawn on a circular wheel. The wheel is divided into twelve segments, called houses. Each of the twelve houses represents a different aspect of the individual, much like the facets of a brilliantly cut stone. The houses depict different environments, such as home, school, and work. The houses also represent roles and relationships: parents, friends, lovers, children, partners. In each environment, individuals show a different side of their personality. At home, you may represent yourself quite differently than you do on the job. Additionally, in each relationship you will project a different image of yourself. For example, your parents may rarely see the side you show to intimate friends.

Symbols for the planets, the Sun, and the Moon are drawn inside the houses. Each planet represents a separate kind of energy. You experience and express each energy in specific ways. The way you use each of these energies is up to you. The planets in your chart do not make you do anything!

Signs of the Zodiac

The twelve signs of the zodiac indicate characteristics and traits that further define your personality. Each sign can be expressed in positive and negative ways. What's more, you have all twelve signs somewhere in your chart. Signs that are strongly emphasized by the planets have greater force. The Sun, Moon, and planets are placed on the chart according to their position at the time of birth. The qualities of a sign, combined with the energy of a planet, indicate how you might be most likely to use that energy and the best ways to develop that energy. The signs add color, emphasis, and dimension to the personality.

The Twelve Signs

Aries	♈	The Initiator
Taurus	♉	The Maintainer
Gemini	♊	The Questioner
Cancer	♋	The Nurturer
Leo	♌	The Loyalist
Virgo	♍	The Modifier
Libra	♎	The Judge
Scorpio	♏	The Catalyst
Sagittarius	♐	The Adventurer
Capricorn	♑	The Pragmatist
Aquarius	♒	The Reformer
Pisces	♓	The Visionary

Signs are also placed at the cusps, or dividing lines, of each of the houses. The influence of the signs on the houses is much the same as their influence on the Sun, Moon, and planets. Each house is shaped by the sign on its cusp.

When you view a horoscope, you will notice that there appear to be four distinct angles dividing the wheel of the chart. The line that divides the chart into a top and bottom half represents the horizon. In most cases, the left side of the horizon is called the Ascendant. The zodiac sign on the Ascendant is your rising sign. The Ascendant indicates the way others are likely to view you.

The Sun, Moon, or a planet can be compared to an actor in a play. The sign shows how the energy works, like the role the actor plays in a drama. The house indicates where the energy operates, like the setting of a play. On a psychological level, the Sun represents who you think you are. The Ascendant describes who others think you are, and the Moon reflects your emotional self.

Astrologers also study the geometric relationships between the Sun, Moon, and planets. These geometric angles are called aspects. Aspects further define the strengths, weaknesses, and challenges within your physical, mental, emotional, and spiritual selves. Sometimes patterns also appear in an astrological chart. These patterns have meaning.

To understand cycles for any given point in time, astrologers study several factors. Many use transits, which refer to the movement and positions of the planets. When astrologers compare those positions to the birth horoscope, the transits indicate activity in particular areas of the chart. The *Sun Sign Book* uses transits.

As you can see, your Sun sign is just one of many factors that describe who you are—but it is a powerful one! As the symbol of the ego, the Sun in your chart reflects your drive to be noticed. Most people can easily relate to the concepts associated with their Sun sign, since it is tied to their sense of personal identity.

Meanings of the Planets

The Sun

The Sun indicates the psychological bias that will dominate your actions. What you see, and why, is told in the reading for your Sun. The Sun also shows the basic energy patterns of your body and psyche. In many ways, the Sun is the dominant force in your horoscope and your life. Other influences, especially that of the Moon, may modify the Sun's influence, but nothing will cause you to depart very far from the basic solar pattern. Always keep in mind the basic influence of the Sun and remember all other influences must be interpreted in terms of it, especially insofar as they play a visible role in your life. You may think, dream, imagine, and hope a thousand things, according to your Moon and your other planets, but the Sun is what you are. To be your best self in terms of your Sun is to cause your energies to work along the path in which they will have maximum help from planetary vibrations.

The Moon

The Moon tells the desire of your life. When you know what you mean but can't verbalize it, it is your Moon that knows it and your Sun that can't say it. The wordless ecstasy, the mute sorrow, the secret dream, the esoteric picture of yourself that you can't get across to the world, or that the world doesn't comprehend or value—these are the products of the Moon. When you are misunderstood, it is your Moon nature, expressed imperfectly through the Sun sign, that feels betrayed. Things you know without thought—intuitions, hunches, you follow opportunity with energy, dash, enthusiasm, and courage; take big chances; and play your cards wide open.

Saturn

Saturn indicates the direction that will be taken in life by the self-preserving principle that, in its highest manifestation, ceases to be purely defensive and becomes ambitious and aspiring. Your defense or attack against the world is shown by the sign position of Saturn in the horoscope of birth. If Saturn is in the same sign as the Sun or Moon, defense predominates, and there is danger of introversion. The farther Saturn is from the Sun, Moon, and Ascendant, the better for objectivity and extroversion. If Saturn is in the same sign as Mercury, there is a profound and serious reaction to sensory impressions; this position generally accompanies a deep and efficient mind. If Saturn is in the same sign as Venus, a defensive attitude toward emotional experience makes for apparent coolness in love and difficulty with the emotions and human relations. If Saturn is in the same sign as Mars, confusion between defensive and aggressive urges can make a person indecisive. On the other hand, if the Sun and Moon are strong and the total personality well developed, a balanced, peaceful, and calm individual of sober judgment and moderate actions may be indicated. If Saturn is in the same sign as Jupiter, the reaction to opportunity is sober and balanced.

Uranus

Uranus in a general way relates to creativity, originality, or individuality, and its position by sign in the horoscope tells the direction in which you will seek to express yourself. In the same sign as Mercury or the Moon, Uranus suggests acute awareness, a quick reaction to sense impressions and experiences, or a hair-trigger mind. In the same sign as the Sun, it points to great nervous activity, a high-strung nature, and an original, creative, or eccentric personality. In the same sign as Mars, Uranus indicates high-speed activity, love of swift motion, and perhaps love of danger. In the same sign as Venus, it suggests an unusual reaction to emotional experience, idealism, sensuality, and original ideas about love and human relations. In the same sign as Saturn, Uranus points to good sense; this can be a practical, creative position, but more often than not it sets up a destructive conflict between practicality and originality that can result in a stalemate. In the same sign as Jupiter, Uranus makes opportunity, creates wealth and the means of getting it, and is conducive to the inventive, executive, and daring.

Neptune

Neptune relates to the deep subconscious, inherited mentality, and spirituality, indicating what you take for granted in life. Neptune in the same sign as the Sun or Moon indicates that intuitions and hunches—or delusions—dominate; there is a need to rigidly hold to reality. In the same sign as Mercury, Neptune indicates sharp sensory perceptions, a sensitive and perhaps creative mind, and a quivering intensity of reaction to sensory experience. In the same sign as Venus, it reveals idealistic and romantic (or sentimental) reactions to emotional experience, as well as the danger of sensationalism and a love of strange pleasures. In the same sign as Mars, Neptune indicates energy and intuition that work together to make mastery of life—one of the signs of having angels (or devils) on your side. When in the same sign as Jupiter, Neptune describes an intuitive response to opportunity along practical and money-making lines. In the same sign as Saturn, Neptune indicates intuitive defense and attack on the world, which is generally successful unless Saturn is polarized on the negative side; then there is danger of unhappiness.

Pluto

Pluto is a planet of extremes, from the lowest criminal and violent level of our society to the heights people can attain when they realize their significance in the collectivity of humanity. Pluto also rules three important mysteries of life—sex, death, and rebirth—and links them to each other. One level of death symbolized by Pluto is the physical death of an individual, which occurs so that a person can be reborn into another body to further his or her spiritual development. On another level, individuals can experience a "death" of their old self when they realize the deeper significance of life; thus they become one of the "second born." In a natal horoscope, Pluto signifies our perspective on the world, our conscious and subconscious. Since so many of Pluto's qualities are centered on the deeper mysteries of life, the house position of Pluto, and aspects to it, can show you how to attain a deeper understanding of the importance of the spiritual in your life.

Astrological Glossary

Air: One of the four basic elements. The air signs are Gemini, Libra, and Aquarius.

Angles: The four points of the chart that divide it into quadrants. The angles are sensitive areas that lend emphasis to planets located near them. These points are located on the cusps of the first, fourth, seventh, and tenth houses in a chart.

Ascendant: Rising sign. The degree of the zodiac on the eastern horizon at the time and place for which the horoscope is calculated. It can indicate the image or physical appearance you project to the world. The cusp of the first house.

Aspect: The angular relationship between planets, sensitive points, or house cusps in a horoscope. Lines drawn between the two points and the center of the chart, representing the earth, form the angle of the aspect. Astrological aspects include the conjunction (two points that are 0 degrees apart), opposition (two points, 180 degrees apart), square (two points, 90 degrees apart), sextile (two points, 60 degrees apart), and trine (two points, 120 degrees apart). Aspects can indicate harmony or challenge.

Cardinal Sign: One of the three qualities, or categories, that describe how a sign expresses itself. Aries, Cancer, Libra, and Capricorn are the cardinal signs, believed to initiate activity.

Chiron: Chiron is a comet traveling in orbit between Saturn and Uranus. It is believed to represent a key or doorway, healing, ecology, and a bridge between traditional and modern methods.

Conjunction: An aspect or angle between two points in a chart where the two points are close enough so that the energies join. Can be considered either harmonious or challenging, depending on the planets involved and their placement.

Cusp: A dividing line between signs or houses in a chart.

Degree: Degree of arc. One of 360 divisions of a circle. The circle of the zodiac is divided into twelve astrological signs of 30 degrees each. Each degree is made up of 60 minutes, and each minute is made up of 60 seconds of zodiacal longitude.

Earth: One of the four basic elements. The earth signs are Taurus, Virgo, and Capricorn.

Eclipse: A Solar Eclipse is the full or partial covering of the Sun by the Moon (as viewed from the earth), and a Lunar Eclipse is the full or partial covering of the Moon by the earth's own shadow.

Ecliptic: The Sun's apparent path around the earth, which is actually the plane of the earth's orbit extended out into space. The ecliptic forms the center of the zodiac.

Electional Astrology: A branch of astrology concerned with choosing the best time to initiate an activity.

Elements: The signs of the zodiac are divided into four groups of three zodiacal signs, each symbolized by one of the four elements of the ancients: fire, earth, air, and water. The element of a sign is said to express its essential nature.

Ephemeris: A listing of the Sun, Moon, and planets' positions and related information for astrological purposes.

Equinox: Equal night. The point in the earth's orbit around the Sun at which the day and night are equal in length.

Feminine Signs: Each zodiac sign is either "masculine" or "feminine." Earth signs (Taurus, Virgo, and Capricorn) and water signs (Cancer, Scorpio, and Pisces) are feminine.

Fire: One of the four basic elements. The fire signs are Aries, Leo, and Sagittarius.

Fixed Signs: Fixed is one of the three qualities, or categories, that describe how a sign expresses itself. The fixed signs are Taurus, Leo, Scorpio, and Aquarius. Fixed signs are said to be predisposed to existing patterns and somewhat resistant to change.

Hard Aspects: Hard aspects are those aspects in a chart that astrologers believe to represent difficulty or challenges. Among the hard aspects are the square, the opposition, and the conjunction (depending on which planets are conjunct).

Horizon: The word *horizon* is used in astrology in a manner similar to its common usage, except that only the eastern and western horizons are considered useful. The eastern horizon at the point of birth is the

Ascendant, or first house cusp, of a natal chart, and the western horizon at the point of birth is the Descendant, or seventh house cusp.

Houses: Division of the horoscope into twelve segments, beginning with the Ascendant. The dividing line between two houses is called a house cusp. Each house corresponds to certain aspects of daily living, and is ruled by the astrological sign that governs the cusp, or dividing line between the house and the one previous.

Ingress: The point of entry of a planet into a sign.

Lagna: A term used in Hindu or Vedic astrology for Ascendant, the degree of the zodiac on the eastern horizon at the time of birth.

Masculine Signs: Each of the twelve signs of the zodiac is either "masculine" or "feminine." The fire signs (Aries, Leo, and Sagittarius) and the air signs (Gemini, Libra, and Aquarius) are masculine.

Midheaven: The highest point on the ecliptic, where it intersects the meridian that passes directly above the place for which the horoscope is cast; the southern point of the horoscope.

Midpoint: A point equally distant to two planets or house cusps. Midpoints are considered by some astrologers to be sensitive points in a person's chart.

Mundane Astrology: Mundane astrology is the branch of astrology generally concerned with political and economic events, and the nations involved in these events.

Mutable Signs: Mutable is one of the three qualities, or categories, that describe how a sign expresses itself. Mutable signs are Gemini, Virgo, Sagittarius, and Pisces. Mutable signs are said to be very adaptable and sometimes changeable.

Natal Chart: A person's birth chart. A natal chart is essentially a "snapshot" showing the placement of each of the planets at the exact time of a person's birth.

Node: The point where the planets cross the ecliptic, or the earth's apparent path around the Sun. The North Node is the point where a planet moves northward, from the earth's perspective, as it crosses the ecliptic; the South Node is where it moves south.

Opposition: Two points in a chart that are 180 degrees apart.

Orb: A small degree of margin used when calculating aspects in a chart. For example, although 180 degrees form an exact opposition, an astrologer might consider an aspect within 3 or 4 degrees on either side of 180 degrees to be an opposition, as the impact of the aspect can still be felt within this range. The less orb on an aspect, the stronger the aspect. Astrologers' opinions vary on how many degrees of orb to allow for each aspect.

Outer Planet: Uranus, Neptune, and Pluto are known as the outer planets. Because of their distance from the Sun, they take a long time to complete a single rotation. Everyone born within a few years on either side of a given date will have similar placements of these planets.

Planet: The planets used in astrology are Mercury, Venus, Mars, Jupiter, Saturn, Uranus, Neptune, and Pluto. For astrological purposes, the Sun and Moon are also considered planets. A natal chart, or birth chart, lists planetary placements at the moment of birth.

Planetary Rulership: The sign in which a planet is most harmoniously placed. Examples are the Sun in Leo, Jupiter in Sagittarius, and the Moon in Cancer.

Precession of Equinoxes: The gradual movement of the point of the spring equinox, located at 0 degrees Aries. This point marks the beginning of the tropical zodiac. The point moves slowly backward through the constellations of the zodiac, so that about every 2,000 years the equinox begins in an earlier constellation.

Qualities: In addition to categorizing the signs by element, astrologers place the twelve signs of the zodiac into three additional categories, or qualities: cardinal, mutable, or fixed. Each sign is considered to be a combination of its element and quality. Where the element of a sign describes its basic nature, the quality describes its mode of expression.

Retrograde Motion: The apparent backward motion of a planet. This is an illusion caused by the relative motion of the earth and other planets in their elliptical orbits.

Sextile: Two points in a chart that are 60 degrees apart.

Sidereal Zodiac: Generally used by Hindu or Vedic astrologers. The sidereal zodiac is located where the constellations are actually positioned in the sky.

Soft Aspects: Soft aspects indicate good fortune or an easy relationship in the chart. Among the soft aspects are the trine, the sextile, and the conjunction (depending on which planets are conjunct each other).

Square: Two points in a chart that are 90 degrees apart.

Sun Sign: The sign of the zodiac in which the Sun is located at any given time.

Synodic Cycle: The time between conjunctions of two planets.

Trine: Two points in a chart that are 120 degrees apart.

Tropical Zodiac: The tropical zodiac begins at 0 degrees Aries, where the Sun is located during the spring equinox. This system is used by most Western astrologers and throughout this book.

Void-of-Course: A planet is void-of-course after it has made its last aspect within a sign but before it has entered a new sign.

Water: One of the four basic elements. The water signs are Cancer, Scorpio, and Pisces.

Using This Book

This book contains what is called Sun sign astrology; that is, astrology based on the sign that your Sun was in at the time of your birth. The technique has its foundation in ancient Greek astrology, in which the Sun was one of five points in the chart that were used as focal points for delineation.

The most effective way to use astrology, however, is through one-on-one work with a professional astrologer, who can integrate the eight or so other astrological bodies into the interpretation to provide you with guidance. There are factors related to the year and time of day you were born that are highly significant in the way you approach life and vital to making wise choices. In addition, there are ways of using astrology that aren't addressed here, such as compatibility between two specific individuals, discovering family patterns, or picking a day for a wedding or grand opening.

To best use the information in the monthly forecasts, you'll want to determine your Ascendant, or rising sign. If you don't know your Ascendant, the tables following this description will help you determine your rising sign. They are most accurate for those born in the continental United States. They provide only an approximation, but can be used as a good rule of thumb. Your exact Ascendant may vary from the tables according to your time and place of birth. Once you've approximated your ascending sign using the tables or determined your Ascendant by having your chart calculated, you'll know two significant factors in your chart. Read the monthly forecast sections for both your Sun and Ascendant to gain the most useful information. In addition, you can read the section about the sign your Moon is in. The Sun is the true, inner you; the Ascendant is your shell or appearance and the person you are becoming; the Moon is the person you were—or still are based on habits and memories.

Also included in the monthly forecasts is information about the planets' retrogrades. Most people have heard of "Mercury retrograde." In fact, all the planets except the Sun and Moon appear to travel backward (retrograde) in their path periodically. This appears to happen only because we on the earth are not seeing the other planets from the middle of the solar system. Rather, we are watching them from our own moving object. We are like a train that moves past cars on the freeway that are going at a slower speed. To us on the train, the cars look like they're going backward. Mercury turns retrograde about every four months for three weeks; Venus every eighteen months for six weeks; Mars every two years for two to three months. The rest of the planets each retrograde once a year for four to five months. During each retrograde, we have the opportunity to try something new, something we conceived of at the beginning of the planet's yearly cycle. The times when the planets change direction are significant, as are the beginning and midpoint (peak or culmination) of each cycle. These are noted in your forecast each month.

The "Rewarding Days" and "Challenging Days" sections indicate times when you'll feel either more centered or more out of balance. The rewarding days are not the only times you can perform well, but the times you're likely to feel better integrated! During challenging days, take extra time to center yourself by meditating or using other techniques that help you feel more objective.

The Action Table found at the end of each sign's section offers general guidelines for the best times to take particular actions. Please note, however, that your whole chart will provide more accurate guidelines for the best time to do something. Therefore, use this table with a grain of salt, and never let it stop you from taking an action you feel compelled to take.

You can use this information to gain an objective awareness about the way the current cycles are affecting you. Realize that the power of astrology is even more useful when you have a complete chart and professional guidance.

Ascendant Table

Your Sun Sign	Your Time of Birth					
	6–8 am	8–10 am	10 am–Noon	Noon–2 pm	2–4 pm	4–6 pm
Aries	Taurus	Gemini	Cancer	Leo	Virgo	Libra
Taurus	Gemini	Cancer	Leo	Virgo	Libra	Scorpio
Gemini	Cancer	Leo	Virgo	Libra	Scorpio	Sagittarius
Cancer	Leo	Virgo	Libra	Scorpio	Sagittarius	Capricorn
Leo	Virgo	Libra	Scorpio	Sagittarius	Capricorn	Aquarius
Virgo	Libra	Scorpio	Sagittarius	Capricorn	Aquarius	Pisces
Libra	Scorpio	Sagittarius	Capricorn	Aquarius	Pisces	Aries
Scorpio	Sagittarius	Capricorn	Aquarius	Pisces	Aries	Taurus
Sagittarius	Capricorn	Aquarius	Pisces	Aries	Taurus	Gemini
Capricorn	Aquarius	Pisces	Aries	Taurus	Gemini	Cancer
Aquarius	Pisces	Aries	Taurus	Gemini	Cancer	Leo
Pisces	Aries	Taurus	Gemini	Cancer	Leo	Virgo

Your Sun Sign	Your Time of Birth					
	6–8 pm	8–10 pm	10 pm–Midnight	Midnight–2 am	2–4 am	4–6 am
Aries	Scorpio	Sagittarius	Capricorn	Aquarius	Pisces	Aries
Taurus	Sagittarius	Capricorn	Aquarius	Pisces	Aries	Taurus
Gemini	Capricorn	Aquarius	Pisces	Aries	Taurus	Gemini
Cancer	Aquarius	Pisces	Aries	Taurus	Gemini	Cancer
Leo	Pisces	Aries	Taurus	Gemini	Cancer	Leo
Virgo	Aries	Taurus	Gemini	Cancer	Leo	Virgo
Libra	Taurus	Gemini	Cancer	Leo	Virgo	Libra
Scorpio	Gemini	Cancer	Leo	Virgo	Libra	Scorpio
Sagittarius	Cancer	Leo	Virgo	Libra	Scorpio	Sagittarius
Capricorn	Leo	Virgo	Libra	Scorpio	Sagittarius	Capricorn
Aquarius	Virgo	Libra	Scorpio	Sagittarius	Capricorn	Aquarius
Pisces	Libra	Scorpio	Sagittarius	Capricorn	Aquarius	Pisces

How to use this table: 1. Find your Sun sign in the left column.

2. Find your approximate birth time in a vertical column.

3. Line up your Sun sign and birth time to find your Ascendant.

This table will give you an approximation of your Ascendant. If you feel that the sign listed as your Ascendant is incorrect, try the one either before or after the listed sign. It is difficult to determine your exact Ascendant without a complete natal chart.

2014 at a Glance

The really big news in Astrology Land this year is an ongoing Clash of the Titans, a testy square between startling Uranus and unrelenting Pluto. These two first began locking horns years ago, and they'll continue to irritate each other throughout 2014, especially in April and December. Freedom of speech versus censoring online information for security reasons will continue to be an issue, and probably won't be resolved just yet.

After two and a half years in Scorpio, Saturn will move into Sagittarius in late December—but not until he and Pluto have created some major religious and political scandals. With Saturn in Scorpio, Pluto's sign, and Pluto in Capricorn, Saturn's sign, the two have been in cahoots—astrologically known as "mutual reception"—for the duration of Saturn's trek through this sign, so these two planets will continue to be especially potent throughout the year. Saturn usually holds on, but in Scorpio, he'll urge us to take stock of what's not working and let it go. Pluto, on the other hand, insists that we let go—but in Capricorn, he insists that we only eliminate what's obsolete or useless. These two potent planets aren't famous for the gentleness of their tactics, so depending on where they land, goodbyes are a definite possibility for us all. On a larger scale, however, secrets in worldwide institutions will continue to be uncovered, challenging our faith in The System. The good news is that by the time Saturn moves on, much of what's no longer appropriate to the society we've become will have been tossed out. Expect new laws on controversial subjects.

Jupiter, as per usual, will have a fine time livening up our lives and encouraging us to expand our horizons. From his spot in home and family-loving Cancer until July, he'll also attempt to restore some good, old-fashioned family values, and the foreclosure epidemic in the United States will continue to taper off. In July, when he enters Leo, a sign known for entertainment and theater, celebrity lifestyles will be in the news, and several rather dramatic celebrity scandals could keep the media well fed for months.

Mars will spend an unusually long time in Libra during 2014, a sign he's not usually very fond of. Libra loves to compromise and reconcile, but Mars's job is to inspire assertion and aggression. As a result, in one way or another, we'll all be feeling a bit more likely to speak our minds, regardless of the consequences, especially with respect to relationship issues we've been trying to keep under wraps. Libra loves partnerships, but Mars is a lone wolf, so finding a happy medium will definitely keep us all busy until he leaves this sign behind on July 25.

The heavens are in the mood for change. Your mission is to figure out what you need to change and use these celestial allies to get the job done.

2014 SUN SIGN BOOK

Forecasts by

Kim Rogers-Gallagher

Aries

The Ram
March 20 to April 19

♈

Element: Fire

Quality: Cardinal

Polarity: Yang/masculine

Planetary Ruler: Mars

Meditation: I build upon my strengths

Gemstone: Diamond

Power Stones: Bloodstone, carnelian, ruby

Key Phrase: I am

Glyph: Ram's head

Anatomy: Head, face, throat

Colors: Red, white

Animal: Ram

Myths/Legends: Artemis, Jason and the Golden Fleece

House: First

Opposite Sign: Libra

Flower: Geranium

Keyword: Initiative

The Aries Personality

Your Strengths and Challenges

First to arrive, first to leave, and always ready to accept a challenge. That's you, Aries! Impatient? Impulsive? Trigger-happy at times? Oh, maybe just a touch. But you're so much fun to be around, no one really minds—with the possible exception of your waitress, who'll undoubtedly get an earful if she takes more than 37.5 seconds to take your order, process it, and deliver it!

Your energy is comparable to a spark plug, Aries, or a red-hot bullet. The thing is, you don't always aim before you turn the key or fire all of your substantial energy at a target. Of course, slowing down, being patient, or just taking your time is out of the question, but if you can count to five (certainly not ten—that would take far too long!), you may actually be able to waste less of your energy and time and conquer one of the things your sign is famous for: starting and not finishing!

Of course, you will always be more likely to begin something than to see it through, which is why you are often the "idea person" or initiator on the job. You are the first of the three fire signs, and just as a match lights up immediately after being struck, your energy, when stimulated, is off and running, with a vengeance. But it only makes sense since your ruling planet is Mars, the "red planet," the guy who fuels us when we set off to pursue something we want. You can even hear the fire in his keywords: aggression, assertion, anger, red! Any questions?

Your Relationships

Getting involved with you on any level requires a lighthearted spirit, a willingness to act spontaneously and often without much regard for The Rules (which are only "suggested guidelines" in your book), and a serious thirst for adventure. Every moment with you is a passionate, exciting one, no encounter is without sparks, and every move you make comes with a complimentary serving of adrenaline. The good news is that this makes you a much sought-after companion, especially for the other fire signs, Leo and Sagittarius, as well as your air-sign cousins, Gemini, Libra, and Aquarius.

Romantically speaking, when you are partnered with another fire sign, you are quite literally "in your element," and it shows! When with another Aries, you two are out to take the world by storm, and obstacles simply do not exist. But with any fire companion, your passion for each other will be obvious in every word, gesture, and touch—and in every heated argument! Fortunately, as long as you express yourself, anger does not last long, which is a big plus in any relationship. Remember, though, that while being with Leo or Sagittarius is comfortable, it's also combustible.

When you find yourself in the company of one of the three air signs, you are even more prone to "going off," for better or worse. This, too, makes sense, if you think about how air reacts with fire on a physical level. Air fans fire into action, and fire helps air to move more quickly. It's one of the matches made in the heavens for you!

When it comes to the earth and water signs—especially Cancer, Capricorn, and Scorpio—while there may be a very powerful initial attraction, you often seem to be at cross-purposes, or simply not on the same page, as far as your goals and hopes for the future go.

In all, Aries, you need a partner who is not just an equally ardent lover, but a worthy opponent!

Your Career and Money

While it would be easy to see you as a spendthrift, Aries, oddly enough, that's not usually the case. In fact, you tend to watch your finances quite carefully. That's not to say that you won't pull out the plastic impulsively if the mood is right and you can afford it, but being physically comfortable is very important to you, and you do everything you can to ensure you'll have what you need—just as soon as you need it! The good news is that you're not afraid to work hard, physically or mentally, to get what you're after—and as with all else, once your fuse is lit, you are absolutely unstoppable. You are best suited to quick movements and short tasks, however, and have an extremely low tolerance for routine, so large projects or long-term projects tend to become tedious to you almost immediately. You need stimulation on a daily basis, so in order to be professionally and financially successful, make sure you are never bored.

Your Lighter Side

When it comes to having fun, Aries, movement, excitement, and freedom are absolutely essential. You love to feel your heart pound and you have no fear, so rollercoasters, skydiving, and even bungee jumping are definitely not out of the question on a Sunday after-noon—especially if you have a playmate on hand who is willing to take a risk, just for the fun of it!

Affirmation for the Year
Aim before you fire! Please!

The Year Ahead for Aries

The ongoing square between startling Uranus and intense, unwaver-ing Pluto that began back in 2011 will continue to hover above us all for several years, Aries, but it will most certainly keep your sign on its toes this year, most especially if you were born between March 27 and April 7, in which case your Sun, the very core of your being, will be highly stressed. These two planetary titans have been locked in a testy square for years now, irritating each other and the natal planets they touch into action—and, in general, activating a very high level of ten-sion down here on Planet Number Three. In your case, the focal point of their cosmic argument has been a collision between your solar tenth house of higher-ups and your solar first house of personality. So in a nutshell, you may be finding that your urge to earn your daily bread by doing what feels "right" to you is at odds with what others seem to be insisting you do. That goes double for authority figures, who will no doubt be far too demanding of your time and energy, and not at all willing to pass out even the tiniest bit of thanks and praise, much less raises, bonuses, or rewards.

The good news is that the tension between these two will turn up the heat on your need to free yourself from any restrictions, either on the job or domestically, and that urge will rise to a fever pitch this year. Crack open the champagne, then, because ruts are about to become a thing of the past—and when it happens, it will happen without warn-ing! You can probably already feel this brewing inside you, and you may have to do some fancy side-stepping to get yourself out of old rou-tines and break habits, but you most certainly have the right team on hand to do it. In the meantime, expect a visit from one of your oldest comrades: Stress, with a capital "S"! Fortunately, if anyone knows how to deal with this, you do. Give yourself a difficult or physically strenu-ous task to accomplish so that you actually fall into bed tired at night, rather than feeling wired and ready to pop.

Now, speaking of feeling wired, let's talk about Uranus, the ruling planet of electricity, who is currently on duty in your very own sign and your solar first house of personality and appearance. This rebellious planet has probably already inspired you to make drastic, sweeping shifts in your appearance, but over the next year or two, you can certainly expect to be bored and restless, and feel an intense need for change on a daily, if not hourly, basis—no matter when you were born, whom you are currently spending your time with, or what you do for work. Again, your best bet is to give in to those urges and to free yourself from anything—or anyone—personally or professionally that is stopping you from reaching your personal goals. Remember, Uranus is the heavens' "rebel," and no needed revolution, personal or societal, can occur without his unpredictable energy. You are the warrior. Use him to defend yourself against falling into a rut—and to dig yourself out of one, in no uncertain terms.

With all this red-hot and often abrupt activity and personal change on your astrological agenda, you will definitely need to find a safe place to retreat to, Aries, and trustworthy companions to hide out with. Fortunately, that is where woozy Neptune comes in. This dreamy, sensitive planet, the ruler of intuition and altered states of all kinds—from sleep to depression to trance states and meditation—has taken up residence in your solar twelfth house of Privacy, Please, urging you to hang a sign with those words on your doorknob and to be unafraid to shut that door and keep the world out, especially in times of extreme tension. You really should give in to her influence, whenever and wherever the need arises. Everyone knows that you are as bold and brave as a sign could possibly be, but even Aries natives need some downtime every now and then. Take comfort in dim lights and soft music whenever possible, and never, ever subject yourself to negative situations, influences, or people.

Now, speaking of negativity, Aries, let's talk about Saturn, the planetary ruler of lead, the heaviest metal. This disciplined, hard-working planet is the best celestial ally of all when it comes to working hard, following the rules, and making a name for ourselves—but too much work and no play can get pretty depressing, in a hurry! Your mission this year, with Saturn on duty in your solar eighth house of joint finances—oh, and sexuality, by the way—is to never lose sight of the light at the end of the tunnel, and to do absolutely everything that is required of you—even if it means going it alone, intimately speaking, for a while. Remember, Saturn's motto has always been "Quality, not quantity."

When it comes to quantity, however, Jupiter is in charge. He's the heavens' answer to Santa Claus, Aries, the kind of energy everyone just loves to see coming to visit. The good news is that he brings abundance wherever he lands, so if you aim your energies in that direction, you will have all that you want and more! The problematic side of this planet only occurs when we use this generosity to create excess, which is also quite possible. In your case, this urge to "expand," enlarge, and grow will occur first in your solar fourth house of home, family, and domestic matters, if it has not already, and next, as of July 16, in the realm of fun times, love affairs, and romance—everyone's favorite place! You may have already changed your domestic situation to include someone new—perhaps even a child—but know that over the coming year, all good things will come to you, emotionally and recreationally, if you remain open to new experiences—and learn from the old ones!

What This Year's Eclipses Mean for You

There will be four eclipses in 2014, Aries. The first pair will occur in April. The Lunar Eclipse (when the Sun and Moon are opposite, during the Full Moon) will be on April 15, and will plant a seed in partner-oriented Libra and your solar seventh house of one-to-one encounters, urging you to begin a new relationship—which, of course, may mean ending your current situation. If that is the case, since both you and Libra are fast-acting cardinal signs, you will take matters into your own hands and do what needs to be done—without ever once looking back!

By April 29, when the Solar Eclipse (during the New Moon) occurs in sturdy Taurus and your solar second house of values, possessions, and money matters, you will probably have the urge to get your affairs in order. You'll be far more willing to accept any changes in your domestic or financial situation. Since New Moons bring beginnings, if you have recently ended a financial situation with a partner, this eclipse will help you to start over on solid ground.

The second set of eclipses will occur in October. The first, a Lunar Eclipse, will arrive on October 8, all done up in your very own sign. This lunation will usher in a time of fast change and self-discovery—or rediscovery—for you, especially since it will fall in your solar first house of personality and appearance. Expect to feel an overwhelming urge to make big physical changes with an eye toward becoming a "new you." Obviously, this would be a great time to begin a diet, end a bad habit, or simply redo your wardrobe.

The last Solar Eclipse of the year will occur on October 23 in determined Scorpio and your solar eighth house. If you play your cards right and follow your antennae wherever they lead, you will be able to begin transforming your physical image and personal presentation. But you'll also have a whole new outlook on what really matters financially as well as on an intimate relationship level—all of which is just what eclipses in Scorpio absolutely demand!

Saturn

Saturn is a very serious kind of energy, Aries. He rules career, reputation, and professional matters, as well as all our dealings with authority figures—which includes being the authority figure, when the occasion demands it. This rather demanding energy will spend the year in your solar eighth house of intimacy, crises, permanent endings, and joint financial issues. Since Saturn is in Scorpio, a fixed water sign that operates quite differently from your cardinal fire energy, this may not be an easy time for you, especially when it comes to your closest relationships. You may find that you are no longer communicating with your partner, or that something seems to be left unsaid between you two that really needs to be said. This is a house of endings and intense experiences, so you can expect all of that and more, especially in your closest and most intimate relationships. This planet plays for keeps, so whatever passes from your life now absolutely had to go. The good news is that it is the best astrological help in our corner of the Universe when it comes to getting the job done, no matter how unpleasant or tedious that business happens to be, so if you have been feeling stalled or waiting for the best time to take care of a seemingly endless problem, take charge of it now. Put your foot down and use that famous bravery!

Uranus

Back in 2011, Aries, this startling planet entered your very own sign and your solar first house of personality and appearance. Talk about a match made in heaven! Uranus just loves to shock and surprise, and is the heavens' chief purveyor of surprise endings, all of which obviously raise the adrenaline level in our lives—which, of course, is exactly what you live for! With Uranus on duty in this very noticeable place, then, it is easy to see how you have probably made quite a splash in your social circles lately, and raised more than one eyebrow as well. In fact, if you were born between March 20 and April 2, you have probably gone through some drastic changes over the past year or so, all with liberating, positive results. Similarly, if you were born between March 27 and April 7, you will experience that urge to free yourself this year— and you will do it quickly, abruptly, and with absolutely no fear of the future. Do a small favor for the people around you, though, if you can—give them a few hours' warning before you dye your hair purple, walk out on your job, or move to another country!

Neptune

Dreamy Neptune is the planet of inspiration, romance, illusion, and altered states, Aries. Basically, whenever we forget about our physical bodies and tune in to the greater whole of celestial energy, we are under Neptune's influence. She has been quite potent for the past year or so, ever since she entered her own sign, Pisces, the perfect astrological conduit for this woozy, vague, and oftentimes invisible energy. She has been traveling through your solar twelfth house of sub-conscious thoughts and desires ever since, gently prodding you into dreaming—both while you're awake and while you're asleep. If you have been feeling especially intuitive, then, it is no wonder, because your antennae are operating on high. This planet also dissolves the boundaries between "us" and "out there," however, so much like your Piscean neighbors, you have probably also noticed a heightened sensitivity to loud noises, bright lights, and harsh situations. These are Neptune's way of asking you to take some time alone, whenever you can, to retreat and think about what you really "need"—and what you really don't need. You are highly susceptible to outside influences now. Let that intuition run wild, but steer yourself away from negative energies in your choice of companions as well as life situations.

Pluto

Pluto is the planet of intense experiences, Aries, the Lord of the Underworld and the bringer of intimacy in all its forms. If you were born between March 29 and April 1, you are quite familiar with his energies, and if you were born between April 1 and 6, you are about to become quite intimately acquainted with him. This planet absolutely demands that we either devote ourselves completely to our current path or completely let go—and never look back! There are no in-betweens with Pluto, and no gray areas—only "inevitables." In your case, since he will be making a rather testy 90-degree angle—an astrological "square"—to your Sun over the coming year, and since he is currently in Capricorn, the sign of authority figures and responsibilities, you may often feel pressured, both by society and by individuals who have authority over you, both of whom you may also feel absolutely unable to please. The good news is that if you have been thinking of making a complete and total change in your career or public profile, you will most certainly be able to pull it off now. The tough part will only happen if you refuse to give way, if you insist on holding on to what is no longer of any use to you in these most public areas of life. In the meantime, you will certainly feel quite stressed, but if you give in and ride the wave, you will experience the rebirth that only Pluto can bring.

Aries | January

Planetary Lightspots

Managing to make everyone happy as much as possible for as long as possible is certainly not something that would ordinarily make your top ten list, Aries, but this month, you'll be far more inclined to compromise. Relax. You're not losing your edge. You're just growing up. Look to January 11 for an authority figure's thumbs up—or thumbs down.

Relationships

Your mission now is to juggle home and family matters with your career, Aries—but no one says it's going to be easy. Stay determined to finish all professional projects, but don't forget there's someone waiting for you at home. Be careful of getting into one of those "if you loved me, you would" stalemates with your partner on January 16.

Money and Success

Talk turkey about financial matters on January 7. If the support that was promised to you on January 3 and 5 comes through, you won't have any reason to worry. If it doesn't, it's definitely time to reexamine your priorities, with an eye toward trimming the fat—even if that means saying goodbye to someone near and dear to you.

Planetary Hotspots

The New Moon on January 1 in your solar tenth house of career matters will make this a New Year's Day to remember. You may close your eyes at midnight and tap your heels together in hopes of landing a better position—which is certainly not out of the question. Hang in there.

Rewarding Days

1, 11, 17, 19, 22, 23, 24

Challenging Days

2, 3, 4, 6, 7, 16, 25

Aries | February

Planetary Lightspots

Any changes you've been meaning to make will receive quite the added boost on February 14, 15, and 16, but with Mercury traveling retrograde as of February 6, you may need to finish up some leftovers before moving forward, and it may take the whole month to do it. Stay positive.

Relationships

Romance is on the agenda, Aries, and it's going to be hot, heavy, and extremely passionate. If you really can't resist someone who's unavailable, be sure you lay down the ground rules of the affair. Don't let them escape without knowing exactly what you're after—and what you're not interested in.

Money and Success

Whatever you set out to do to improve or enhance your resumé now, rest assured that it will work. You may need to wait until February 24 to see material evidence of your success, and even then, it won't come easy. But when all is said and done, you'll know you did everything you could possibly do. Let the issue rest, and spend some time with loved ones. They miss you!

Planetary Hotspots

If there are goodbyes to be said this month, a square between the Sun and stoic Saturn will urge you to say them on February 11. You may have to assert your position again on February 19 or 26, but even if a certain someone insists that you aren't thinking clearly, if you're sure, go for it.

Rewarding Days
5, 9, 14, 15, 16, 23, 24

Challenging Days
10, 11, 12, 18, 19, 25, 26

Aries | March

Planetary Lightspots

You've been trying very hard for a very long time to restore peace the best way you can—by letting dear ones know that the time spent away from them isn't pleasant, but in the long run, it will better your collective lifestyle. Well, congratulations. They'll get it around March 13. Say hallelujah! Say amen!

Relationships

Feeling a bit woozy, Aries? Like you'd rather be anywhere else but here on Planet Number Three? Well, it's no wonder. A pack of Pisces planets in your solar twelfth house of Privacy, Please have conspired to lure you inward—not your usual state of affairs. Look for finalizing news of the very best kind on March 13. Expect a reunion.

Money and Success

Talk about a change of fortune! You may wake up on March 17 or 18 tingling, and if you're on your way to a money-oriented deal, there's no wonder. You're on your way to changing reality as you know it, with only a vision and your own determination to get the job done. Not to worry, though. The Universe has your back.

Planetary Hotspots

Arguments about Who Said What to Whom will arise around March 11, and you may need to be very specific to make your point as crystal clear as you thought it was the first time you presented it. The good news is that you'll have allies on hand you never would have expected.

Rewarding Days

1, 5, 13, 14, 15, 28

Challenging Days

2, 3, 10, 11, 21, 22, 29

Aries | April

Planetary Lightspots

The Sun is already holding court in your very own impulsive, impractical, yet irresistible sign, Aries, and on April 7, chatty Mercury will join him. Will you be the star of the show? Oh, you bet. You'll also be wittier and funnier than you've been for quite some time. Take a bow! It's your turn to shine.

Relationships

What You Want vs. What They Want may be a bone of contention this month, Aries, but oddly enough, it may be you who wants to settle on a reasonable course of action. No, compromise isn't what you're usually famous for, but every now and then, even you get to settle out of court. You may not be entirely satisfied, but you'll know the verdict was fair.

Money and Success

You're not known for being careful, Aries, not in any area of life, and that certainly does go for money matters. Even if you think you're being good, others probably see you as an impulse buyer. Your mission now is to avoid giving in to the smooth talk of a seasoned salesperson on April 25, 26, 27, or 30.

Planetary Hotspots

Relationship issues may be especially testy around April 1, 2, 3 and April 22 and 23, Aries, but with your own planet, fiery Mars, in the mood to compromise by virtue of his presence in fair-minded Libra—well, the worst scenario has you apologizing for saying something too quickly. Fortunately, everyone who knows you will be able to forgive.

Rewarding Days

1, 2, 7, 13, 14, 22

Challenging Days

3, 4, 8, 15, 16, 23, 24

Aries | May

Planetary Lightspots

You're never feeling better than when you know you're free to be you, Aries, and while you're quite skilled at it, the Universe doesn't often see fit to let you get away with being a rebel—at least, not as often as you'd like. Between May 14 and 16, however, a parade of passionate planets in fire and air will conspire to free you up.

Relationships

Your solar third house of siblings and neighbors is filling up with well-meaning, gossipy planets in Gemini, so someone who belongs to one of those groups may insist you need to meet the person they're sure is perfect for you. Don't refuse—no matter what happened last time. You never know. This time, they just might be right.

Money and Success

If you're dealing with real estate ventures, Aries, you'd do well to look to May 2, 3, 5, 6, and 9 to finalize the deal. Several planets in earthy, grounded Taurus and your solar second house of personal finances will be happy to negotiate any land-related deal. Taking care of debts, owed or owing, will be another priority. Combine the wisdom of your experience with intuition.

Planetary Hotspots

Self-control may be an issue for you this month, Aries, especially if you've been a little too free with your rhetoric lately. Around May 2, chatty Mercury and responsible Saturn will call you on the carpet, and later in the month you might need to make a bit of a scene to make your point. How sad—right?

Rewarding Days

3, 4, 5, 12, 15, 16

Challenging Days

9, 10, 13, 14, 17

Aries | June

Planetary Lightspots

You're always on the lookout for a person who'll let you be yourself, Aries. Your brusque manner scares off most new admirers, but if you use your intuition this month, you'll be able to spot the one person in the room who'll appreciate you and love you "because of" rather than "in spite of."

Relationships

Talk about being a magnet, Aries! Once loving Venus set off for your sign and your solar first house of personality and appearance last month, you were beating your admirers off. Around June 13 or 14, however, you might do better to talk to them before you call the authorities. One never knows what they might let slip, after all...

Money and Success

Any financial matters that have to do with your home or domestic situation may be challenging now, but if you reach out to powerful friends on June 7 or 8, you'll likely find that the issue won't go any further. On June 13 or 14, The Powers That Be may be less than cooperative, but don't let them have their way without a fight.

Planetary Hotspots

From June 6 to 8, you'll be "enjoying" the company of several planets in cardinal signs like your own, all of whom will be determined to push your buttons and see exactly how far you're willing to go to keep the peace. Better warn anyone who decides to try you out, though, especially around June 14 or 25.

Rewarding Days

3, 4, 8, 17, 18, 23, 29

Challenging Days

6, 7, 13, 14, 15, 24, 25, 26

Aries | July

Planetary Lightspots

Wonderful, benefic Jupiter is about to enter your solar fifth house of lovers for the coming year, Aries, and your list of admirers will undoubtedly lengthen during his stay. The good news is that you won't be bored, not for a moment. The tough part will be waving adieu to those dear ones when they board the plane homeward.

Relationships

Your focus will shift to home and domestic matters this month, Aries, but that doesn't mean that your ruling planet, fiery Mars, won't be doing his best to shake things up in your solar seventh house of one-to-one relationships. He'll be on his way as of July 25. Hold on to any relationship that's worth the effort. Let the rest go, gladly.

Money and Success

If you're in the mood to try your hand at investing, Aries, you'd be best off to do it with the green light of a trusted counselor. Wait to act until after fortunate Jupiter enters your solar fifth house of speculation on July 15. Be careful with your personal money matters in general now. It would be easy for someone to mislead you, and you'll be mad at yourself if you fall for it.

Planetary Hotspots

You won't believe how far you're willing to go to defend your family now, Aries, so urgent events around July 18, 19, and 20 will have you rolling your eyes and wondering where you were when all that happened. The good news is that you'll be completely exonerated by the testimony of the innocent bystanders you helped out of the line of fire. Oh, don't look confused. You know what I mean.

Rewarding Days
7, 9, 18, 19, 21, 23, 24, 28

Challenging Days
8, 12, 13, 15, 16, 22, 31

Aries | August

Planetary Lightspots

Loving Venus will pass into Leo, your fire-sign cousin, on August 12, and just a week later, she'll meet up with outgoing, benevolent Jupiter. This pairing reflects the heavens' most generous planets in one of the most generous signs. With all this going on in your solar fifth house of lovers, dealings with children, and creativity, you'll undoubtedly be the star of the show. Enjoy!

Relationships

Mighty Jupiter and the Sun have been keeping the home fires burning from their positions in your solar fifth house of lovers, Aries, and since they're all done up in Leo, the most romantic sign of all, it's easy to see how you might not have time for friendships right now. Don't desert them entirely. You might need them in the not-so-distant future.

Money and Success

Once loving Venus passes into your solar fifth house of speculation, Aries, you'll be quite tempted to gamble, even with those hard-earned resources you've been holding on to for so long. Remember that luck is fickle, but credit card bills are extremely regular. Don't jeopardize your future for a few thrills. Likewise when it comes to taking chances on new admirers who seem to be too good to be true.

Planetary Hotspots

Talk about a good time! The Sun and Mercury, the cosmic Messenger, will get together on August 8 in Leo and your solar fifth house of lovers and recreational activity. With mighty Jupiter already holding court there, the stage has been set for you to fall in love, but there could be a couple of false alarms. Easy there!

Rewarding Days
2, 3, 11, 12, 17, 18, 19

Challenging Days
1, 7, 23, 24, 25, 26, 29

Aries | September

Planetary Lightspots

Relationships may take up a lot of your time now, Aries. With the exception of a possible power struggle with a higher-up around September 8 or 9, however, the reasons you're so focused should be quite pleasant. In fact, by the end of the month, you may be making plans with a sweetheart to take things one giant step forward.

Relationships

By the end of the month, Aries, three planets will be on duty in your solar seventh house of one-to-one relationships, all done up in balance-loving Libra. Could this mean you'll finally be willing to compromise on an issue that's been a sticking point between you two for a while now? Maybe. You might decide to forgive and forget and start over with a clean slate, too.

Money and Success

Venus rules love and money matters, Aries, and as of September 5, she'll be on duty in your solar sixth house of health and work-related matters. If you're under the weather, a loved one will definitely be dishing out some serious TLC. At work, you'll be able to make great strides toward promoting your goals with the help of an authority figure around September 14.

Planetary Hotspots

Emotions will run high with the Full Moon on September 8—so much so that if you're still stewing the next day, you'll arrange a confrontation. Be careful not to let it become too heated. Being calm and reasonable yet totally firm is the only way to put this issue to bed for good.

Rewarding Days

2, 3, 13, 14, 24, 25, 29

Challenging Days

7, 8, 9, 12, 20, 21

Aries | October

Planetary Lightspots

Outgoing Jupiter's presence in your solar fifth house will continue to make your encounters with the kids extra enjoyable. This is a terrific time for a spontaneous day trip with the family. With your ruling planet, Mars, currently on duty in fun-loving Sagittarius, recreation and leisure-time activities are an absolute must. Expect to be contacted by at least one long-distance friend or lover, too.

Relationships

Your solar seventh house of one-to-one relationships will continue to play host to a pack of Libran planets, Aries, all of them intent on convincing you to settle your differences. The longer this dispute goes on, the harder it will be to find a happy medium, and that's exactly what you need to do—so make it quick!

Money and Success

Matters involving business partnerships will heat up around the Lunar Eclipse on October 8, Aries. Controlling Pluto will get into a testy square with Venus that same day, who just so happens to be in charge of finances. No matter what you're arguing about, remember that anger won't solve it. Call in a professional if you need help.

Planetary Hotspots

Just as the Lunar Eclipse arrives on October 8, loving Venus in your solar seventh house of one-to-one relationships will square off with intense Pluto. Yes, this sure could be a difficult day, especially if you're angry about being manipulated, controlled, or just plain used by someone you cared for. Do yourself a favor. Stay calm and make arrangements to simplify your life by month's end.

Rewarding Days

5, 13, 14, 15, 26, 27, 28

Challenging Days

3, 4, 10, 11, 16, 17, 23

Aries | November

Planetary Lightspots

A joint financial issue you have been working on for months stands every chance of working out now, thanks to the input of the Full Moon in Taurus and your solar second house of money matters on November 6. Your mission is to take what you need, and nothing more. You can emerge from all negative situations with a brand-new attitude if you're willing to try, just this once, to be patient.

Relationships

By mid-month, there will be four planets on duty in your solar eighth house of intimate partners and joint resources, Aries. One of those planets is Saturn, so at times you may feel overburdened and over-whelmed, but by month's end, a pack of lighthearted Sagittarius planets will arrive to help you relax, unwind, and maybe even take a trip.

Money and Success

Several lucky breaks could come your way on the work front this month, Aries, and if you've worked hard and paid your dues, you'll have the full support of authority figures. Many of them will reach out with advice, and one may offer to take you under their wing or make you an apprentice.

Planetary Hotspots

Expansive Jupiter will touch base with loving Venus in sexy Scorpio on November 9, inspiring you to pull out all the stops and make a very big show of your feelings. If you can afford it, why not? Go first class all the way. That urge to go overboard will come up again around November 13 and 22, however, so don't spend it all in one place.

Rewarding Days

1, 2, 3, 16, 22, 27, 28, 29

Challenging Days

8, 9, 10, 12, 18, 25, 26

Aries | December

Planetary Lightspots

With generous, benevolent Jupiter in your solar fifth house of love affairs, recreation, and dealings with kids, you're already primed to have some serious fun, Aries. But this month, several planets in Jupiter's favorite sign, Sagittarius, will join in—and Sagittarius planets are all about love, laughter, and good times. Enjoy the good feelings!

Relationships

You certainly won't be bored this month, Aries. In fact, you may have more invitations and offers than you can accept. If you're not attached, someone with quite an interesting accent and several great stories to share will be along shortly. Whether or not you get involved is up to you, and you should definitely trust your antennae—but let's just say that things look pretty darned good.

Money and Success

If you're careful not to overspend around December 3 or 4, you could run into The Real Deal while you're out shopping. Don't take the first product that's offered to you. Ask a lot of questions and make sure you get the answers. If you've been pulling for a promotion at work that involves a long-distance move, hang on to your hat.

Planetary Hotspots

Startling Uranus in your own sign and your solar first house of personality and appearance will once again square off with intense, controlling Pluto this month, Aries. If matters between you and an authority figure seem to have gone as far as they can and you aren't willing to put up with the situation anymore, you'll be tempted to walk. Be sure you have other prospects before you do.

Rewarding Days
3, 4, 5, 12, 14, 21

Challenging Days
1, 15, 16, 19, 20, 24, 25

Aries Action Table

These dates reflect the best—but not the only—times for success and ease in these activities, according to your Sun sign.

	JAN	FEB	MAR	APR	MAY	JUN	JUL	AUG	SEP	OCT	NOV	DEC
Move	15			6, 9		18, 27						
Start a class					7, 12, 15, 28	6, 23					1, 16, 22, 27	8, 12, 14
Join a club	11, 30		5									1, 4, 20
Ask for a raise	7, 11, 12				24, 25				3, 15, 21			21, 25
Look for work			15, 16					15, 21, 25				
Get pro advice			13	2		8	8		3, 14			1, 20
Get a loan	11	24								14	6, 8, 9	
See a doctor			29						7, 17			20
Start a diet					2, 10							
End relationship						11, 12, 14		25, 26		11	12	
Buy clothes			18	26								
Get a makeover			20, 30				7	1		8, 27, 28		
New romance	8	14		25, 26			19, 24, 26	7–9, 12, 18	24, 29			
Vacation		26			6, 18, 24		13		13, 21		1, 13	

Taurus

The Bull
April 19 to May 20

♉

Element: Earth

Quality: Fixed

Polarity: Yin/feminine

Planetary Ruler: Venus

Meditation: I trust myself
and others

Gemstone: Emerald

Power Stones: Diamond, blue
lace agate, rose quartz

Key Phrase: I have

Glyph: Bull's head

Anatomy: Throat, neck

Color: Green

Animal: Cattle

Myths/Legends: Isis and Osiris,
Ceridwen, Bull of Minos

House: Second

Opposite Sign: Scorpio

Flower: Violet

Keyword: Conservation

The Taurus Personality

Your Strengths and Challenges

Well, Taurus, let's get right to the heart of the matter: that famous stubborn streak. It influences everything in every facet of your life, from work to relationships. There's just no denying it. You are as determined as the day is long, capable of focusing completely on what's important to you. So what's wrong with that? Your steady, grounded nature makes you a sought-after catch—romantically, professionally, and emotionally—because others come swiftly to realize that when you make a promise, you keep it, no matter what. If that's being stubborn, it's a shame more of us aren't. Okay, so you do occasionally get "stuck" in a situation that isn't good for you because you don't want to throw away the time, effort, or emotions you've invested. In your mind, holding on to what you've got is far better than risking it all to try something new. In other words, you believe that the devil you know is better than the one you've yet to meet.

That doesn't mean you're absolutely anti-change of any kind, however. If you see futility in a current circumstance, especially if you are losing more than you are gaining, you will put your foot down and walk away—permanently. There is no such thing as a second chance for you. If it didn't work once, it won't work twice. That solid, sensible approach to life in general makes you an excellent advisor and confidant and an even better long-term friend or partner.

Your Relationships

Speaking of relationships, let's talk about Venus, your ruling planet, who just so happens to be in charge of love, comfort, and money, all of which you, Taurus, absolutely must have to be truly happy. Venus's influence will simply not allow you to spend your time with those who do not pull their own weight in some way. You admire and respect commitment and a strong work ethic, and you tend to surround yourself with those who feel the same. You know what you're worth, and if others don't appreciate you, you're gone, especially with regard to acquaintances who have yet to prove themselves.

There is one exception to that rule, however, which only occurs when you meet someone who is just too physically delicious to ignore—someone you immediately want to call your own. Mercury may rule the senses in general, but Venus decides what makes each of them feel best—our appetites, that is. And since you folks are the undisputed Touch-Meisters—the most sensual, comfort-loving creatures on the planet—when you spot someone who arouses your urge to get up close and personal, sense and sensibility often fly out the window, much to the amazement of those who know you to be far more practical. The good news is that once you're attached to a partner, you stop looking. The tough part is allowing them to live their own lives. You like to take charge—and you're good at it, too—but that may be interpreted as possessiveness or excessive jealousy. Telling you to hold on with an open palm is impossible—but do try to let your partner make their own choices, for better or worse. After all, what you really want is someone as solid and sturdy as yourself, and that gift is earned most memorably through experience.

Your Career and Money

When it comes to work, Taurus, your affiliation with Venus often brings you to Venusian places and situations. Your knack for what looks like making money effortlessly makes you the perfect financial advisor, investment analyst, or banker, but if you tend more toward the aesthetic side of your ruling planet's territory, you may opt for a career in beauty, art, or music. Regardless of which you choose, you will throw yourself into it, full speed ahead, and not stop until you are firmly situated at the very top of your field. Once that's done, you'll set about expanding your assets according to a cautious, calculated plan that doesn't allow for backtracking or mistakes.

Giving up what you love and have worked hard to have is just about impossible, which often extends not just to savings, but to possessions as well. When you're trying to force yourself to let an object or attachment go, remember that getting rid of what has become obsolete creates space for something new and better—something you can proudly show off to envious others.

Your Lighter Side

Pleasure and creature comforts, Taurus—that's what life is all about for you. So ideally, your perfect situation includes the absolute fulfillment of all your senses. Good music, beautiful surroundings, and a physically desirable companion are the essential elements to total happiness—along with a nice, fat bank account to help you feel secure and allow you to live every day with a solid safety net in place.

Affirmation for the Year
*Allowing myself to change my belief system
helps me evolve into the person I really am.*

The Year Ahead for Taurus

You'll be dealing with change this year, Taurus, and while we all know that's not your favorite state of affairs, you may surprise even yourself with how well you cope—and actually flourish, as well. To start with, serious Saturn, the Cosmic Taskmaster, will continue on his journey through intense Scorpio and your solar seventh house of one-to-one relationships, pushing, prodding, and pulling until you pay attention to what's lacking in this tender department. Scorpio planets are relentless, so don't expect any problems that arise between you and your significant other to just go away. But whether it's a family member, a friend, or a partner, prepare to make a choice, and know that it's going to be permanent. In the meantime, do what you do best: evaluate the situation, assess the damage, and determine whether or not it's worth the time and energy you've already invested to stay put. If you can't honestly say it is, move on. Cut your losses and put your energy into situations that are positive, practical, and realistic.

The good news is that just about every outer planet will be on your side this year, providing you with opportunities to change not just the way you relate to others, but how you live your life as well. In particular, Pluto will turn your attention to The Big Picture, demanding that you dig deep into your beliefs and face facts. Are you really committed to the political party or religion you've been adhering to, or have you been sticking with it because it's how you were raised and what's familiar? Under Pluto's influence, what was once comfortable could now become obsolete, and you'll be just as adamant about defending your new positions as you were unwilling to even listen to opposing thoughts before. In the process, you'll encounter those who are far more in tune with you on a deeper, more meaningful level—and that's the only level you'll be willing to settle for.

Neptune's continued journey through your solar eleventh house of friendships puts this invisible but highly powerful energy in a position to subtly guide you toward friendships and group affiliations that are more appropriate for your long-term goals. Along the way, you may need to gradually let go of dear ones who no longer share your dreams—but don't worry. Neptune will provide you with faith for the future, and anyone who's worthy of your affection will be back once they've completed their own missions. In the meantime, let them go with your blessings.

Speaking of completing a mission, let's talk about Uranus, who'll stay on duty in your solar twelfth house of solitude and privacy throughout 2014. Now, Uranus is already quite impulsive, but he's currently wearing Aries, a sign that's known to be every bit as spontaneous and impetuous. This ultra-freedom-oriented energy will urge you to step back and make changes from behind the scenes on a deep, internal level. Just like Pluto, Uranus will challenge your beliefs, and you may make some extremely sudden decisions to ensure that your lifestyle reflects The Real You. The good news is that you won't be bored. Wherever Uranus is, it's impossible to remain in a rut, no matter how comfortable that rut happens to be.

Outgoing, benevolent Jupiter will spend half the year in your solar third house of conversation and communications, and from his position in instinctive Cancer, he will inspire you to make choices based on your gut feelings. You are a highly responsible sign and tend to follow the rules by which you were raised, but it's time to broaden your horizons, explore your options, and take risks. Fortunately, Jupiter will provide you with all the enthusiasm and optimism you'll need to get the job done. Once Jupiter enters fiery, fixed Leo and your solar fourth house of home, family affairs, and emotions on July 16, you'll be ready, willing, and able to incorporate those internal changes into your domestic life.

Fiery Mars will spend an unusually long time in Libra and your solar sixth house of work, routine, and health habits. On duty here until July 25, he'll push you to act impulsively, but planets in Libra live to restore balance. How to do that without ruffling any feathers? Impossible. Anything that's unfair or unjust about your current work situation simply won't do, and arguments over major issues could come up with coworkers. If you've done all you can to smooth them over and keep things on an even keel, consider that you may have stayed put long enough in a no-win situation, and prepare yourself for the possibility that one day, you may simply walk out. Mars gives us initiative, so you may also start a business or end a work-related relationship, especially if you've been putting in more than you've been getting back.

Healthwise, if you're looking to quit a bad habit, you'll be able to do it cold turkey, and as stubborn as you are, it will take. Just don't start any habits now that aren't healthy—because those will take, too!

What This Year's Eclipses Mean for You

There will be four eclipses this year, Taurus—two solar and two lunar. Solar Eclipses are high-energy New Moons that herald new beginnings. Lunar Eclipses are potent Full Moons that put the Sun and Moon on opposite sides of an issue and often bring power struggles or tugs-of-war into our lives.

The first will occur on April 15, a Lunar Eclipse in partner-oriented Libra and your solar sixth house of work and coworkers. This could mean you're ready to take on a business partner, or that you're suddenly part of an on-the-job team. You may decide to pursue a business with your significant other, too. The balance-oriented nature of Libra will insist that you incorporate cooperation, compromise, and equality into all your work-related relationships.

Then, on April 29, the first Solar Eclipse of the year will arrive in your own sign, activating your solar first house of personality and appearance. This meeting of the Sun and Moon will urge you to hold on to what's dear—and that most certainly includes your significant other, best friends, and family members. If any of these important relationships has been undergoing a testing period, you will need to make a final decision now. Hang tough or let go? Only you can decide, and you'll be equally committed to either course of action. Take all the time you need to arrive at a decision you're comfortable with. This eclipse involves fixed signs, and they play for keeps. Don't be rushed into premature judgment by someone else's agenda.

The second Lunar Eclipse will occur in me-first Aries on October 8. This time, your solar twelfth house of Privacy, Please will play host to the Moon, and your solar sixth house of work will hold the Sun. If you felt pulled in two directions during April, circumstances will arise now that are quite similar. The only difference is that now you'll be willing to stand alone if necessary, even if it means estranging yourself from others. If someone you care for quite deeply doesn't understand your need for solitude or privacy, you'll be moved to bring the situation to an end, and it will be permanent.

The last eclipse of the year will arrive on October 23, a Solar Eclipse that's all done up in sexy Scorpio. This meeting of the Sun and Moon will occur in your solar seventh house of one-to-one relationships, demanding that you take all your encounters to a deeper, more meaningful level. If you're getting the intensity you need, you'll be satisfied. If not, you'll experience the uncharacteristic urge to ditch the whole thing and move on. This is a time of closure, so you may also put an end to a relationship that has been long and difficult. No matter how tough the going gets, remember that Scorpio is Pluto's agent, and Pluto never leaves a void in our lives for long.

Saturn

If you were born between April 11 and 21, your Sun will receive a visit from Saturn this year, from his spot in your solar seventh house of one-to-one relationships. Now, from this spot, Saturn will influence all your vis-à-vis encounters, no matter how casual, but he'll turn his focus most especially on whomever you think of as "yours." It doesn't matter whether it's a family member, best friend, or romantic partner. If you use the word "my" before you describe the person, that's a relationship that will probably undergo a testing period this year. Those that last will be tougher, stronger, and far more committed. Those that end were simply no longer useful to you. Saturn doesn't remove what's working, only what's holding us back, and while it's not your style to throw your hands up and walk away, change is sometimes inevitable. If you've officially had it, don't think about ending the relationship as "quitting." Think of it as quitting while you're ahead. Take comfort in the knowledge that you've done everything you can, then move on and don't look back.

If you're single and looking, you may be drawn toward someone substantially older or younger than yourself, or from an entirely different walk of life. You may also become involved with someone whose lifestyle or geographic location makes it hard for the two of you to spend time together. One way or the other, there will be roadblocks, but again, this planet just loves to test us. If you decide the person is worthy of the effort, you'll be determined to make a commitment, and you'll do everything you can to keep your promise.

Uranus

If you were born between April 29 and May 8, this startling planet has been on duty in your solar twelfth house for several years. Now, this place deals with secrets, but it's also where we keep the side of us that only comes out when we're completely alone or in the company of someone we trust implicitly. With Uranus in this private spot, you have probably been privy to more than one juicy bit of gossip lately, but you may also have been the subject of gossip or scandal yourself. It's important that you not react to what's being said by retreating for an extended period of time. You will definitely need privacy frequently during this transit, if for no other reason than to relax, let loose, and forget about what the neighbors think, and you should take that time alone. The good news is that Uranus brings along awakenings, so you'll find that your greatest "aha" moments will occur more often now when you're feeling safe and sheltered, far from the maddening crowds. Uranus's affinity with computers means that you'll probably spend a fair amount of time home alone on the computer, and again, the motivation could be secret. Be careful not to become involved in clandestine online relationships that could threaten the security of the life you've built. Have some fun with this energy instead. An online alias will allow you to express yourself freely but still maintain your anonymity.

Neptune

If you were born between April 23 and 28, the lovely lady Neptune has been holding court in your solar eleventh house of groups, friendships, and social acquaintances since 2012. Over the course of this time, your choice in what you consider kindred spirits has already begun changing, but this year, Neptune will make contact with your Sun, a far more personal astrological encounter. Friends you have known forever may slowly disappear from your life, a little at a time, and while it's okay to miss them, don't try to hold on. Anyone who leaves your life now will likely do so on positive terms, and chances are good they'll be back. Neptune's mission is to subtly guide you toward a more spiritual, religious, or metaphysical peer group so that you can find your true calling. Group meditation, yoga, or Wicca may call to you, and you'll want to be with those who share your beliefs, not just your daily habits. You'll be willing to open up, so twelve-step groups aren't a bad idea, and volunteer work will appeal to you, too. As with all Neptune transits, it's important that you don't allow yourself to be taken advantage of. If you don't trust someone's motives, back off and let your intuition be your guide.

Pluto

If you were born between May 1 and 4, you have been hosting this potent planet in your solar ninth house of long-distance travel, education, and politics, but over the coming year, Pluto will directly contact your Sun. Since this is an easy trine, all the best of Pluto's gifts will come easily to you: determination, depth, and endurance in particular. Now, those are qualities you already possess by virtue of your earth-sign heritage, but with Pluto urging you on, you'll be unstoppable. Once you set your mind to any course of action, failure will absolutely not be an option. Your self-discipline and willpower will be running on high, so if you need to break unhealthy habits or start a new physical regime, this is a great time to do it. Taking that long-distance trip you've been putting off for years is another terrific idea. Separating yourself from the mundane and investigating different places, people, and ideas will broaden your perspective like nothing else now, and you'll undoubtedly emerge from the experience feeling renewed, rejuvenated, and restored. You may also become involved in politics, and the more strongly you feel about an issue, the harder you'll fight for it—or against it. As with all Pluto transits, the danger lies in the possibility of obsession, however, so if your loved ones begin to gently suggest that you might be a tad over-involved, listen up. Take a step back and examine your motives. Think of all possible outcomes. You're the proverbial force to be reckoned with right now. Aim this energy in a positive direction.

Taurus | January

Planetary Lightspots

A pack of planets moving through career-oriented Capricorn and your solar ninth house of long-distance relationships could put you in touch with someone from out of town who'll be only too happy to help you, Taurus—at least for as long as they're around. If you've been mooning over The One Who Got Away, stop mooning and call them.

Relationships

A tug of war between home-oriented Jupiter in Cancer and several planets in serious Capricorn could mean you'll be feeling quite torn at times this month, Taurus, between doing what your loved ones want you to do now and planning for their future. Only you can make the decision, but why not try a bit of juggling?

Money and Success

A New Moon in hard-working Capricorn on New Year's Day will get the show on the road for you, Taurus, especially with regard to career matters. With intense Pluto on duty in this same sign, however, your accomplishments may not arrive without a price. You may need to relocate or return to school. Be prepared to spend the month proving yourself—and to emerge victorious.

Planetary Hotspots

On January 16, the Full Moon in Cancer will join forces with loving Venus in an irritating square with passionate Mars, the stuff that "If you loved me, you would" syndrome is made of. Don't fall prey to anyone who's trying to rope you into doing their bidding by guilt, jealousy, or bribery.

Rewarding Days

10, 11, 17, 21, 23, 24

Challenging Days

1, 2, 8, 9, 16, 25, 26

Taurus | February

Planetary Lightspots

Your axis of home and career-related matters will be illuminated by a Full Moon on February 14, Taurus. Yep. Just in time for Valentine's Day. With the added influence of an easy trine between the Sun and red-hot Mars, passion of the nicest kind will be on tap—as long as you two can turn off your phones and get a sitter.

Relationships

Saturn has been on duty in your solar seventh house of one-to-one relationships for almost two years, Taurus, so you've probably gotten used to either being alone or carrying all the weight for your primary partner. This month, however, several planets in impulsive, freedom-loving Aquarius will insist that you take a stand and get yourself out from under it all.

Money and Success

Your own planet, Venus, is the ruler of not just love but also money, Taurus. You're quite susceptible to her moods, so seeing that she's on duty in hard-working Capricorn at the moment, you're probably putting your nose to the grindstone without any hesitation. Expect rewards to arrive around February 23 or 24.

Planetary Hotspots

When it comes to conflict, Taurus, your usual line of defense—and offense, for that matter—is to dig in your heels and cross your arms. You may not need to do that as much this month, but around February 19, a major work or money-oriented decision could force your hand. Don't hold back.

Rewarding Days

4, 9, 13, 14, 16, 20, 22, 23

Challenging Days

10, 11, 15, 18, 19, 25, 26, 27

Taurus | March

Planetary Lightspots

Your ruling planet, Venus herself, will set off for startling Aquarius and your solar tenth house of career matters on March 5, Taurus. She'll urge you to be a bit more daring at work and a lot more daring personally, but don't give in entirely. Remember, you still have to explain yourself to that image in the mirror every morning.

Relationships

The Full Moon due to occur on March 16 will illuminate your axis of friends and lovers. If you've been spending more time than usual with someone you usually only think of platonically, you might be surprised to learn that they're not on the same page. Surprise! Love often hides where we'd least expect it.

Money and Success

You'll have valuable allies on duty with regard to your professional life this month, Taurus—but they'll probably turn up in the oddest possible shapes and forms, and you'll be quite surprised by where you'll run across them, too. Your mission is to remember not to judge a book by its cover.

Planetary Hotspots

With the exception of arguments around March 11 or 29, Taurus, you should probably get through this month without blowing your cork. You may, however, feel a bit restless. Isn't it time for you to take a vacation? Even if it's just a long weekend, indulge yourself, and don't you dare answer the phone if it's work calling!

Rewarding Days

1, 12, 13, 14, 18, 21, 22, 28

Challenging Days

9, 10, 11, 16, 29, 30

Taurus | April

Planetary Lightspots

There's been quite a bit of activity lately in your solar twelfth house of Privacy, Please. Now, if anyone understands the concept of sanctuary, it's you, Taurus, so you've probably been a bit off your game without it. By the end of the month, however, the astrological culprits will move on and you'll be able to withdraw and retreat for some much-needed solitude.

Relationships

A Lunar Eclipse in partner-oriented Libra on April 15 will make relationships a focus for many of us, Taurus, but along with a testy opposition between chatty Mercury and red-hot Mars the very next day, an argument over exactly what your responsibilities are—and aren't—on the job could be inevitable. The good news is that this issue really did need to come to the surface, and if you handle it well, your workload will lighten.

Money and Success

Opportunities to make contact with those who have already made it in your chosen field will be plentiful, Taurus, so don't turn down any invitations to attend group events, especially if they're being hosted by like-minded others. You'll find support and advice from sympathetic sources—and you may even find someone you're romantically interested in.

Planetary Hotspots

The Solar Eclipse on April 29 will occur in your very own sign, Taurus, and in your solar first house of personality and appearance. Together with an easy trine between communicative Mercury and sexy Pluto, this may be a very productive time. If you're interested in someone, you'll want to look and feel your best.

Rewarding Days

2, 5, 10, 11, 17, 18, 19, 25

Challenging Days

1, 7, 8, 14, 16, 21, 22, 23

Taurus | May

Planetary Lightspots

Now, this is the kind of astrological weather you can live with, Taurus! The Sun in your sign will set the stage for lots of recognition and more than a few added perks. And with mighty Jupiter on duty in your solar third house of conversation and communications, it's easy to see how you'll be able to make yourself heard, possibly for the first time in a long time.

Relationships

With serious Saturn on duty in your solar seventh house of one-to-one relationships for the past couple of years, Taurus, nothing's been easy in that life department. Well, relief is on the way. The Sun in your own sign will conspire with sexy Pluto on May 3 and mighty Jupiter on May 6 to see to it that at least one fortunate encounter comes along.

Money and Success

Fickle Mercury will move into his favorite sign on May 7—chatty, mischievous Gemini. This puts the Trickster in an excellent position to wreak havoc on your hard-won financial gains, Taurus, and to turn any effort to move ahead into a battle of wits. Fortunately, you'll be up for the challenge, but do be sure you've got expert witnesses to back you up.

Planetary Hotspots

If you feel that you've been caught up in an emotional crossfire around May 14, Taurus, don't worry that you've lost your mind, but do stay out of the line of fire. This thing has been silently brewing, and while not many folks have noticed, you certainly have. If you have to say goodbye—temporarily at least—well, then, that's what has to happen.

Rewarding Days

8, 9, 12, 15, 23, 24, 28

Challenging Days

2, 3, 10, 11, 14, 18

Taurus | June

Planetary Lightspots

June 4, 8, and 18 are tailor-made for you, Taurus. Your ruling planet, Venus, will make contact with Neptune, Pluto, and Jupiter, triggering all kinds of blessings in several areas of life. In particular, however, you might want to direct your thanks at siblings, neighbors, and those who have spoken up on your behalf.

Relationships

If you're still somehow miraculously single, Taurus, someone delicious who shares your belief system, values, and priorities could be along as soon as June 4 or 8. You may need to do a bit of finagling to get your schedules to work, but no one needs to tell you to keep at it. Your determination and patience will pay off.

Money and Success

If you're investing in a new business or considering striking out on your own, Taurus, this is definitely the month to pursue the funding you need. Your ruling planet, loving Venus, will make the job easy for you, increasing your charm and turning up the volume on that earthy, grounded quality that people—especially prospective lenders and investors—just love.

Planetary Hotspots

You're due for just one ripple this month, Taurus, and it will probably take the form of an argument with a coworker on June 14. The good news is that you have certainly paid your dues, so your position will be understood by the higher-ups. Your mission is to let go of any petty differences that may have fueled this thing.

Rewarding Days
4, 6, 8, 17, 18, 21, 29

Challenging Days
7, 12, 13, 14, 24, 25

Taurus | July

Planetary Lightspots

After three weeks of moving retrograde, thoughtful Mercury will turn direct on July 1, Taurus. He's been on duty in your solar second house of money matters for the duration, so more than one confusing or problematic financial issue has probably come up. The good news is it's time for it to be resolved. Look to July 13 for good news to arrive.

Relationships

Your relationships with siblings and neighbors will go quite well this month, Taurus, thanks to the Sun, Mercury, and benevolent Jupiter in nurturing Cancer. These three will see to it that you're able to finally see why others do what they do—and to be quite sympathetic to their problems as well.

Money and Success

Venus will bring you several chances to make money in odd or unusual ways this month, Taurus. Even if an offer doesn't sound like any job opportunity you've ever been presented with before, don't turn it down without a second look. One never knows where fame and fortune will come from, but coincidental encounters are often part of the story.

Planetary Hotspots

What we say we believe and what we truly believe are often two different things, Taurus. Whether we realize it or not, all that programming from childhood really does play a part in our team's colors. If you suddenly feel the need to at least investigate the other side's story with regard to a major issue—say, politics, religion, or education—don't resist.

Rewarding Days
7, 9, 10, 12, 13, 18, 20

Challenging Days
4, 8, 19, 22, 23, 24, 28, 29

Taurus | August

Planetary Lightspots

The New Moon of last month was in your solar fourth house of home, family, and domestic matters, Taurus, so a great deal of your time and energy has gone into keeping things running on an even keel. You'll have help with that mission this month on August 8 and 18, when what seemed like large problems can be solved without all that much fuss.

Relationships

Jupiter, Mercury, and Venus will join the Sun in your solar fourth house of home, family, and domestic matters this month, Taurus, urging you to use their Leonine energy to shine. That might mean it's time for you to take a leading role in the life of a child, or you might simply be in the mood to entertain at your place. Either way, Leo planets insist that you have fun!

Money and Success

It's time to listen to a family member or domestic partner who's been nagging at you to meet someone they're sure will be able to help you career-wise, Taurus. First of all, they may be right, but also, the Universe is in the mood to arrange fortunate encounters now. Don't look any gift horse in the face.

Planetary Hotspots

Like it or not, Taurus, we all have to step into the spotlight every now and then. The good news for you this month is that your personal spotlight will be operated by several planets in appreciative Leo and your solar fourth house of family members. Don't be afraid of the applause. You've certainly earned it.

Rewarding Days
8, 14, 16, 21, 24, 25

Challenging Days
1, 2, 17, 18, 26, 28, 29

Taurus | September

Planetary Lightspots

The Sun and loving Venus, your ruling planet, will spend most of the month in your solar fifth house of lovers, dealings with children, and creative moments, all done up in Virgo, your earth-sign cousin. On September 3 and 14, this pair will contact Pluto, who just so happens to be on duty in your solar ninth house of deeply held beliefs. If your work isn't in sync with your ideals, take a look around. Something better might be waiting for you to uncover it.

Relationships

It may be the end of summer, Taurus, but the fun is just beginning for you. If you're attached, you two should consider a spontaneous outdoor outing. Where have you always wanted to go together—and what's the holdup? Make plans to spend some quality time alone together. Yes, that means no phones and no kids.

Money and Success

Opportunities to rub elbows with those who can give you a leg up will arise all month, Taurus, but the most stable contact will probably occur on September 21. If you've been looking for a mentor or guru, let your intuition guide you. When fiery Mars enters your solar eighth house of joint resources on September 13, an old loan or dispute over inheritances could surface.

Planetary Hotspots

You do love your schedule, Taurus, and have never been fond of having it disrupted, especially if there's money involved. This month, however, you may need to deal with a bump in the road to success, especially around September 13, when chatty Mercury and impulsive Uranus team up with passionate Mars. Your mission is to keep quiet until you're sure of the facts.

Rewarding Days
2, 3, 5, 14, 15, 20, 21, 25

Challenging Days
6, 7, 9, 12, 13

Taurus | October

Planetary Lightspots

Mercury will turn retrograde on October 4, Taurus, and when he does, he'll be on duty in your solar seventh house of one-to-one relationships. Retrogrades are all about redoing things, so if you're single and someone from the past comes back into your life, you may be tempted to give it a second shot. Be sure you have new solutions to old problems.

Relationships

Your solar seventh house of one-to-one encounters will host Mercury this month, Taurus, and since he'll be moving in reverse from October 4 through October 25, it may be tough to get your schedule to work with your significant other's. If worse comes to worst, forget any fancy plans and resolve to meet up at your place. Peace and quiet isn't so bad, is it?

Money and Success

Last-minute emergencies could come up at work around October 8 or 11, Taurus, and you'll need to decide whether you can give up yet another evening to your job. The good news is that your efforts won't go unnoticed. The tough part will be explaining to your partner and family why you're missing dinner.

Planetary Hotspots

A Solar Eclipse in intense Scorpio and your solar seventh house of one-to-one relationships will occur on October 23, Taurus, a highly charged New Moon with enough energy to change any relationship at a moment's notice. Telling you to stay calm is impossible, but rehearsing what you want to say couldn't hurt, and might keep you from saying anything you'll regret.

Rewarding Days

5, 13, 14, 15, 26, 27, 28

Challenging Days

4, 7, 8, 16, 22, 23

Taurus | November

Planetary Lightspots

The Full Moon on November 6 will shine its light into your solar first house of personality and appearance, Taurus, urging you to take a good, long look at your lifestyle and, in particular, at how your habits are influencing your health. If you don't like what you see, it's time to make some plans. Quit smoking, go on a diet, or break out of a rut. It will all go easier if you have a companion, or at least someone to check in with on a daily basis.

Relationships

The Full Moon on November 6 will be in your sign, Taurus, but it will also activate your relationship axis, asking you to do a personal inventory. Think of everyone who's in your life right now, and decide who should stay and who should be gradually phased out. You've probably been thinking about this for a while, but it's time to put your silent plans into motion.

Money and Success

The Sun and Mercury will slip into your solar eighth house of joint resources on November 22 and 27, Taurus, all done up in generous Sagittarius. This sign loves to help but can't keep from going overboard, no matter what it's doing, so be warned. You may be asked to loan more than you comfortably can, but think before you do, and don't feel bad about refusing.

Planetary Hotspots

It's time for a serious heart-to-heart chat with a dear one, Taurus. You may give it a try on November 9 or 13, but if you've done all you can and they just won't listen, wash your hands of the situation. By the time November 18 rolls around, you'll have plenty of reasons to understand why it's best to back off and let them make their own mistakes.

Rewarding Days
1, 3, 6, 10, 17, 21

Challenging Days
8, 9, 12, 13, 18, 25, 26

Taurus | December

Planetary Lightspots

A series of lovely trines will occur this month, Taurus, between generous Jupiter and the Sun, Mercury, and Venus in Sagittarius in your solar eighth house of shared resources and intimate partners. With Jupiter in your solar fourth house of emotions, making all your feelings bigger than life, it will be impossible to resist the urge to get closer to a playmate. You might also devote a bit of time to going over your checking account.

Relationships

You've been dealing with serious Saturn in your solar seventh house of one-to-one relationships for two and a half years now, Taurus, and it probably hasn't been easy. Whoever left your life really did have to go, as you've no doubt already gathered. This could mark the beginning of a time of withdrawal for you, but don't run away from it. You need to rethink your relationship priorities.

Money and Success

The Full Moon in Gemini on December 6 will occur in your solar second house of money matters, Taurus, and could point to a need to gather some information for a financial matter. If you're applying for a loan, especially if it's related to a trip or a return to school, do it before December 23, when Saturn could make things a bit tougher for you.

Planetary Hotspots

Uranus and Pluto are at it again, forming yet another in a series of testy squares. These two superpowers will pit your solar twelfth house of Privacy, Please against your solar ninth house of politics, religion, and views on The Big Picture. Pluto demands time alone to brood before making decisions, so make a space in your schedule for a few minutes of meditation, and be sure to do it every day.

Rewarding Days

1, 3, 4, 5, 12, 14, 19, 27

Challenging Days

1, 6, 15, 20, 23, 24, 25

Taurus Action Table

These dates reflect the best—but not the only—times for success and ease in these activities, according to your Sun sign.

	JAN	FEB	MAR	APR	MAY	JUN	JUL	AUG	SEP	OCT	NOV	DEC
Move	1, 7, 11	14	1, 17, 22			18	18, 26	2, 18				
Start a class			28	24	28						1, 9	
Join a club	30		28								11	
Ask for a raise				17, 25	12					15		
Look for work			1, 2				12, 13	24, 25	24	16		
Get pro advice		24, 25	13	25	24							20
Get a loan	11	24						25	27			23, 25
See a doctor			3, 29									21
Start a diet	12			29							12, 18	
End relationship	25	19	11	16	2, 10	12		26		23		
Buy clothes							7				9	
Get a makeover				19, 23, 29								
New romance	11		16				8, 24		5, 14, 21	23	6	
Vacation	11, 12	24		17		13, 18					22	

Gemini

The Twins
May 20 to June 20

♊

Element: Air

Quality: Mutable

Polarity: Yang/masculine

Planetary Ruler: Mercury

Meditation: I explore my inner worlds

Gemstone: Tourmaline

Power Stones: Ametrine, citrine, emerald, spectrolite, agate

Key Phrase: I think

Glyph: Pillars of duality, the Twins

Anatomy: Shoulders, arms, hands, lungs, nervous system

Colors: Bright colors, orange, yellow, magenta

Animals: Monkeys, talking birds, flying insects

Myths/Legends: Peter Pan, Castor and Pollux

House: Third

Opposite Sign: Sagittarius

Flower: Lily of the valley

Keyword: Versatility

The Gemini Personality

Your Strengths and Challenges

Your ruling planet is Mercury, Gemini—which really explains a lot. He's the guy with the wings on his head and his feet (think "FTD logo"), known as the Messenger of the Gods, and those wings are the perfect equipment for a sign that loves to think on its feet—literally. It's no wonder you're a mental gymnast who also knows every shortcut in town. But Mercury is also known as the Trickster, so be honest—you certainly do love practical jokes, don't you? The only thing that might be more fun is being able to figure out someone else's trickery. That's why you love puzzles, word games, movies with twisty-turny plots, and intelligent conversation with quick-witted others, which you sometimes enjoy all at once! Mercury's jurisdiction over the five senses makes you the ultimate multitasker, able to do at least three things at once, and to get them all done, too. Well, unless you're distracted, which happens a lot, and understandably so. Every single message every one of your senses sends you is equally fascinating. The good news is that you absolutely do not ever miss a trick, so someone trying to pull the wool over your eyes—at any time, on any subject—truly has their work cut out for them. You won't be satisfied until you have all the details right where you want them—right on the tip of your tongue, ready to be shared with the next lucky person you decide to charmingly chat up. And with you, Gemini, there's always a whole lotta chattin' goin' on.

Your Relationships

As fond of new information and constant movement as you are, Gemini, you are undeniably the perfect playmate and the life of every party. This knack for making everything fun makes you quite the sought-after guest and keeps your social life full, which is just how you like it. A constant parade of interesting friends of any age or affiliation and either sex keeps your mind fed, so naturally, you just love meeting new people. Yes, you are quite the social butterfly, and a charming companion, too. Your only requirement is that whomever you choose to share your time with can never, ever bore you. That's the one thing your otherwise incredibly adaptable sign absolutely can't tolerate. That need to be intellectually stimulated at all times is tough for just one person to pull off—hence your attitude about monogamy, which you tend to avoid at all costs, unless and until you meet up with someone you see as nonstop fascinating. You tend to be drawn to the other air signs (Libra and Aquarius), since communication is their specialty, too. Librans, who are every bit as chatty as you, and Aquarians, whose favorite word is "interesting," often make the perfect mates, but your opposite sign, fiery Sagittarius, is also right at the top of the list, with a curiosity and thirst for new experiences that rival your own. Virgos can be fun, too—at first, anyway, until they start editing over your shoulder and asking you to get to the point of a juicy story with tons of delicious tidbits. You were gifted with an everlasting fascination for every facet of life. No matter whom you choose to share yours with, be sure they can keep up!

Your Career and Money

Mercury's influence makes you a skilled and tireless communicator, Gemini, so you are often drawn to careers that allow you to talk or write. Whether you do that one on one, with a group of coworkers, or by sharing your views onstage with an audience really doesn't matter. The important thing is that your innate restlessness needs to be fed if you're going to stay interested long enough to complete any task. You adore working on computers, too—just as long as yours is absolutely the fastest available at the moment. Your fondness for movement and natural ability to find shortcuts make you the perfect candidate for the travel business, too.

Financially speaking, you tend to be a tad on the impulsive side (mostly for entertainment reasons, but you also have quite the selection of gadgets), and since you aren't fond of tedious tasks, your bank account may leave a bit to be desired. Even if money matters aren't well organized, however, the fact remains that you are quick-witted and resourceful enough to always come up with a brilliant plan to find the cash you need to trade for the experience you want.

Your Lighter Side

Everyone loves to play, Gemini, but few signs are as good at it as you are. To keep your mind well oiled, you often turn to puzzles, word problems, and lively banter with friends. You're also quite fond of movement in general, so dancing, gymnastics, and socializing make you happy, with the added bonus of making you tired long enough to keep your body and brain still for a few well-needed hours of rest.

Affirmation for the Year

Knowing what matters is the first step toward having it.

The Year Ahead for Gemini

Fiery Mars will keep you busy from January until July 25, Gemini, but chances are good that you'll love every passionate, exhausting minute. This energetic planet will be on duty in partner-oriented Libra and your solar fifth house of love affairs, recreation, and activities with children for the duration of this unusually long transit. Now, Mars is nothing if not impulsive, so you'll want to forget about anything even remotely resembling work and live life to its fullest—with one special person by your side. If you're single, however, that may not be the case for long. Your social calendar will be jammed with all kinds of invitations and offers, so you'll have plenty of opportunities to meet new admirers. Oh, and during April, the Lunar Eclipse in this same relationship-loving sign will flip a switch, so you may run across them under unusual or supposedly "coincidental" circumstances. Of course, Mars is as easily bored as you are, believe it or not, so you may go through prospective partners quickly. What you'll really be after is excitement, and you'll have it. Mars brings one adrenaline rush after another, but if he's operating from your house of lovers, how bad can it be? Well, remember that this fiery planet loves to stir the pot, so you may be more argumentative and assertive than usual. While you're interviewing prospective lovers, someone who's always been a worthy adversary may also catch your eye.

Now, let's talk about everybody's favorite planet, good old Uncle Jupiter, the heavens' answer to Santa Claus. This fun-loving, gener- ous—okay, and extremely excessive—planet will spend the first half of 2014 in home-oriented Cancer and your solar second house of finances and money matters. You may decide to dig in to your piggy bank to invest in a new home or to expand some facet of your domes- tic life. Another child? A new pet? A marriage or new live-in partner? Maybe. You might also add on to your current residence. Jupiter just loves travel, too, so if you're ready to move, it could be another state, coast, or even country you'll consider. If you stay put, your home will be a source of great comfort for you, and you'll appreciate family and children even more than before. This can be a truly positive time, with windfalls arriving from out of the blue. Still, remember the excessive side of this planet. Don't spend money you really don't have or over-extend your credit.

On July 16, Jupiter will enter entertaining Leo, a fire sign you've always enjoyed. He'll set up shop in your solar third house of communications and conversations, and since you're already quite the talker, there'll be a whole lotta chattin' goin' on for the next year. If you're a teacher, your dealings with students, especially children, will be especially rewarding, and it won't be hard to keep their attention. In this dramatic sign, you'll be the star of the show whenever you utter a sound, and that could be great fun, but that spotlight could also work against you. Be careful not to say too much about your private life or indulge in idle gossip. Secrets are tough to keep when Jupiter is in the neighborhood. Of course, there are lots of ways to communicate. If you're a writer, this is a great time to pour all that energy into a book, or if you've thought about acting, joining a local theater group now would be a terrific way to put this playful energy to positive, productive use.

Saturn will spend yet another year in your solar sixth house, insisting that you tend carefully to work and health-related matters. This planet is a strict taskmaster, and your daily schedule will continue to include an awful lot of responsibilities, which could lead to stress, so you'll need to find a way to fit in some exercise to work off that energy. Saturn loves structure, however, so once you commit to a regime, he'll help you to keep at it, and your determination to stick to a diet or quit a bad habit will be quite intense.

Unpredictable Uranus will continue on his path through impulsive Aries and your solar eleventh house of friendships and group affiliations. You may be put in charge of a group situation quite suddenly, but you'll love every minute. Your natural ability to mingle, network, and socialize will be running on high, so there will likely be lots of new, interesting, and "different" individuals in your life. Remember, however, that new friends who enter your life now may not be permanent fixtures. Uranus sends his "representatives" into our lives to deliver a message or make a point, usually about personal freedom and independence. Once their job is done, they may be on their merry way, off to inspire someone else. It's definitely time to hold on with an open hand.

Neptune's continued presence in your solar tenth house of career and reputation may inspire you to follow your true calling, possibly through religious, spiritual, or metaphysical work, but this planet often lulls us into believing we already have what we want. In short, don't quit your day job until you're sure your new vocation can produce the income you need.

Intense Pluto will stay put in your solar eighth house, and dealings with intimate partners, joint resources, and debts or inheritances may take up a great deal of your time and energy. Pluto's "mutual reception" with serious Saturn could mean you'll be dealing with courts or authority figures, and if that's the case, you'll need to be completely honest and act with integrity at all times. This team demands that you take responsibility, but once that's done, you'll have exactly what you deserve.

What This Year's Eclipses Mean for You

Four eclipses will occur in 2014, Gemini. Two will occur in April and two in October. Solar Eclipses are high-energy New Moons with potent transformational potential. Lunar Eclipses put the Sun and Moon opposite in an equally powerful Full Moon, and tend to act out through relationships or emotional tugs of war. So when the first Lunar Eclipse arrives on April 15 in partner-oriented Libra and your solar fifth house of lovers, creativity, fun, and dealings with children, you can expect some excitement. Libra's love of one-to-one relationships could mean it's time for a new love, and if so, the Sun in your solar eleventh house of friendships may point to someone you've known for some time. Feelings you've been harboring for that person may demand to be expressed, or you may be startled by a revelation of affection from someone you hadn't ever thought of romantically. Whatever you do creatively will go best if you do it with a partner, and you won't want to socialize without a companion.

When the Solar Eclipse of April 29 arrives in earthy, sensual Taurus and your solar twelfth house of secrets and Privacy, Please, you may decide to withdraw—but chances are good you won't be spending much time alone. Someone sensual and delicious who has recently caught your eye will likely be a frequent behind-the-scenes companion. If you're attached and seeing someone on the side, be careful, and think about the consequences of your actions. If you're single—well, this could most definitely be Stage Two of the delightful flirtation the Lunar Eclipse inspired back on April 15.

On October 8, a second Lunar Eclipse, this one in passionate Aries, will get the show on the road in your solar eleventh house of groups and friendships, once again linking this house with your house of lovers. Just as was the case back in April, someone from one of these life areas may change sides. Then again, Aries loves to be in charge, so you may be offered the reins to a group that has recently lost a leader, or you may lead the charge to oust someone who's using their power and control unfairly. Either way, be sure not to get too fond of that control yourself!

On October 23, the final Solar Eclipse of the year will occur via a high-energy New Moon in Scorpio. While this lunation will go to work invisibly to wake you up in your solar sixth house of work, it will also activate your solar twelfth house of secrets, and you may feel as though you're living an instant replay of April's events. It's time to let the world know what you've been tending to behind the scenes and to call on favors you've earned from coworkers. Pull a few strings if you need to.

Saturn

If you were born between May 10 and 21, Saturn will spend the year aspecting your Sun from his spot in your solar sixth house of work and health matters, Gemini. Now, Saturn is a serious planet, and his visits aren't known for being fun-filled, but his job is to test your existing structures, point out what's wrong, and force you to make changes. Healthwise, this would be a great time to take stock of how your daily habits are affecting your lifestyle. If you need to cut back, diet, or quit a negative habit, this is the time to do it. On the job-related front, you may find that you've just about had it with someone who is over-bearing, especially if they've been shirking their responsibilities and handing them over to you. In that case, Saturn will urge you to move on, but remember, this planet loves nothing more than preparation. Don't make a move until you know you've covered all your bases and have a definite new employment situation ready.

Fortunately, Pluto in your solar eighth house of joint resources will be locked into a powerful but cooperative relationship (called "mutual reception") with Saturn this year, so if you feel taken advantage of or misused by an employer or coworker, you'll be more than well equipped to deal with them appropriately. It may mean a long battle (perhaps even a long legal battle), but in the end, you will have your due—and so will they.

Uranus

If you were born between May 30 and June 7, you'll get a wonderful, stimulating boost from startling Uranus this year, Gemini. This unpredictable planet will stay on duty in impulsive Aries and your solar eleventh house of group affiliations, friendships, and future goals all during 2014, forming a fun, easy sextile to your Sun. Now, sextiles cause planets to "fall in love." As curious, lighthearted, and changeable as your Sun is, then, imagine how much you'll adore this visit from a planet so fond of surprises. Speaking of surprises, expect lots of them to come your way. You may have sudden, "coincidental" meetings with others who'll end up inspiring you, by their example, to change your life for the better. Or you may bump into a long-lost loved one at the grocery store, or find the perfect pet right outside your door. It's all possible now, so keep your eyes open and your wits sharp. Most importantly, you'll be moved to take action as soon as you're motivated, and the way you'll tackle problems will be nothing less than innovative. Anything that seemed unsolvable in the past will suddenly be a lot less intimidating as you come to realize that what you said you'd never do was exactly what you knew you had to do. Let go of "shoulds" and "coulds" and go with your heart.

Neptune

If you were born between May 24 and 29, your Sun is currently being squared by Neptune from her spot in your solar tenth house of professional matters. The woozy, dreamy nature of this planet is often underestimated, but that doesn't mean her influence on you will be any less powerful. Neptune's passage through this career-oriented house is a time of spiritual awakening, when we come to realize that the path we're on either benefits the larger whole or doesn't. If it doesn't, Neptune will do her best to silently remove any structures that are keeping you away from your true calling in life. Along the way, you can expect to be pulled toward spiritual, metaphysical, and religious groups, and there is a great deal to be learned from them. The danger is that you may become so taken up with devoting your life to your cause that you forget about your own personal needs, as reflected by the Sun. Your compassion and empathy for all living creatures will be running on high. Use your intuition to find a realistic way to make those feelings work for you, and don't quit your day job to become an artist until you've made a solid name for yourself.

Pluto

If you were born between May 29 and June 4, you are due for quite the reality check, Gemini, courtesy of intense Pluto in your solar eighth house of intimate partners and joint finances. Not to worry, however. Pluto's mission is to get your attention and compel you to take a good, hard look at what really matters. In the process, he may pry away anything that doesn't matter, but the good news is that this planet temporarily affords us with a "superpower" of sorts: the ability to hear what isn't being heard, see what isn't obvious, and understand the true motivations of others. So you might expect to operate as a detective, analyst, and accountant this year—on your own behalf. If there's anything unsavory going on within an intimate partnership, you'll smell it a mile away and end the situation. Anyone who tries to take advantage of you or yours financially will have a war on their hands, and you'll fight for as long as it takes to set things right. You'll have what you deserve once the dust settles, along with a keen eye to spot similar situations in the future and nip them in the bud.

Now, Pluto is quite fond of the eighth house. This is his natural territory, and when he's "at home," his energy is quite potent. Pluto rules The Inevitable. He's in charge of all those topics that aren't well suited to the dinner table—and matters of life and/or death, too. He's an all-or-nothing kind of energy, and he'll be impossible to ignore. In fact, the more you try to pretend everything's just fine, the more ungently Pluto will force you to sit up and pay realistic attention. So, over the coming year, all your most personal relationships will come to the forefront of your life, for better or worse, as will matters of joint finances, inheritances, legacies, and loans. Do yourself a favor, and don't leave the details to others. Go over the fine print in all legal and financial matters personally, and make sure any difficult endings in personal relationships are overseen by unbiased, objective third parties.

Gemini | January

Planetary Lightspots

You always have been fond of Aquarius energy, haven't you, Gemini? Here, finally, is a sign you can relate to. Aquarius is every bit as curious as you, just as skilled on the computer, and a whole lotta fun to boot! So when your ruling planet, Mercury, passes into this cerebral cousin on January 11, the pace of life—and your favorite, conversations—will definitely pick up.

Relationships

There will be several tugs of war going on this month, Gemini, and while most of them will involve your axis of money matters, with four planets in your solar eighth house of shared finances, you may find yourself having more than one rather heated chat over What's Mine and What's Yours. If it's time to set stricter guidelines, look to January 11 to do it peacefully.

Money and Success

The Full Moon on January 15 in family-oriented Cancer will illuminate your axis of money matters, Gemini, and along with all those planets in Capricorn and your solar eighth house of shared resources, news about an ancient monetary dispute may surface. Your mission is to remain calm and unemotional, no matter what comes up. Generous Jupiter has your back, so not to worry.

Planetary Hotspots

A pack of planets in hard-working, ethical Capricorn has taken over your solar eighth house of joint finances and intimate encounters, Gemini, so expect to be ever so much more cautious than you usually are with regard to both. If you're ready to seal a deal, be sure to check with a seasoned pro around January 11, and get their take on the fine print.

Rewarding Days

6, 7, 11, 12, 17, 19, 24, 30

Challenging Days

1, 2, 3, 5, 16, 25

Gemini | February

Planetary Lightspots

You'll be in the mood for lively chatter, puzzles, and interesting new acquaintances around the Full Moon in Leo on February 14, Gemini. By all means, you really should indulge yourself. If you're single, one never knows who'll come along and peek over your shoulder with the answer to 23-Across, but they certainly won't be boring.

Relationships

All those planets in Aquarius and your solar ninth house of long-distance communications will no doubt inspire you to reach out to someone you haven't seen or heard from in far too long, Gemini. The good news is that they'll be just as happy as you are to finally reestablish contact. Check out social media if you can't find them.

Money and Success

No matter what type of business venture you're thinking of, Gemini, if you can possibly wait until February 24 to sign on the dotted line, you'll be using the combined energy of stable Saturn and Venus, the Goddess of Love and Money. Yes, this is definitely the team you want on board when you're making financial decisions. Stall if you need to, or bribe someone. (Just kidding.)

Planetary Hotspots

You and that certain higher-up you've been feeling repressed by are about to get into it, Gemini, and if they challenge you around February 11 or 19, you will need to decide whether to keep the peace or assert yourself. What a decision—especially since all those planets in Aquarius at the moment have never been fans of cowering or buckling to authority.

Rewarding Days

8, 9, 15, 16, 20, 22, 23, 24

Challenging Days

10, 11, 14, 18, 19, 25, 26, 28

Gemini | March

Planetary Lightspots

Your ruling planet, Mercury, started the month in a station, Gemini, which means he was virtually stopped in his tracks, and not transmitting at his usual mega-speeds. Around that time, you might find you're not getting the information you need, or that your plans for school or travel seem to have been waylaid by bureaucratic blunders. Be patient. Hold back for a week or so.

Relationships

On March 1, passionate Mars will stop to turn retrograde, Gemini, which is plenty of reason for many of us to spend the next few weeks revisiting a recent decision. In your case, however, he'll be in your solar fifth house of lovers, recreation, and encounters with kids, so if you don't have as much energy or initiative as usual when you're out playing, don't call in the medics.

Money and Success

The good news is that generous Jupiter is still holding court in your solar second house of finances, Gemini. The tough part will be deciding what to do with any little windfall that comes your way. Your first instinct will be to spend it on the family, but think about it. When was the last time you actually bought something for yourself—and your partner?

Planetary Hotspots

A Full Moon on March 16 in your solar fourth house of home and domestic matters will shine her light on a recent issue that your dear ones have been pouting over: you're working too much, at least for their tastes. Sit them down and have a chat—as only you can do. The good news is that the pressure at work is about to let up.

Rewarding Days

1, 2, 12, 13, 14, 18, 27, 28, 29

Challenging Days

10, 11, 15, 16, 17, 22, 23

Gemini | April

Planetary Lightspots

Friends, lovers, kids, and playmates. That's what the month looks like for you, Gemini, and as per usual, you'll love every minute of it. You may not be quite so amused if someone you're working with tries something you see as less than forthright around April 11, and you'd do well to wait it out.

Relationships

There will be conflict just about everywhere you look this month, Gemini, especially when it comes to moving forward and/or sitting tight because it's easier. You're usually pretty easygoing about relationships, but you may need to make a decision now, and it's going to be final—not to mention sudden.

Money and Success

Keep a very careful watch on your finances after April 5, Gemini. You already have risk-loving, extravagant Jupiter in your solar second house of finances, but once Venus takes off for woozy, dreamy Pisces on April 5, there'll be a little bit more water hovering around above you than you'd like. Your dreams will be quite prophetic, though—even your daydreams.

Planetary Hotspots

Several planets in Aries and your solar eleventh house of friendships and group affiliations will face off with aggressive Mars this month, who's still on duty in your solar fifth house of lovers. It seems apparent that dividing your time between your BFFs and your current flames may be a problem. Why not introduce them? This may not be the time, but if you must, try your luck on April 17.

Rewarding Days

2, 10, 11, 16, 17, 25, 26, 29, 30

Challenging Days

3, 14, 15, 21, 22, 23, 24

Gemini | May

Planetary Lightspots

Once your ruling planet, chatty Mercury, sets off for your own sign on May 7, Gemini, he'll be on duty where he just loves to be—in your solar first house of personality and appearance. Yes, you're talkative, and yes, you get on quite well with just about anybody from any walk of life, but your ability to reach across and touch someone will be truly amazing now.

Relationships

The New Moon in your sign and your solar first house of personality and appearance will arrive on May 28, Gemini, and with it, an urge to change the way you come off to others. If that means trimming down or quitting something that's not good for you, so much the better. Internally speaking, however, this is just the beginning.

Money and Success

You have another month or so until generous Jupiter leaves your solar second house of personal finances behind, Gemini. That might be a blessing, if you've been out of control and not sure how to tame your spending, but if things have been going well, don't let Jupiter get away without one last favor. On May 24, anything money-oriented you decide to do will probably go well. Write that down.

Planetary Hotspots

You haven't ever been known for being the jealous type, Gemini, so when the green-eyed monster attacks, you're often at a loss as to how to handle it. Well, prepare yourself, because one of those uncustomary bouts of jealousy might just rear its ugly little head on May 14, and together with the Full Moon that same day, you won't be playin'.

Rewarding Days

3, 6, 9, 12, 15, 16, 23, 24, 28

Challenging Days

2, 10, 11, 14, 18, 19

Gemini | June

Planetary Lightspots

With your ruling planet, Mercury, moving retrograde for most of the month, you'll be less than delighted with communications, short trips, and even the outcome of casual conversations. The good news is that once the Venus-Jupiter sextile arrives on June 18, you'll at least be able to laugh things off with a good friend.

Relationships

Prepare yourself, Gemini, because as of June 23, when Venus, the Goddess of Love, enters your sign and your solar first house of personality and appearance, you're going to turn into a veritable magnet for the attention of delicious new others. If you're single, think of this as a romantic buffet. If not, be gracious, but be firm.

Money and Success

You're one of the heavens' most famous geniuses, Gemini, along with startling Uranus, who inspires that trait. So on June 6, when the Sun in your sign forms an exciting sextile to Uranus, one never knows what new invention, innovation, or breakthrough you'll have. Do us all a favor and write it down before it disappears.

Planetary Hotspots

Your ruling planet, Mercury, the Messenger of the Gods, will turn retrograde on June 7, and from his spot in your solar second house of finances, he'll draw your attention toward taking care of outstanding money matters. The good news is that you may actually have had it with being nice to someone who has owed you a lot for far too long. If they haven't made any effort, it's time to crack that whip.

Rewarding Days
3, 4, 6, 17, 18, 28, 29

Challenging Days
7, 8, 12, 13, 14, 19, 24, 25

Gemini | July

Planetary Lightspots

Startling Uranus and intense Pluto are still going at it via their years-long square, which puts your solar eleventh house of friendships and groups at odds with your solar eighth house of intimate partners and joint resources. No, this wouldn't be a good time to lend money to a friend, Gemini, especially if it's not pocket change. Any urge to change The System from the roots up will be met with resistance, too. Take comfort in what's familiar.

Relationships

Red-hot Mars will spend one last month in your solar fifth house of lovers, Gemini, urging you to stalk over to yet another lovely new person and say hello. If you haven't met anyone exotic over the past seven months, this is prime time, so get dressed. If you have, don't stress about keeping them entertained. Turning the lights out will suit them just fine!

Money and Success

The Sun, Mercury, and Venus will all spend time in your solar second house of personal finances this month, Gemini, urging you to spend time, money, and resources on family matters and home and domestic situations. Expect something quite unpredictable to prompt you to drag out your plastic on July 8, 19, or 24. A scratch ticket—and I do mean *one*—might not be a bad idea on July 24. Windfalls are possible now, too.

Planetary Hotspots

Around July 4, 22, and 28, some arguments about What's Yours vs. What's Mine may come up, and if you're already splitting from someone you were living with or financially attached to, things could get quite contentious. Your mission is to hire a professional to see what you can't see in the fine print.

Rewarding Days

7, 12, 13, 30

Challenging Days

3, 4, 8, 18, 19, 22, 24, 28

Gemini | August

Planetary Lightspots

As of August 12, both loving Venus and generous Jupiter will be on duty in Leo and your solar third house of conversations and communications, Gemini. Now, these two planets are the heavens' most benevolent energies, and when they're together, anything is possible. If you're trying to talk someone into something, give it your best shot around August 18. Bet you won't fail.

Relationships

All those planets currently on duty in romantic Leo are currently holding court in your solar third house of communications, Gemini, making you even more charming than usual, and even more persuasive—which is kind of scary. Everyone knows you can talk anyone into anything, especially you. Be fair, though, and don't take advantage of anyone less cerebrally equipped.

Money and Success

Jupiter may have left your solar second house of personal finances behind as of last month, Gemini, but that doesn't mean the blessings he brought won't still be in effect. Look to August 1 for sudden news about a long-distance venture to bring a smile to your face. Relocating may be an issue now, but you'll be primed and ready to go!

Planetary Hotspots

Any planet that squares off with Uranus takes its life into its own hands, Gemini, so when Venus, the Goddess of Love, does just that on August 1, something major could happen to change your financial situation or your love life. Your mission is to remain calm and roll with the punches.

Rewarding Days
2, 3, 12, 15, 20, 21

Challenging Days
1, 7, 8, 18, 24, 25, 26, 29

Gemini | September

Planetary Lightspots

Libra and Virgo are the two signs most concerned with making nice, Virgo, and when planets in those signs affect us, we're equally inspired. So on September 2, when your ruling planet, chatty Mercury, heads off into balance-loving Libra, your willingness to compromise will be a thing of legends. And on September 5, when loving Venus heads off into precise Virgo and your solar fourth house of home, you'll want to devote all your energy to making yours the perfect family.

Relationships

Your ruling planet, Gemini, is in partner-loving Libra at the moment, and just about everyone you've crossed paths with has been terrific, talkative company. If you have somehow miraculously managed to stay single up until this point, Gemini, once the Sun and Venus enter your solar fifth house of lovers, on September 23 and 29, you should pay particular attention to someone who's really listening.

Money and Success

Venus, the Goddess of Love and Money, will spend most of the month in Virgo and your solar fourth house of home, emotions, and domestic situations, bringing her grace, tact, and discretion into all your dealings. If you're after a partnership or a loan to start a business, talk the situation over sometime between September 5 and 28.

Planetary Hotspots

The Full Moon on September 8 will occur in Pisces and your solar tenth house of career and authority figures, Gemini, but it will also activate your solar fourth house of home. You may feel as if you're being tugged in two directions now—at least two—but if you pay attention, you'll not only find a way to advance yourself, you'll also discover just how little time it takes to keep your loved ones happy. The secret is uninterrupted attention. A little beats none.

Rewarding Days

2, 3, 5, 11, 14, 21, 25

Challenging Days

6, 7, 8, 9, 13, 30

Gemini | October

Planetary Lightspots

If anyone adapts well to change, it's you, Gemini. So when loving Venus and the Sun take turns aspecting Uranus on October 7 and 11, you'll probably be better equipped than most to handle the pair. The thing is, oppositions tend to act out in our relationships, and in your case, that might mean deciding whether a friend is really a lover—or if a lover would make a better friend.

Relationships

The Sun and Venus are on duty in your solar fifth house of lovers at the moment, Gemini, and since they're all done up in charming Libra—well, let's just say there are worse fates. But on October 10, Mercury will reenter Libra in reverse, so even if you've been having the time of your life with a new flame, information could arrive that will cause you to rethink your relationship.

Money and Success

If you're in business with a partner, Gemini, or even if you're just contemplating it, you need to have that follow-up financial sit-down soon. Too many important details may have been missed, and this time, it would serve you well to hire a seasoned yet neutral professional to oversee the negotiations.

Planetary Hotspots

Getting Into It in your world means having an extremely heated yet intellectual debate, Gemini, and this month, the Universe seems to be setting you up for that possibility at least once. Prepare yourself for some fireworks, especially around October 15. The good news is that if you don't take yourself too seriously, you might end up laughing about it in the end.

Rewarding Days
5, 13, 14, 15, 25, 27, 28

Challenging Days
4, 6, 7, 11, 23, 26

Gemini | November

Planetary Lightspots

By the end of the month, a parade of planets will have assembled in lighthearted Sagittarius, your opposite but often favorite sign. They'll infiltrate your solar seventh house of one-to-one relationships, urging you to have some serious fun with an interesting playmate, and not to worry about the future. Don't listen to them. No one's saying you can't have fun, but don't forget about consequences.

Relationships

You may be a bit more willing to experiment with your partners later this month, Gemini. A pack of planets in devil-may-care Sagittarius will invade your solar seventh house of one-to-one relationships, urging you to boldly go where no one has gone before. That may mean you're suddenly interested in that exotic stranger with the sexy accent, but if you're happy with your current situation, behave yourself.

Money and Success

For the first half of the month, Venus will be on duty in Scorpio and your solar sixth house of work, Gemini. This ultra-charming energy will be a terrific asset for you, especially if you have been trying to wheedle your way into an interview for a better position. You may also decide it's time to take better care of your health. Start off slow with any exercise regime.

Planetary Hotspots

The New Moon in Sagittarius and your solar seventh house on November 22 will most definitely get the show on the road for you in terms of relationships, Gemini. New Moons bring beginnings, so this could be a really good time, especially if you're single. If you're not, prepare yourself for a major change with regard to at least one of your primary relationships.

Rewarding Days
1, 2, 3, 11, 17, 21, 27

Challenging Days
8, 9, 12, 13, 22, 26

Gemini | December

Planetary Lightspots

The Full Moon due on December 6 in your own sign will combine efforts with an easy trine between startling Uranus and curious Mercury in equally inquisitive Sagittarius. This team will undoubtedly inspire you to explore different ways of handling monogamy, Gemini, but you might also develop an interest in dealing with couples. Ready or not, it might be time to get that degree in counseling.

Relationships

All one-to-one encounters will take precedence in your life now, Gemini, and you might end up feeling as if you're missing out on something. That's quite common when planets in "Grass Is Greener" Sagittarius transit our solar seventh house of relationships, as they're doing in your chart. Your mission is to decide whether anything better really is out there.

Money and Success

With sociable Venus, the planetary holder of the purse strings, on duty in your solar seventh house of relationships, you'll be ready to pick up any tab to please your partner until December 10. At that point, she'll move into serious Capricorn and your solar eighth house of shared resources, loans, and debts, and you may need to pull back just a tad in the department of entertainment.

Planetary Hotspots

Once again, right around December 15, unpredictable Uranus will get into a testy, action-oriented square with intense Pluto. This clash of the astrological Titans will pit your solar eighth house of joint resources against your solar eleventh house of groups. What's possible? Well, with Uranus involved, just about anything, to be honest. You won't stand for being censored in any way, however, personally or with regard to your cause.

Rewarding Days

1, 4, 5, 12, 13, 14, 26, 27

Challenging Days

15, 16, 19, 20, 23, 24, 25

Gemini Action Table

These dates reflect the best—but not the only—times for success and ease in these activities, according to your Sun sign.

	JAN	FEB	MAR	APR	MAY	JUN	JUL	AUG	SEP	OCT	NOV	DEC
Move			16		9			15, 21, 25				
Start a class	11, 17, 19	28	14			6, 23		10				
Join a club	24								25	8, 11		
Ask for a raise		26			23–25			25				
Look for work		24, 25	13				20				18, 25	
Get pro advice		24				18						
Get a loan	15		28		24	8	12, 13	18	14, 21	26		1, 20
See a doctor				24, 25					21			
Start a diet	11, 12										18, 25	
End relationship	25, 26				2, 10	14, 15		26, 27			22	6
Buy clothes		26			28		18, 24					
Get a makeover							24					
New romance			22	17, 25			25		24	5, 15		6, 8, 14
Vacation		14, 16	14, 18, 28									

Cancer

The Crab
June 20 to July 22

Element: Water

Quality: Cardinal

Polarity: Yin/feminine

Planetary Ruler: The Moon

Meditation: I have faith in the promptings of my heart

Gemstone: Pearl

Power Stones: Moonstone, chrysocolla

Key Phrase: I feel

Glyph: Crab's claws

Anatomy: Stomach, breasts

Colors: Silver, pearl white

Animals: Crustaceans, cows, chickens

Myths/Legends: Hercules and the Crab, Asherah, Hecate

House: Fourth

Opposite Sign: Capricorn

Flower: Larkspur

Keyword: Receptivity

The Cancer Personality

Your Strengths and Challenges

Your planet is the Moon, Cancer, the Queen of Emotions herself. She waxes, wanes, disappears entirely every two weeks, then becomes the star of the show when she's full. So are you moody? Of course you are! It's your job. But while you may be changeable, just like the Moon, you're also quite predictable in the eyes of those few carefully selected others who are lucky enough to know you well. The energy of the Moon isn't as obvious as that of her partner, the Sun, but just like the ocean tides she controls, she's quietly powerful and a force to be reckoned with. Sound familiar? It should. When you're on a mission, especially if it involves nurturing, defending, or protecting a child or other loved one, you can be extremely intimidating. Whether you realize it or not, you exude a quiet power that's quite formidable—which might be why family members and even your kids will only push you so far.

Now, speaking of family, let's talk about home. Your symbol is the crab, a creature so cautious it carries its home with it wherever it goes, and so vulnerable its shell also doubles as protection. Similarly, your home is your sanctuary—your nest—and anyone or anything who lives under your roof can't help but feel safe there. But you also make it clear right from the git-go that your home is definitely your castle, and you are definitely King or Queen.

Your Relationships

When you love someone, Cancer, there's absolutely no way they can possibly miss it. You tend their wounds, listen to their problems, feed them comfort food, and always, always have their back. Anyone who enjoys that kind of treatment from you won't come by it easily, however. You are cautious and private, and you take your time getting to know others. If and when you let your guard down, it's a tremendous compliment. In exchange for all that, you ask only that you are respected and that your rules are obeyed in your home.

Your family members are nearest and dearest to your heart. They come before anyone or anything else. That goes double for your children, the light of your life. You treat your pets as kids, too, and lavish them with the same TLC your human children enjoy.

Now, your highly emotional nature means your feelings can easily be hurt, although often unintentionally. That's when you sidle off and disappear for a while to lick your wounds and "moon" over the offense. As you get older, you tend not to take everything quite so personally, but as a young adult, you are often extremely sensitive. In fact, it may take years for you to literally come out of your shell and give friendships or romance a try.

The Moon's influence also makes you quite instinctive, and you usually operate on feelings rather than facts, trusting your gut above all else. So while you're searching for your soul mate, you move quickly from one possible candidate to the next. Those keen antennae of yours tell you almost immediately whether or not there's a reason to stick around. Sturdy Taurus and responsible Capricorn often fit the bill just fine when it comes to long-term relationships, and you'll feel an instant bond with perceptive Scorpio and intuitive Pisces.

Your Career and Money

As home-oriented as you are, Cancer, your ideal job situation will always be working from home. But if that's not possible, you'll need to find a work environment that feels like home. In that case, you end up thinking of your coworkers as part of your extended family. Occupations that deal with real estate, children, or domestic situations are a nice fit for you, but you might also enjoy the food-service industry, especially if it's one of your own secret recipes that's served up. Financially speaking, as with many other areas of life, security is very important. Your home is precious to you, and you know the value of having a safety net in place to be sure you keep it. You have no problem putting money aside for a rainy day, and when you do pull out your wallet or credit card, it's usually because you've found The Real Deal—or because one of the kids has finally worn you down!

Your Lighter Side

Having your family and dearest friends over to your place is what you love best, Cancer, and if they're gathered cozily around the dinner table or in front of the fireplace, so much the better. Either way, you're a gracious and generous host. When you leave your nest in pursuit of some fun, it's often to share activities with your children.

Affirmation for the Year
I am solely in charge of my future.

The Year Ahead for Cancer

To start with, Cancer, let's talk about Jupiter, the heaven's answer to Santa Claus. This benevolent planet will continue on the trek he began late last June, and will spend the first half of 2014 in your very own sign and your solar first house of personality and appearance. You have been, and will continue to be, generous to a fault, and a bit on the ultra-excessive side at times, especially when home, family, or children are involved. Your dealings with these individuals will continue to be loving and warm, and they'll return your attention and affection many times over. Just be careful not to do too much for your loved ones. Remember, if they are not taking responsibility for themselves, you will not be doing them a favor by helping them to avoid the issue. A little "tough love" might be in order, but if you continue to give them your support even while you demand that they are accountable for their actions, you will truly be giving them a gift. You can pass along a bit of advice you've gleaned from similar experiences and offer to guide them through their troubles, but refuse to make decisions for them.

With Jupiter in this spot, you will also be feeling quite positive and optimistic about the future, which will make you a fun, easygoing companion others will want to have around. Expect your social calendar to expand in leaps and bounds, including encounters with new, interesting others, some of whom will no doubt be from another state, coast, or country, and all of whom will have exciting tales of their adventures to report. Long-distance travel with family or to visit your childhood home is also a possibility, and either will be truly emotionally rewarding.

On July 16, Jupiter will tap at the door of your solar second house of money, values, and personal resources, all done up in fiery, creative Leo. This will begin a year-long period of increased attention to your financial situation, and while Jupiter certainly does love to give, he also inspires us to be excessive—and Leo loves to show off. In short, it would be wise for you to resist the urge to make purchases or investments that aren't financially sound simply to impress someone with what you've got. Leo rules pride, which often goes before the fall, as they say. Don't let your pride harm your credit rating. Make careful purchases and even more cautious investments through trusted advisors. Remember, slow and steady wins the race.

Then there's Saturn, Jupiter's opposite planetary energy. Saturn is a taskmaster who is just as pessimistic and practical as Jupiter is optimistic and reckless. Saturn will hold court in Scorpio, a water-sign cousin, nicely balancing Jupiter's energy with a strong dose of practicality and personal responsibility. And since Saturn will do it all from his spot in your solar fifth house of lovers, you may decide that a casual relationship has evolved into something far more profound. In that case, taking the relationship a few steps toward monogamy may be on tap. The good news is that while Saturn has a reputation for withholding frivolities, he's equally well known for giving us what we've earned. So if you've invested time and energy into getting to know someone, you will be rewarded now with the knowledge that you can settle down with them without any worries. As with all situations in your life, however, you must trust your antennae, Cancer. After all, when have they ever let you down?

As unpredictable Uranus continues on his way through your solar tenth house of career, reputation, and dealings with authority, you may feel the urge to cut yourself loose from any occupation or public situation that makes you look bad or feel oppressed. This planet just loves to act suddenly, so while you may have been stewing over what to do for some time now, if and when you decide to make changes in this department, you'll do it quickly, and others probably won't see it coming. Uranus also rules sudden reversals, so before you leave a solid, secure position behind, be sure you might not have been better off to wait just a while. A promotion could be taking shape behind the scenes, and it would be a shame to lose that chance by being too impulsive.

Remember, too, that Uranus is currently working with Pluto, who'll turn up the depth and intensity in all your encounters from his spot in your solar seventh house of one-to-one relationships. These two in cahoots are a formidable pair, and they'll be causing quite a bit of stress between career matters and partnerships of all kinds. If your primary relationships become stretched to what seems like the breaking point, try to wait it out. This pair will keep the pressure on for several years, and if you give in and act too radically every time they hit, you'll be jeopardizing the security you've just recently found.

Dreamy Neptune in her favorite sign, Pisces, will spend yet another year in your solar ninth house of education, travel, and growth-oriented experiences. You will feel quite wistful and nostalgic for what you might have had "if only...." Don't give in to daydreaming about yesterday so much that you give up on today—and tomorrow. You are well equipped to put that vague wistfulness to work for you by listening to the voice of your subconscious and being realistic about what would really make you happy and fulfilled. Returning to school or taking a long-distance trip may be just the ticket to change your perspective and open your eyes to the full range of possibilities in your world.

Now, let's talk about fiery Mars, the ancient God of War, who'll be on duty in your solar fourth house of home and family matters until July 25. This assertive, aggressive guy usually zips through a sign in about six weeks, so during this extended visit he will insist that you act firmly and decisively in domestic situations, but all done up in balance-oriented Libra, he'll also make you far more willing to make a compromise—as long as it's fair and fast. Mars is confrontational, however, so you might also expect arguments and debates with children, family, and domestic partners to arise more frequently than in the past. Again, compromise is really the best way to go.

What This Year's Eclipses Mean for You

There will be four eclipses in 2014, Cancer. The first will occur on April 15, when a Lunar Eclipse activates your solar fourth house of home and family matters, wearing partner-oriented Libra. Along with Saturn's stabilizing transit of your solar fifth house of love affairs, this may be the time you decide to move in with someone, make a commitment, or even get married. Your partner may be substantially older or younger than you and may even be a higher-up or authority figure, but any age difference will be far less important than what the two of you share.

On April 29, a Solar Eclipse in solid, sturdy Taurus and your solar eleventh house of friendships and goals for the future will help you put together a five-year plan, and if you get to work on it now, it will eventually provide you with the grounded, secure lifestyle you have always craved. This lunation may also activate your solar fifth house of lovers, so someone you care for platonically may make it clear that they think of you as far more than a friend. On the other hand, you may decide that your current flame makes a better pal than partner.

The Lunar Eclipse on October 8 will light up your solar tenth house of career matters, reputation, and dealings with authority. It will occur in fiery, impulsive Aries and, together with startling Uranus's passage through the same sign and house, could mean you'll suddenly have the urge to walk out on a job situation you're not happy with. While hanging in there for even one more day may be tough once you've made your decision, give it a shot. Things change suddenly with eclipses, so you may be considered for a raise or promotion just as you've reached the end of your rope, especially if you've been working hard to impress the higher-ups.

The final eclipse of the year will be solar, occurring in detective-like Scorpio on October 23 in your solar fifth house of lovers. New information about your current flame or playmate could mean there's about to be a drastic change in your feelings. If you feel deceived or betrayed, you will take steps to end the situation, and you won't look back.

Saturn

Saturn will remain in Scorpio until December 23, and will influence your Sun directly during 2014 if you were born between July 9 and 22. The good news is that this transit will link Saturn with your Sun in an easy, positive trine, so you can expect to enjoy all the steadiness and quiet determination this planet provides. The best news is that Saturn will be operating on you from his spot in your solar fifth house of love affairs, recreational pursuits, and dealings with children. You may finally feel secure enough to take a formerly casual affair to a new, committed level, or you may meet someone you immediately know you can trust, who will easily draw you out of your shell.

If you have been pursuing a hobby that you would love to make your main source of income, this is a terrific time to put that process into motion. Beginning slowly, perhaps part-time at first while maintaining your current job, is the best way to accomplish these goals.

You may also feel financially secure enough to begin planning a family or welcome an addition to your current domestic situation. Either way, all your encounters with family members will take on a deeper, more respectful tone. Since you are so home-oriented, you may also decide to invest in a nest of your own. With Saturn operating as an astrological safety net, you will make rational, practical decisions and refuse to extend yourself further than you know you should. This is generally a time of peace, stability, and tranquility. Enjoy it!

Uranus

Expect to raise some eyebrows this year, especially if you were born between June 30 and July 9, when unpredictable Uranus will contact your Sun from his spot in your solar tenth house of career, reputation, and professional matters. This planet has absolutely no regard for rules and regulations and loves nothing more than rebelling against authority. In an action-oriented square with your Sun, Uranus will demand that you free yourself up from restrictive or stagnating career situations, and get out from under the thumb of authority figures you feel are trying to control you. The more repressed you feel, the more suddenly you'll take action.

The time period directly after this transit is often uncertain and unsettling, but carries with it a feeling of liberation. Your life may be a bit unstable for a while, but the personal freedom you'll regain will make it all worthwhile. You'll discover strengths you never knew you had, and be willing to experiment with occupations you'd never before considered. As a result, you'll emerge from this period feeling like you're an entirely new person.

Now, Uranus and Pluto are both all-or-nothing energies, and they'll be operating in concert this year. When both are affecting the Sun, the very core of our being, it's easy to shock others with sudden, drastic behaviors. If you've been at the end of your rope in a personal or professional situation, walking away may be the solution, but try to hold on long enough to come up with Plan B before you storm off into the sunset.

Neptune

If you were born between June 25 and 29, your Sun will enjoy a visit from Neptune during 2014 from her position in your solar ninth house of beliefs, education, and travel. Neptune's influence will be benevolent but easy to miss, since the aspect is an easy trine and Neptune operates virtually invisibly. Fortunately, you are quite an intuitive, instinctive creature, so you will notice her at work more easily than many of us might. The "symptoms" of this transit include an increased sensitivity to harsh sounds, bright lights, and negative situations. You'll find that your compassion for others is running on high, and you will need to retreat or withdraw often to recharge your psychic batteries. Neptune dissolves boundaries and turns us into psychic sponges, so it's important to only allow yourself external experiences that are positive. A terrific use of this transit is to investigate spiritual paths or become involved with meditation or metaphysical study groups. Traveling to water destinations is also favored, and you may even find yourself drawn to living on a lake or seacoast.

Pluto

If you were born between July 2 and 5, your Sun will be contacted by an opposition from Pluto during 2014. This aspect typically influences relationships in a very powerful way, and while chances are good you're well aware that something has been brewing, you can expect matters to come to a head. Now, one of Pluto's demands is closure and finality, so if you have been thinking of extricating yourself from an unproductive, unhealthy, or obsessive relationship, whether it is platonic, romantic, or professional, this is the time to do it. It may not be easy—in fact, it may be a tough process, especially if your affairs are tightly woven together— but it is a necessary one, and the relentless nature of Pluto won't let you rest until you've ended it. You need to regain control of your life. There is simply no two ways about it.

It's important to remember, however, that while you may feel a sense of loss for a while, once you have given in and let go of the past, Pluto always brings something new along—and it's usually a much better something. This planet rules the process of life, death, and rebirth, so acceptance of the inevitable and a determination to move forward will eventually put you on a much more positive path. Pluto's lessons are tough, but again, they're necessary. Cooperate, and you will assist the process, emerging stronger from the experience.

Of course, throughout the year, Pluto will remain in a square aspect to transiting Uranus, a testy relationship that could also bring change to your professional life quite abruptly. The good news is that squares demand action and change, so no matter what difficulties arise, you'll be willing to take matters into your own hands.

Cancer | January

Planetary Lightspots

Tensions between you and just about everyone close to you could be running high this month, Cancer, especially around the Full Moon in your own sign on January 15. You'll righteously assert yourself in all your encounters, possibly for the first time in a long time. Sounds like you're fed up and not willing to back down. Well, good for you! You've spent plenty of time worrying about others' feelings—but not enough time considering your own.

Relationships

Several planets in no-nonsense Capricorn will move through your solar seventh house this month, Cancer, and not one of them will allow you to hide what you're feeling from your partner. You might think you're doing a great job of keeping quiet, but your attitude will say it all. Why bother trying to hide it at all? Have a serious chat on January 7, when loving Venus and chatty Mercury will come together to help you say it nicely.

Money and Success

Business relationships will be passionate this month, and at times, it will be tough to find compromises. The thing is, compromise is the best way for you to get ahead right now. This isn't an impossible dilemma. Express yourself, but keep a cool head. Set up important meetings around January 11, when others will be more willing to negotiate.

Planetary Hotspots

Your feelings will be quite close to the surface this month, Cancer, and especially obvious to significant others and relatives. With fiery Mars on duty in your solar fourth house, one of the emotions you'll be expressing quite freely will likely be anger, at least around January 2, 8, and 16. If an elder family member seems to be trying to run your life, consider that it may only be out of genuine concern for you.

Rewarding Days
1, 10, 11, 12, 17, 23, 24

Challenging Days
2, 3, 4, 5, 8, 15, 16, 25

Cancer | February

Planetary Lightspots

If you've been looking for the right time to bring closure to an emotional situation in a caring, sympathetic way, Cancer, there's no finer time than February 24 to give it a shot. Loving Venus in your solar seventh house of one-to-one relationships will form an easy, productive bond with realistic, protective Saturn, ensuring that you're able to either let go or set down firm, non-negotiable ground rules.

Relationships

Valentine's Day will be an especially emotional day for you, Cancer. Your ruling planet, the emotional Moon, will reach her full stage on February 14, and as per usual, you'll react by wearing your heart on your sleeve. The good news is that an easy trine between the Sun and Mars will bring along passion, too—of the nicest kind.

Money and Success

Mercury will retrograde back into your solar eighth house of shared resources on February 12, Cancer, and until he turns direct on the last day of the month, you may find yourself quite consumed with taking care of business—for at least the second time. If paperwork has been confusing, incomplete, or even missing in action, this is your chance for a redo. Take advantage of it.

Planetary Hotspots

From February 5 through February 12, as thoughtful Mercury moves retrograde through Pisces and your solar ninth house of long-distance people and places, you may find yourself sighing and staring wistfully out the window. If you're distracted because you miss someone, it's time to restore contact—no matter what happened the last time you saw one another.

Rewarding Days

3, 4, 5, 14, 20, 22, 23, 24

Challenging Days

10, 11, 15, 18, 19, 25, 26

Cancer | March

Planetary Lightspots

There will be two New Moons this month, Cancer. The first will occur on March 1, all done up in Pisces. Your natural instinct will be added to by Pisces' gift of psychic intuition, so you really must trust your gut at this time. On March 30, a second New Moon will set up shop in fiery Aries and your solar tenth house of career matters, urging you to make a brand-new start. How about a home-based business?

Relationships

Far-off loved ones will once again be on your mind this month, Cancer, thanks to the Sun and thoughtful Mercury, who'll pass through your solar ninth house. You'll be especially nostalgic and sentimental around March 1, 22, and 28, and memories from childhood will definitely play a part in your decisions. Look to March 13 for an old flame to reach out, hoping for a second shot at the title.

Money and Success

You may need to break into your piggy bank this month, Cancer, for urgent or at least unexpected family matters—and it may not be for the first time. Passionate Mars will spend the month retrograding through your solar fourth house of home and domestic matters, turning up the thermostat on all your relationships with relatives and children. Make it clear that this is absolutely the last time.

Planetary Hotspots

You've spent a lot of time over the past few months making your position clear on the home front, Cancer, and some of it has gotten through. There may still be some misunderstanding about what you expect from anyone living under your roof, however—including your long-term lover—and it will need to be dealt with around March 11 or 29. You really can't back off now. Stick to your guns.

Rewarding Days

1, 3, 12, 13, 17, 22, 23, 28

Challenging Days

10, 11, 16, 20, 29, 30, 31

Cancer | April

Planetary Lightspots

Here's another passionate, high-activity month, Cancer, so if you're already feeling stressed, better double up on your vitamins and get yourself into an exercise regimen that will allow you to blow off some steam. You'll definitely need an outlet around April 15, when a Lunar Eclipse in partner-oriented Libra will activate a major tug of war between your house of home and your house of career matters.

Relationships

Several testy oppositions will occur this month, Cancer, and all of them will rock the main beams of your solar chart. Crises involving self-assertion, home-related issues, one-to-one relationships, and career matters will seem insurmountable at times, and you'll spend more than one sleepless night wondering what you did to cause this. Stop that. You're not on the planet alone, and you're not responsible for the actions of others.

Money and Success

The Sun and Mercury will join startling Uranus in impulsive Aries and your solar tenth house of higher-ups, urging you to rebel against any authority you see as stifling or restrictive. This may not do wonders for your relationship with your boss, and if you want to keep working, you'll have to smile, nod, and swallow your pride. It's time to intensify the job hunt. Seriously.

Planetary Hotspots

Uranus and Pluto have scheduled their latest battle for April 21, Cancer, pitting your solar seventh house of one-to-one relationships against your solar tenth house of career matters. You've been trying very hard to be good, and to cross your t's and dot your i's, but you may need to take a personal day to tend to a very personal matter. Don't feel bad about it. You're entitled to a life outside of work.

Rewarding Days

2, 17, 18, 19, 25, 26, 29

Challenging Days

1, 3, 8, 14, 16, 20, 21, 22, 23

Cancer | May

Planetary Lightspots

After all the conflicts you've had to deal with lately, Cancer, a little break in the action would be nice—and it's certainly not like you haven't earned it. Well, relief is on the way. An easy trine between Pluto and the Sun in Taurus on May 3 will give you a chance to catch your breath while someone else actually steps in to take charge, just when you're at the end of your rope.

Relationships

Jupiter is the heavens' version of Santa Claus, Cancer, and he's on duty now in your sign and your solar first house. You're in the mood to give, give, and give some more, and you've done your best to make everyone around you feel loved, appreciated, and cared for. Well, finally, at long last, someone will thank you for your efforts. Look to May 6 or 24 for a grateful hug and heartfelt gratitude.

Money and Success

Your personality will be your best asset this month, Cancer, as outgoing, positive Jupiter continues to pass out goodies from his spot in your solar first house. Whether you need a loan or just a few words of advice from someone more experienced, you'll have all the support you need—thanks to all the good things you've done for others in the past. See? Payback can be a good thing.

Planetary Hotspots

The New Moon on May 28 will occur in your solar twelfth house, Cancer, and since it's all done up in communicative Gemini, you may end up hearing some confidential information. What should you do about it? Trust your antennae. If you know there's someone out there who needs to hear the truth, so be it. If the news would be more hurtful than helpful, keep it to yourself.

Rewarding Days

3, 4, 6, 9, 15, 24, 25, 29

Challenging Days

1, 2, 10, 11, 14, 16, 18, 28

Cancer | June

Planetary Lightspots

Happy days are here again, Cancer. A New Moon in your sign on June 27 will bring the Sun together with your ruling planet, the Moon. For once, everyone out there will understand what it's like to be you—to be under the influence of this highly emotional energy. You'll be better able to deal with it than most of us, so while you'll definitely be amused by others' reactions, try not to gloat. Not too much, anyway.

Relationships

You've always been quite fond of Taurus, your earth-sign cousin, Cancer, so with loving Venus on duty in that solid, stable sign and your solar eleventh house for most of the month, it's a given you'll be feeling quite safe and secure in most of your friendships. If jealousy becomes an issue around June 12, it will be up to you to call a state-of-the-relationship meeting and settle your differences.

Money and Success

Taurus is a money magnet, Cancer, and with Venus in this sign and your solar eleventh house of groups, it's easy to see how making beneficial financial contacts will be easy for you this month. Your mission is to accept all invitations to mingle, even with competitors, especially around June 4, 8, and 18. Turn on the charm and listen closely to seemingly casual conversations.

Planetary Hotspots

Your ruling planet, the emotional Moon, will get into it with fiery Mars and unpredictable Uranus on June 7, Cancer, just as talkative, thoughtful Mercury stops to turn retrograde in your very own sign. Needless to say, the information you have at this time may not be entirely accurate, and you may not know the truth until July 1. In the meantime, don't say anything you might end up regretting.

Rewarding Days

3, 4, 6, 8, 18, 21, 27, 29

Challenging Days

7, 12, 14, 17, 19, 24, 25, 26

Cancer | July

Planetary Lightspots

The Full Moon on July 12 will occur in Capricorn and your solar seventh house of one-to-one encounters, Cancer, and as per the influence of this righteous sign, it will be tough for you to keep quiet if you see someone being unfairly held back from getting what they deserve. If it's you you're seeing as the victim, you'll be absolutely unstoppable until you have what you know you've earned.

Relationships

Your ruling planet is the emotional Moon, Cancer, and you're extremely susceptible to all her moods, so when she's full, your feelings are usually pretty darn tough to conceal. On July 12, then, when she arrives in her full glory in your solar seventh house of one-to-one relationships, whatever you've been mulling over will demand to be expressed. The good news is that since Full Moons are so fond of bringing matters to a head, you might decide to take your casual relationship one step closer to monogamy.

Money and Success

Your ruling planet, the Moon, will plant a creative seed in Leo and your solar second house of money matters on July 26, Cancer, and an opportunity to turn a hobby into a business could be along shortly. Your mission is to market yourself, which isn't always easy for you, but if you think of it as a way to finally make your living at home, you might be a better salesperson.

Planetary Hotspots

Mercury, Venus, and the Sun will take turns passing through your sign and your solar first house, Cancer, all of them determined to accentuate the positive qualities of your already emotional nature. The urge to care for, nurture, and protect those you love will be especially strong. Lucky them!

Rewarding Days
7, 13, 14, 18, 23, 25, 26

Challenging Days
3, 4, 8, 12, 19, 22, 24, 28

Cancer | August

Planetary Lightspots

A Full Moon on August 10 in your solar eighth house could activate a tug of war in your life, Cancer, and the subject will be money. Joint finances, inheritances, and unpaid or past-due loans could be involved, in which case you'll need to spend more time than you'd like untangling the details. But with Mercury on duty in your solar second house, you'll have plenty of energy to tackle the job.

Relationships

Sexy Mars in Scorpio set off for your solar fifth house just before the month began, Cancer, marking the beginning of an extremely passionate, intimate six weeks. If you've been seeing someone casually up until now, a handshake and a kiss goodnight might not cut it for much longer. It's time to find out what you two really have. Is it the stuff that long-term relationships are made of?

Money and Success

All those planets in creative Leo that are currently marching through your solar second house aren't in the mood to make money for anyone else right now, Cancer. In fact, they're not in the mood to deal with anyone's rules on the job, either. That will hold true in your life around August 1, 8, and 9, when startling Uranus will step in, urging you to strike out on your own and work for yourself, even if it's just part-time.

Planetary Hotspots

Red-hot Mars has tiptoed off into sexy, secretive Scorpio and your solar fifth house, Cancer, urging you to take a casual relationship to a whole new level. If you decide to share anything other than quality time alone with them, you'd better get all it all down in writing. You may be taken in by someone's slightly dangerous reputation, but before you hand over anything substantial, be sure that reputation hasn't been underplayed.

Rewarding Days
7, 8, 14, 15, 18, 21, 23

Challenging Days
9, 10, 19, 25, 26, 28, 29, 30

Cancer | September

Planetary Lightspots

We're due for a Full Moon on September 8, Cancer, and in your case, it will occur in your solar ninth house of education, politics, and religion. In short, all The Big Issues will be especially near and dear to your heart now, especially if they involve elders, kids, or animals. This is a terrific time to get involved with your favorite cause.

Relationships

Mars's continued presence in your solar fifth house will turn up the thermostat on all your encounters with casual lovers, playmates, and kids, Cancer. The good news is that there won't be an awful lot of drama this month in that department, and relationships should chug along at a sociable, if somewhat intense, pace. And with charming Venus in your solar third house, even if disputes arise, you'll be well equipped to manage them practically and efficiently.

Money and Success

After urging you to spend—and spend big—on anything that sounded like a fun time last month, loving Venus will enter discreet Virgo on September 5, a meticulous, discerning energy that will inspire you to not just cut back, but to count your pennies carefully. You probably need a few hours alone with your checkbook, and getting to know your credit card statement wouldn't be a bad idea, either.

Planetary Hotspots

On September 24, a New Moon will silently inspire you to start looking for a better domestic situation—one that's better suited to keeping everyone happy. If it's a move to a different school district or a better neighborhood you're after, a casual comment you make to an acquaintance that day could be the first step. Watch and see.

Rewarding Days

3, 4, 5, 10, 14, 15, 25

Challenging Days

8, 9, 12, 13, 20, 21, 22, 29

Cancer | October

Planetary Lightspots

Mercury will back up into your solar fourth house on October 10, Cancer, and right up until he turns direct there on October 25, you'll have a second chance to make things right between you and a family member you've been at odds with lately. The problem may be that you simply haven't had any quiet time alone together to talk things over. Well, there's no time like the present, is there?

Relationships

With Venus, the Goddess of Love, all done up in her most charming Libran outfit and passing through your solar fourth house, your encounters with relatives, kids, and friends you think of as family will go along quite smoothly. In fact, if you need to make amends, this would be a great time to extend your hand. It may take a while, but your efforts will eventually restore your relationship to its former closeness.

Money and Success

A generous coworker you've always been fond of will step up on your behalf around October 5, Cancer, and won't be shy about touting your virtues to anyone in authority who'll listen. You probably won't hear about it right away, and when you do, you'll wonder what you did to deserve this, but not to worry. You'll get an earful from them shortly—especially if the higher-ups aren't quick enough to reward you.

Planetary Hotspots

There will be two eclipses this month, Cancer. The first will occur on October 8 in your solar tenth house of authority, joined by a testy square between Venus and intense Pluto. You may need to sit down with children to explain why privileges have been taken away, or with a partner to discuss changing financial agreements. Don't let these issues slide. Eclipses don't fool around.

Rewarding Days
5, 6, 13, 14, 15, 23, 27, 28

Challenging Days
3, 4, 7, 8, 11, 16, 24, 26

Cancer | November

Planetary Lightspots

The heavens have a distinctly Plutonian flavor to them at the moment, Cancer, thanks to the Sun, Venus, and Mercury in Scorpio, all of which will bump into Saturn in that same intense sign. With Pluto himself on duty in your solar seventh house of one-to-one relationships, you've been a bit more likely to blow emotional situations out of proportion, but the real danger now is obsession. Watch for signs that one or both of you is far too focused on the other.

Relationships

Two days that could be very difficult for you and your current flame are scheduled this month, Cancer, so be on guard against inciting an already volatile situation. On November 10, aggressive Mars will collide with intense Pluto in your solar seventh house, urging you to do whatever it takes to make your point to your partner—including cutting them entirely out of your life. Similar circumstances may arise on November 18 or 25, and you'll be even less likely to compromise.

Money and Success

Ready to shop for the holidays, Cancer? Well, be careful with your plastic on November 8 and 9, when Venus will square off with extravagant Jupiter, urging you to forget about your budget, thanks to the festive mood you're enjoying. Remember, your love and your company are the best gifts of all, and the ones folks will remember the most fondly.

Planetary Hotspots

You don't have to prove anything to anyone, Cancer, so if someone challenges you around November 10, 12, or 13, you won't take kindly to it. In fact, you may confide to a dear one that you're done trying to gain respect from a certain person who seems to enjoy making you squirm. Don't let them get away with it. You've done your best. Now, make your escape.

Rewarding Days
1, 2, 3, 6, 11, 20, 21

Challenging Days
7, 8, 9, 10, 12, 13, 18, 22, 26

Cancer | December

Planetary Lightspots

Mercury will square off with dreamy, romantic Neptune around December 1, Cancer, and suddenly, all those intimate details you've been trying to forget about The One Who Got Away will suddenly come flooding back into your memory. Your mission is to realize that you just might have a case of selective memory. Take a few days to remember it all—not just the good times.

Relationships

A New Moon in respectable Capricorn on December 21 will join forces with the planetary station of Saturn on December 23 to make Doing the Right Thing the only way to go. That may mean you've decided to make an honest man or woman of the person you've been living with or seeing exclusively for a while now. If you're already attached, a business partnership that's offered now might be just what the doctor ordered.

Money and Success

When it comes to winning, Cancer, luck often comes in handy more than skill. Keep that in mind around December 4 and 14, when Venus and the Sun will set up appointments with generous Jupiter. If you're a gambler, this wouldn't be a bad time to invest in a few lottery tickets. Don't take chances with your health, however, and try not to overdo it on food, drink, or other goodies.

Planetary Hotspots

Once again, rebellious Uranus and intense Pluto have gotten themselves into a fiery, irritating square, Cancer, and this time out, you won't be able to avoid getting involved. Venus, the Goddess of Love and Money, will get into it with both these Titans on December 20, and from her spot in your solar seventh house of one-to-one relationships, it's a given she'll incite some type of dispute. If money is the issue, don't let anyone push your preferences aside. Stand your ground!

Rewarding Days

2, 3, 4, 5, 8, 12, 14, 19, 21

Challenging Days

1, 7, 15, 16, 20, 23, 24, 25

Cancer Action Table

These dates reflect the best—but not the only—times for success and ease in these activities, according to your Sun sign.

	JAN	FEB	MAR	APR	MAY	JUN	JUL	AUG	SEP	OCT	NOV	DEC
Move	15				19	27–29					22	
Start a class			13, 22, 28						21			
Join a club							7, 8			5, 15	6	
Ask for a raise	30					12		8, 9, 18, 24		18		
Look for work									13, 21		22	
Get pro advice	7, 11		9		2, 10							12, 14
Get a loan	11	11, 19					23, 24					
See a doctor		26, 27	1, 29					24, 25	7, 17			
Start a diet												
End relationship				1, 21–23		7, 14, 18, 25	26			4, 8		
Buy clothes			1					2, 12, 18				
Get a makeover	13, 15			1			18		5			
New romance	2, 15, 16				14	27					8, 13	21
Vacation		23			11, 28	4, 8, 18				27–29		1, 4, 14, 20

Leo

The Lion
July 22 to August 22

♌

Element: Fire

Quality: Fixed

Polarity: Yang/masculine

Planetary Ruler: The Sun

Meditation: I trust in the strength of my soul

Gemstone: Ruby

Power Stones: Topaz, sardonyx

Key Phrase: I will

Glyph: Lion's tail

Anatomy: Heart, upper back

Colors: Gold, scarlet

Animals: Lions, large cats

Myths/Legends: Apollo, Isis, Helios

House: Fifth

Opposite Sign: Aquarius

Flowers: Marigold, sunflower

Keyword: Magnetic

The Leo Personality

Your Strengths and Challenges

You, Leo, are fixed fire, the astrological equivalent of a roaring bon-fire. It is absolutely impossible to ignore you—and why would anyone want to? You're a star, and anyone who spends time with you feels like they've won the lottery. Like the lion, your symbol, you're also fiercely loyal and extremely brave. Courage, generosity, and playfulness are the qualities you strive to cultivate and search for in others. As entertaining as you are, you're rarely lonely, and fans are easy to come by. In fact, you usually have quite the entourage in tow wherever you go, and you can turn absolutely anywhere into your own personal stage. All you need is a bit of positive reinforcement and a dollop of attention and you're good to go.

Your kinship with the lion also makes you quite proud—as well you should be. The lion was a highly regarded crest in medieval times and a symbol of royalty that easily drew preferred treatment for the owner. You do love being treated like you're special, and you live for applause, but what you're willing to trade is well worth the price of admission.

Of course, you don't get praised, applauded, or admired if you don't conduct yourself accordingly, so your reputation is extremely important to you, and you'll take great pains to demonstrate your worth and value in all areas of life, but most especially on the job and in your personal relationships.

Your Relationships

Talk about a good time! You're entertaining, fun-loving, and outgo-ing, Leo, a perfect playmate and an amazingly attentive partner. Your planet is the Sun, and when you focus his light and warmth on others, they melt. Add a little bit of star-quality attention and they feel not just special, but very, very spoiled. When you're in love—and it usually hits you fast and hard—you'll dramatically pull out all the stops to let your beloved know exactly how much you care. Romance is your busi-ness, and you're good at it, so whether it's being driven to dinner at a five-star restaurant in a limo or sharing a picnic lunch you've lovingly prepared, you have a way of presenting it that leaves no misunder-standing. You've decided they deserve a reward for being extraordi-nary, unique, and endlessly fascinating, and as long as you see them that way, the hits will keep on comin'. If your efforts aren't adequately appreciated, however, your ardent attention will fizzle out and you'll be off, once again on the hunt for the perfect mate.

Your relationships with children are a priority, whether they're your own or the offspring of friends or family members. In children, you see unfettered, honest creativity, which you consider the spark of life.

Since you value loyalty so highly, you can become involved with Scorpio or Taurus, fixed signs like yourself who don't take commitment lightly. Those relationships may last a while, but the drastic differences in your natures will often pull you apart, and the ending won't be pretty. You might have better luck with lighthearted Sagittarius or curious Gemini, both of whom will be fascinated with your endless energy and creative spirit.

Your Career and Money

You were born to bask in the spotlight, Leo, so when you choose a career, it often involves a stage of some kind. Like your Leo sister, Madonna, that may mean you live to perform creatively, but you can turn a classroom into a performance setting, too, and along with your fondness for children, teaching certainly has its appeal. Regardless of what you choose to do with your life, you'll need positive reinforcement on a regular basis to perform consistently. Just be sure not to steal the spotlight from others who also deserve it.

You're usually quite careful with your finances, Leo, since meticulous Virgo rules your solar eighth house of money matters and possessions. You prefer to do your own books, balance your own statements, and investigate your investments personally. When you do spend, however, you're quite lavish, tending toward the very best, whether it's an experience or an object. Be sure not to go overboard to impress others with what you have. Who you are is plenty impressive enough!

Your Lighter Side

You love challenges, Leo, and live for the thrill of victory. You can be highly competitive, especially when your reputation is at stake, and you enjoy every minute of the battle. Your softer side shows up in your creativity with art, music, and entertainment. When you need to recharge your batteries and let down your hair, you often do it with children.

Affirmation for the Year

I have the inner strength to create balance in my life.

The Year Ahead for Leo

There's a lot of hard work on the agenda this year, Leo, but a great deal of recognition and rewards as well. Keep that in mind when you feel you're in the middle of a tug of war between advancing your career by impressing the higher-ups and spending much-needed time with your family. Fortunately, if you can force yourself to tend to both for the first six months of the year, a valuable astrological ally will arrive in July, none other than mighty Jupiter himself, who'll enter your sign and your solar first house of personality and appearance on July 16.

This benevolent planet brings blessings, opportunities, and lucky contacts as part of his celestial entourage, and he operates quite well in your sign. So while you may feel the stress and tension of demanding Saturn, Jupiter will be more than happy to step in, increase your confidence and energy, and give you the ability to see the lighter side of even the toughest situations. Jupiter is the heaven's answer to Santa Claus, too, so you'll often be moved to make the dreams and wishes of a loved one come true, and the fixed nature of your sign means you won't stop until they have it all. Jupiter is endlessly generous, often to the point of excess, but you won't hear any complaints. In fact, your dear ones will adore you even more, and a parade of new friends and admirers will arrive. You'll feel truly appreciated, possibly for the first time in a long time.

The best news is that since Jupiter will be emerging from the depths of your solar twelfth house, you'll already have several guardian angels of your own on duty, and they won't be going anywhere during 2014. These mentors, advisors, and prosperous associates you've accumulated over the past year will stay by your side to help you resolve any financial rough spots and counsel you through stressful emotional moments. Be sure to let them know they're appreciated, too.

Speaking of rough spots, let's talk about Saturn, who'll be in Scorpio until December 23, forming a testy square with your sign. This duty-oriented planet will increase your responsibilities at home and push you, at times, to what may feel like the breaking point. The affairs of children and other family members may make you think it's necessary to assume control of some aspect of their lives, and while you will be moved to step in and bail them out, you may not be doing them any favors. Remember, the hard lessons are the ones we remember best, and building character often involves accumulating a few scars.

Saturn also frowns on frivolities and unnecessary expenses, so in order to keep your domestic situation intact, you may have to reel in your spending, either by creating a more frugal domestic budget, moving to a less costly residence, or insisting that family members carry their own financial weight. Even if you aren't feeling the pinch in that department, you should put away some savings for a rainy day, count the blessings you have, and resolve not to spend more than you make. Keeping your credit intact will ensure that you have financial options available when and if you need them.

Uranus's presence in your solar ninth house of beliefs and personal philosophies may mean you experience an epiphany or awakening this year, and in keeping with this rebellious planet's need to question authority, some of your most deeply held beliefs may be challenged. Your views on politics, education, or religion in particular could change drastically, and rather than attempting to hold on to how you were raised and what you were taught, you'll be willing to explore new ideas. The end result will be a totally new you, with a far more open mind and a startling ability to accept unusual opinions and lifestyles.

Your new attitude may arrive because you've returned to school and exposed yourself to different acquaintances, but a long-distance trip or move could also do the trick. When we remove ourselves from our daily routine, we also remove the expectations others have of us. Being in a new environment means operating from a different part of our brains. Regardless of how you open these doors, the changes will be lasting—and they'll definitely raise a few eyebrows, too, which you'll secretly enjoy.

Neptune will continue her journey through your solar eighth house of intimacy and joint resources, casting magical spells along the way and asking that you indulge yourself in dreams and fantasies. Occasional escape from reality is a necessity for us all, but be careful. Neptune makes it all too easy to develop dependencies, so avoid excess. Monitor your alcohol intake, keep prescription drug use to a minimum, and stay out of casinos.

Be wary, too, of those who may see you as an easy touch. You can make donations and help where and when the need is appropriate, but don't be drawn into hard-luck stories or lured into get-rich-quick schemes. Remember, if it seems too good to be true, you could be right. Listen to your intuition, but back it up with solid, practical advice from seasoned professionals.

Pluto will remain on duty in your solar sixth house of health and work this year, and you'll feel his intensity most when it comes to your relationships with higher-ups and coworkers. If you have the feeling there's a lot going on around you that you're not privy to, investigate the situation before you initiate conflict or become embroiled in a work-related scandal. Examine your daily regime carefully. Do you need more exercise, or is a bad habit controlling your life? You can make changes now, but you will need to commit, and take it one step at a time.

Fiery Mars will stay put in your solar third house of communications until July 25, an unusually long visit for this assertive planet. Does this mean you'll be argumentative, aggressive, and tough to reason with? It might, but only if you feel there's an unfair set of circumstances unfolding and consider it your duty to intervene. Mars will spend this time in balance-oriented Libra, the sign of the natural-born negotiator, and your urge to step in and take charge of arguments, disputes, and disagreements will be strong, especially if siblings are involved.

But since this house also relates to neighbors, you may also be at war with someone who lives near you. Disputes over property lines and issues of respect may arise, some of which may need legal intervention to be resolved. You'll be feeling quite assertive, but resist the urge to take matters into your own hands.

What This Year's Eclipses Mean for You

The year 2014 will play host to four eclipses, Leo. The first pair will occur in April, and the second will take place in October. On April 15, a Lunar Eclipse—basically a highly charged Full Moon—will arrive in balance-loving Libra and your solar third house of communications. At this time, you may decide there's a better way to make your thoughts and needs known, especially when dealing with your primary partner. There will definitely be a need for compromise, but you'll be able to understand their point of view, possibly for the first time in a long time. The more you value the relationship, the more willing you'll be to find the middle ground, but don't become self-sacrificing, or one of you may eventually end up feeling resentful.

On April 29, a Solar Eclipse will activate earthy, practical Taurus and your solar tenth house of career matters. You may feel stressed at this time, as the need arises to tend to pressing professional matters while responsible Saturn insists on more of your time and energy from his spot in your solar fourth house of family matters. The good news is that a raise or promotion you have been pushing for could finally become a reality. Try to make it clear to loved ones that the extra time you're putting into your career now will benefit your domestic situation in the long run. When you do spend time with them, turn off your phone and give them your full attention.

On October 8, a Lunar Eclipse will arrive in Aries, your fire-sign cousin. This lunation will occur in your solar ninth house of travel, higher learning, and personal philosophy, turning up the volume on your need for excitement and a break in the routine. But once again, your solar third house of communication will also play a part. If you can manage it, this would be a terrific time to plan a long-distance family reunion. You may also decide it's finally time to go back to school to add new skills or experiences to your resumé, another excellent plan.

The Solar Eclipse on October 23 will be in intense Scorpio, activating your solar fourth house of home for the second time this year, and possibly bringing back that tug of war you first experienced in April. If you need to relocate for work or make improvements to your home, serious Saturn will be on hand to help, bringing you the determination to take care of business—but there may be a few goodbyes along the way.

Saturn

If you were born between August 12 and 23, serious Saturn will visit with your Sun this year, urging you to tighten up your belt in the department of home, family, and domestic matters. This frugal, no-nonsense planet will call your attention to frivolous, unnecessary expenditures of time, energy, and money, and you may need to cut back on expenses or indulgences to maintain your lifestyle. Obviously, stress may be hard to avoid, and you may feel overburdened by financial responsibilities and personal obligations. It's important that you don't overextend yourself. Do what's necessary, even if it's not popular with loved ones. If you need to move to a smaller home or lay down the law with children or other family members, be fair and firm, and explain your decisions thoroughly. Saturn's mission now is to test your foundation on both internal and external levels, and to bring your attention to any weaknesses or flaws. You'll need a great deal of self-discipline and perseverance, but if you work hard, apply yourself, and keep putting one foot in front of the other, you'll eventually be able to look back at this time and be thankful for it.

Saturn's influence will also inspire you to become quite protective of whomever and whatever you care for most, but try not to become controlling or overpossessive in the process, which could end up doing more harm than good. It will be tough to convince yourself to let children and family members live their own lives and make their own mistakes, but rest assured that the lessons they'll learn will stick.

Uranus

If you were born between August 1 and 9, Uranus will liven things up for you this year in surprising but delightful ways. This unpredictable planet is currently positioned in your solar ninth house of long-distance places and people, urging you to travel, seek out new experiences, and learn something new. His contact with your Sun will bring out the brave, adventurous side of your nature, and you may find yourself suddenly fascinated with activities or new people who are different from anyone else you know. If they're living an exciting, freedom-oriented lifestyle, you'll be even more interested. You're craving distractions from routines you find tedious, and Uranus will be more than happy to provide.

This house also has to do with our higher selves, with our opinions and personal philosophies, so another facet of this transit may be a radical change in your beliefs, possibly having to do with politics or religion. Stay open to new ideas and activities and consider all options, including radical lifestyle alternatives you might not have been willing to try in the past. Think of this as a spiritual growth spurt that's going to be great fun, and don't be surprised if you hardly recognize yourself when it's over.

Neptune

If you were born between July 27 and August 1, Neptune will contact your Sun from her place in your solar eighth house of intimate relationships and joint resources. Neptune prefers fantasies to reality any day, and wherever she happens to be working her magic, we tend not to be as realistic or practical as usual. That may mean that finances have suddenly become quite confusing, and you may not be able to pinpoint the reason. It's very important that you don't brush off any warning signs or try to ignore an unpleasant reality. If you don't trust your own judgment, seek out help from an unbiased, objective professional and take their advice to heart. Also, don't sign anything until it's been gone over with a fine-tooth comb by a third party with a solid reputation.

When it comes to intimate relationships, Neptune's influence means you may not be seeing your partner clearly. You're in the mood for romance, and you long to be in love. While you do stand a good chance of finding the perfect lover, you may need to make some adjustments in your lifestyles to stay together, such as a long-distance move or a change in your work schedule.

Pluto

If you were born between August 4 and 9, Leo, your Sun will be directly contacted by Pluto this year. The aspect is a tricky "inconjunct," a relationship between two planets that calls for major adjustments. In your case, since Pluto is currently on duty in your solar sixth house of work and health, and since the Sun rules our life force and creativity, you are being asked by this intense, focused planet to take a good, long look at your lifestyle, habits, and job situation. If any of those aspects of your life are lacking in personal satisfaction or doing you more harm than good because they're unhealthy or unproductive, you will need to honestly face those facts and choose a better path. Granted, this may not be easy, but there are several positive outcomes waiting at the end of the tunnel.

To start with, improving your health may simply involve changing your habits. Put yourself on a new schedule that includes downtime for stress relief and a reasonable amount of exercise. Remember, our habits shape our lives. The good news is that it only takes about three weeks to ditch one habit and become hooked on a new one. Invest a bit of your natural determination, and success is just about guaranteed.

When it comes to work and work-related relationships, times may be tense, and you may feel as if you are being drawn into no-win situations. Try to be objective. Are you contributing to the problem, or are you deliberately sabotaging yourself because you're unhappy? Dig deep, give yourself an honest answer, and take steps to put yourself on a more positive life path.

Leo | January

Planetary Lightspots

As per usual, Leo, you probably aren't ready to stop partying just because the holidays are supposedly over, but the Sun, Mercury, and Venus in your solar sixth house are all done up in responsible Capricorn, insisting that you get back to business. If you apply yourself, especially when projects come up on January 7, 11, and 12, you'll be able to resume your social schedule with a clear conscience. Don't worry. Your friends won't forget you.

Relationships

All work and hardly any play will make socializing more difficult for the first half of the month, Leo, but on January 11, Mercury will dash off into your solar seventh house of one-to-one encounters, and once again, you'll enjoy the company of lighthearted, spontaneous friends. One of those friends may introduce you to someone who's definitely not your usual type around January 17. Oh, why not? Check it out.

Money and Success

You'll have plenty of opportunities to impress the higher-ups by mid-month, Leo, thanks to the Sun, Mercury, and Venus. This team will give you the determination and endurance you need to get any job done, no matter how much you're not enjoying it. Don't complain about it, especially not at work. Someone in a position of authority may be testing you.

Planetary Hotspots

The New Moon on January 30 will mark a turning point in your relationships, Leo, and since it will occur in startling Aquarius, it's tough to say exactly why. Given the rebellious nature of this sign, however, it is safe to say that you might surprise even yourself at the choices you make. So, if friends and family members are a bit taken aback at first, cut them some slack.

Rewarding Days

6, 7, 10, 11, 17, 18, 24

Challenging Days

1, 2, 3, 5, 8, 16, 25, 26

Leo | February

Planetary Lightspots

You certainly won't be bored this month, Leo, but you may be a bit off your game. Once Mercury turns retrograde on February 6, joint resources may need your attention, especially if any financial details were recently overlooked. The good news is that Mercury's duty when he's retrograde is to give us a second chance to get it right. Think of this as an opportunity, not a hindrance.

Relationships

If you're not comfortably settled with your latest romantic fan by February 12, Leo, Mercury retrograde may have a surprise in store for you. From his spot in your solar seventh house of relationships, he'll urge you to return to the past. You might begin noticing a pattern in your relationships, for better or worse. You might also decide to give someone a second shot at the title.

Money and Success

Before you automatically assume that an authority figure is picking on you, Leo, consider that they might be pushing you to see just what you're capable of. Fortunately, charming Venus will linger all month in your solar sixth house of work, urging you to be pleasant, polite, and accommodating. She'll come in handy around February 11, 12, and 19, when tensions—and tempers—on the job could run quite high.

Planetary Hotspots

You may feel that authority figures are challenging your lifestyle and relationship choices around February 11 or 19, Leo, and you won't take it kindly. In fact, the harder they push for you to "just be reasonable," the more you'll set out to shock them. No one's saying you can't make your own decisions—but might there be a shred of truth in what they're saying? Don't be a rebel without a cause at your own expense.

Rewarding Days

13, 14, 16, 20, 23, 24, 28

Challenging Days

5, 6, 11, 12, 18, 19, 26, 27

Leo | March

Planetary Lightspots

You'll have a chance to take back some angry words this month, Leo, and to do it graciously, too. In fact, once assertive Mars turns retrograde on March 1 in your solar third house of communication, you might even begin to wonder why you were so mad to start with. Of course, your pride may not allow you to reach out right away, but chances are good that by March 14, you'll be able to set your ego aside. The good news is that you'll have a most receptive audience.

Relationships

Mercury is slowly moving forward again in your solar seventh house of one-to-one relationships, Leo, so if you've invested the past three weeks in attempting to rekindle an old romance, it will soon be clear whether or not it's possible. But Mars will turn retrograde on March 1 in partner-oriented Libra, and you might decide to defer any decisions for a while. If you have any doubts, backing off for a bit wouldn't hurt. Venus will see to it that you don't lack for company.

Money and Success

You'll need to keep a very careful eye on joint finances this month, Leo, as the Sun and Mercury in Pisces take turns meeting up with vague, dreamy Neptune. Losing money is possible, so don't carry as much with you as you ordinarily might. Keep your PIN numbers to yourself, too, and absolutely do not let anyone use your credit or debit cards.

Planetary Hotspots

That same bone of contention that came up late in January and again last month between you and a higher-up will once again rear its ugly little head this month, Leo. When the issue comes up on March 10 or 11, you'll be totally fed up and finally ready to speak your mind. If you can wait until March 13, however, you can go over the head of this person and appeal to someone who'll end up wielding far more influence.

Rewarding Days

1, 12, 13, 14, 18, 27, 28, 30

Challenging Days

2, 3, 5, 10, 11, 21, 22, 29

Leo | April

Planetary Lightspots

Loving Venus will enter your solar eighth house of intimacy and joint finances on April 5, Leo. She'll be all done up in dreamy, romantic Pisces, a mixed curse and blessing. On the one hand, sexy moments with your sweetheart will take on an almost mystical quality. On the other, it will be especially easy for you to overlook the fine print on contracts and overestimate your financial position.

Relationships

A spring tan might be just the thing right about now, Leo, especially if your long-suffering partner has been especially understanding about your work schedule over the past few months. A chance to jump in the car or board a plane without much notice will arrive, as soon as April 1 or 2, and you really should take it. Whether you actually hit the road or just make plans for the future, all astrological systems are go for a great time.

Money and Success

The Sun, Mercury, and shocking Uranus will shake things up for you during April from their spots in your solar ninth house, Leo, and the urge to see or do something different and possibly even have a real adventure will be just about undeniable. If you're not in the mood for a long trip, a weekend away would be nice. You might also consider going back to school to pad that already impressive resumé.

Planetary Hotspots

You're just dying to get away, aren't you, Leo? If your partner feels the same, it will be tough to resist, but plan to be handy between April 19 and the 24, when job-related responsibilities will drag you back to reality. The good news is that while you may not see it just yet, you're developing the ability to juggle work and play—which will ultimately be the secret to your success.

Rewarding Days

2, 17, 18, 19, 25, 26, 29

Challenging Days

1, 3, 8, 11, 14, 16, 21, 22, 23

Leo | May

Planetary Lightspots

A tug of war between your duties at home and your commitment to your career will probably have you at wit's end more than once this month, Leo. You're building a name for yourself, and as you know, that takes time and devotion. Your mission is to find a way to get that message across to everyone who's complaining about not seeing you. If they simply won't listen to reason, do what you have to do.

Relationships

Venus, the Goddess of Love, will spend most of the month in your solar ninth house, Leo, where long-distance relationships begin. If you've recently met someone from another state, coast, or country and, despite the geographic challenges, you want to pursue the relationship, you'll have plenty of energy to pull it off. If you're single, spicing things up between you two is an absolute necessity—but if anyone can think of a creative way to do it, it's you.

Money and Success

Family members may be spending money as fast or faster than you're making it, Leo, and if that's the case, you won't be willing to put up with it any longer. A warning delivered on May 2 may not take, so on May 10, making your point in more dramatic fashion might be called for. Stay calm. Contact a professional and sit tight. It's almost over.

Planetary Hotspots

A Full Moon will arrive on May 14, Leo, putting the emotional Moon in intense Scorpio and your solar fourth house of home at odds with the Sun, your own planet, in stubborn Taurus and your solar tenth house of career and professional dealings. This is a very important astrological axis, and when it's stimulated by players like these, big changes aren't usually far behind. Your mission is to take your time making major decisions in either department. Fixed energies play for keeps.

Rewarding Days

3, 4, 6, 9, 12, 15, 24, 25

Challenging Days

1, 2, 10, 13, 14, 18, 27, 28

Leo | June

Planetary Lightspots

Mercury's tri-monthly retrograde period will begin on June 7, Leo, and this time it will occur in your solar twelfth house. Old memories are due to resurface, for better or worse, and they'll be tough to ignore. You may begin wondering how your own upbringing has influenced your relationships with loved ones. Your dreams will be especially symbolic, too, so keep a dream journal, and look it over for patterns.

Relationships

Venus will spend most of the month in earthy, practical Taurus, urging one and all to settle down and plant some roots. If you're already involved and happy about it, you might decide to make things official. If you're unattached, look to a business-related event or gathering for the chance to meet someone in your field who's not only delicious, but just as determined as you are to reach the top.

Money and Success

Venus rules love and money, Leo, and she just loves being in Taurus. That's where she is at the moment, and since that puts her in your solar tenth house of career matters, things could be a lot worse for you on the professional scene. In fact, with some effort, you might finally attract the attention of that influential higher-up with the ability to pull you up the ladder.

Planetary Hotspots

Two of the heavens' most volatile energies will get into a testy square on June 14, Leo, and just about all of us will feel the tension. In your case, since Mars and Pluto will force a confrontation between your third solar house of communication and your solar sixth house of work and health, you may end up in a rather heated debate with a coworker or healthcare practitioner. Don't lose your fiery little head. Draw back and regroup.

Rewarding Days

3, 4, 8, 12, 18, 28, 29

Challenging Days

6, 7, 13, 14, 19, 24, 25, 30

Leo | July

Planetary Lightspots

After three long weeks of moving in reverse, Mercury, the Messenger of the Gods, will shift gears on July 1. Yes, there'll be cause for much rejoicing in the kingdom, but you might also feel the urge to carefully pore over the facts that surround a recent pact between members of your current group—and what you find may not be the stuff that celebrations are made of. On the other hand, you'll solve the mystery.

Relationships

A new you will emerge with the New Moon in your sign and your solar first house of personality and appearance on July 26, Leo, and as with everything else you do, your fans will be waiting in the wings to applaud you. You won't settle for niceties now, though. If that's what you think you're getting, you'll ask for the truth around July 19—and heaven help anyone who tries to pull the wool over your eyes.

Money and Success

The Full Moon in Capricorn on July 12 will turn up the volume on your work ethic, Leo, which is already quite substantial. The good news is that all those painstaking efforts to get it right haven't gone unnoticed. The best news is that you may receive a raise, bonus, or promotion, but even if it doesn't happen right away, a pat on the back from a higher-up will keep you on track.

Planetary Hotspots

With expansive Jupiter on duty in your solar twelfth house of secrets, private moments, and subconscious desires, Leo, you've been a lot more introverted lately. In fact, your friends have probably started asking you if there's a problem. Unbeknownst to them, there's no problem at all. You're simply in the mood to spend quality time alone. Still, you may need to allay their fears, so answer your phone on July 4, 19, and 22, even if you don't want to.

Rewarding Days
9, 13, 18, 20, 23, 24, 31

Challenging Days
3, 4, 8, 19, 21, 22, 25, 27, 28

Leo | August

Planetary Lightspots

Venus, Mercury, and the Sun will all spend time this month in your sign, Leo, turning up the heat in your solar first house of personality and appearance. Does this mean your fan base will grow? Oh, you bet. By leaps and bounds, no doubt. Will they stick around? Well, at least one might. You'll know they're worth your time and energy when a confrontation forces sides around August 8.

Relationships

On August 10, Leo, a Full Moon will charge up your relationship axis, and you may decide it's time to tie down that often elusive new lover. If they're on the same page, everything will go well. If not, you'll know it. In this case, let your pride lead you, one way or the other. If you leave, because you can't have what you want, don't maintain any contact whatsoever. Who needs it? Certainly not you!

Money and Success

Once Mercury takes off for your solar second house of personal finances on August 15, you'll be in the mood to make some quick deals, and the better they look, the faster you'll want to move. Don't do that. Woozy, romantic Neptune is on duty in your solar eighth house of joint resources—plenty of reason to avoid signing anything without doing your homework. But if you add in the New Moon on August 25, it's easy to see that The Real Deal won't be available until then.

Planetary Hotspots

A domestic situation that's been brewing for months may come to a boil around August 25, when a New Moon combines energies with feisty Mars and no-nonsense Saturn in your solar fourth house of home. You'll need to take charge, and getting others to cooperate may not be easy. If you put your own special blend of charm and determination into it, however, you can make it work. Piece of cake.

Rewarding Days

2, 3, 7, 17, 18, 21, 23

Challenging Days

8, 9, 25, 26, 27, 29, 30

Leo | September

Planetary Lightspots

Lighthearted Mercury in cooperative, people-pleasing Libra will spend most of the month in your solar third house of short trips, conversations, and daily encounters, Leo. You're already the star of the show wherever you are, but this month, you'll be given the chance to let your audience know you're a real, live person, too. Let your hair—well, mane—down.

Relationships

Love and money matters will be intertwined this month, Leo, thanks to a transit of Venus through your solar second house of personal resources. You'll want to earn more, but when your partner asks you what's more important—your job or your relationship—you'll be hard-pressed to answer. The good news is that you already know what you want to do. The tough part will be admitting you've known it for some time now.

Money and Success

An urgent situation at work around September 9 will demand that someone step up and take the reins, Leo, and if anyone is ready to do it, it's you. The situation may be less than pleasant, but a new beginning is a new beginning, and most abrupt new starts are rough. If you hang tough, you'll be solidly in charge and well grounded in your new position by September 14.

Planetary Hotspots

On September 13, fiery Mars, a planet whose energies you've always enjoyed, will set off for equally fiery Sagittarius and your solar fifth house, Leo. Issues involving love, creativity, leisure-time activities, and children will be in the spotlight, but mostly for pleasant reasons. What a terrific time to take a spontaneous jaunt with the kids, or to suggest a romantic, unplanned weekend rendezvous with your sweetheart!

Rewarding Days
1, 2, 3, 10, 14, 20, 24, 25

Challenging Days
8, 9, 12, 13, 21, 27, 28

Leo | October

Planetary Lightspots

Just about everyone you meet will be in a terrific mood around October 5, Leo, and if you happen to be in the company of a fiery new admirer, life will truly be good. Until you know your Mystery Date a little better, however, you might want to sit tight and put off that trip to Zimbabwe or Sri Lanka or wherever it is you've always wanted to go with a lover. Better safe than sorry, right?

Relationships

If you've made promises to a dear one to keep the peace recently, Leo, you may be called on the carpet around October 4 or 8 to make good on them now. If there's any way you can come through, make it happen, but if you can't, there's only one thing to do: admit defeat and beg forgiveness. No, you're not good at tucking your tail between your legs, but every now and then, it has to happen. Buck up.

Money and Success

Saturn, the ruler of career aspirations, has been on duty in your solar fourth house. He's been urging you to crack the whip, demanding that you put domestic matters first, even if professional duties are more urgent. Well, he'll be moving on next month, but right about October 23, the Sun and Venus will make it clear that all that work was definitely not in vain.

Planetary Hotspots

Mercury will turn retrograde on October 4, Leo, and from his initial spot in your solar fourth house of home and family matters, he'll see to it that you revisit a recent executive decision you made with an eye toward loosening up—but just a touch. That's fine, but be sure your inmates/captives understand that this is only a trial run, and their freedom can be curtailed again in a moment's notice.

Rewarding Days
5, 13, 14, 15, 16, 25, 27

Challenging Days
4, 6, 7, 23, 26, 28, 29

Leo | November

Planetary Lightspots

Venus will set off for Sagittarius on November 16, Leo, a sign you've always gotten on well with. This puts the Goddess of Love in your solar fifth house of fun-time activities for a full month, so prepare to use up your sick days and personal days. No, it won't be easy to go to work now, especially if you're not happy there, but your mission is to stay put until another opportunity comes along—which it will.

Relationships

If you've somehow managed to remain single up until now, Leo, the Universe may have an alternate plan in mind this month. The New Moon on November 22 will get something started in your solar fifth house, and new playmates may be on the agenda. If you're happy with your current flame, not to worry. You two will keep those home fires burning. A new arrival may even be the proof.

Money and Success

It's a good time to straighten out disputes involving inheritances, unpaid loans, and outstanding debts of any kind, Leo, but you won't enjoy the confrontations necessary to get the job or jobs done. Someone who has been avoiding you quite efficiently will get up the guts to face you as soon as November 1, but you may not be receptive until November 11. In the meantime, leave the door open just a crack.

Planetary Hotspots

What they've seen is what you'll get on November 12, Leo, so if you've been putting the finishing touches on a work-related plan to climb that ladder, pay attention to the feedback you receive from higher-ups. If it's good, you're on the right track. If it's skeptical, maybe rein in that rhetoric. Just a touch.

Rewarding Days

1, 2, 3, 11, 16, 17, 20, 21

Challenging Days

8, 9, 10, 12, 13, 18, 22, 26

Leo | December

Planetary Lightspots

After two and a half years of travel in your solar fourth house of home and domestic matters, serious Saturn in Scorpio will finally move on, Leo. This will mark the beginning of a new type of freedom and surety in family matters, but you'll also feel far more secure about the home base you've created. Saturn's next mission is to get you to tighten up the old belt when it comes to frivolities, however, so start now with a savings account or secret stash—at least.

Relationships

Fiery, rebellious Mars will enter your solar seventh house on December 4, Leo, urging you to make it extremely clear to one and all that you're not like them. Over the next few weeks, however, you may cross paths with those you'll now consider members of your tribe. Finding new peer groups is important to personal growth, but be sure you're not getting swept up in others' enthusiasm.

Money and Success

It's hard to go wrong financially when you've got Venus, the Goddess of Money, on duty in your solar sixth house of work, and you probably won't. In fact, if the Uranus-Pluto square on December 15 tries to work its disruptive energy early, you'll be more than well equipped to handle it.

Planetary Hotspots

After all is said and done, Leo, and all the fighting is through, you'll emerge victorious in a work-related situation, right around December 20. Talking yourself into believing that you've earned this won't be a problem. Resisting the urge to gloat, which you so deserve after all this time, may be a little tougher.

Rewarding Days

2, 3, 4, 5, 8, 12, 13, 14

Challenging Days

1, 6, 15, 16, 19, 20, 23, 24, 25

Leo Action Table

These dates reflect the best—but not the only—times for success and ease in these activities, according to your Sun sign.

	JAN	FEB	MAR	APR	MAY	JUN	JUL	AUG	SEP	OCT	NOV	DEC
Move					24	27			29			
Start a class			30		7, 12, 28	23	1					
Join a club										11		
Ask for a raise	11, 12					18		11, 21, 25	21			
Look for work			13, 28	1			12	15, 25	3, 5, 14			
Get pro advice				25	24	8					12, 21	
Get a loan		24								27		
See a doctor								10				
Start a diet	11, 12											10, 16
End relationship	16, 25	11, 19			2, 10		9, 26					
Buy clothes												
Get a makeover		14						8, 18				
New romance	24	14	14, 29					18		14	16	4, 12, 14
Vacation			30	7			7			5		

Virgo

The Virgin
August 22 to September 22

♍

Element: Earth

Quality: Mutable

Polarity: Yin/feminine

Planetary Ruler: Mercury

Meditation: I can allow time for myself

Gemstone: Sapphire

Power Stones: Peridot, amazonite, rhodochrosite

Key Phrase: I analyze

Glyph: Greek symbol for containment

Anatomy: Abdomen, gallbladder, intestines

Colors: Taupe, gray, navy blue

Animals: Domesticated animals

Myths/Legends: Demeter, Astraea, Hygeia

House: Sixth

Opposite Sign: Pisces

Flower: Pansy

Keyword: Discriminating

The Virgo Personality

Your Strengths and Challenges

You're probably quite tired of hearing about how picky you are, Virgo, especially since you just don't see it that way. Doesn't everyone organize and reorganize what's important to them on a daily basis, aiming to make it perfect? Doesn't everyone see the flaws you do? Well, unfortunately, they don't, but that doesn't mean your particular brand of meticulous attention to detail isn't much needed in the world. It's what gives you an edge in health-related careers, where precision is an absolute must, and what motivates you to pore over a list of numbers until you find the mistake. Most of us don't have the patience or interest to keep going on either of those tasks, but you do. In fact, it's fun. Your ruling planet is Mercury, who just loves puzzles, and unlike your Gemini cousins who also adore details, you know which are necessary and important and which aren't.

Now, how about that reputation for obsessive-compulsive neatness? Are you really all Felixes in a world of Oscars? Well, some of you are most definitely over the top when it comes to keeping things in their proper order, and that may extend to your home and to your way of dealing with others. The thing is, you only devote that intense attention to the things that matter to you, so most often you're a complete slob, preferring to devote your time to perfecting one special area of life—and it's usually work—and letting the other more insignificant things slide.

Your Relationships

You bring your eye for detail and your urge to create perfection into all your relationships, Virgo, and you tend to get involved with others who fulfill those requirements by being almost exactly, but not quite, perfect. Initially, you see only potential. In your eyes, they're diamonds in the rough, simply in need of a fixer-upper, and you're sure you can provide that. You can see what's wrong and come up with caring solutions so you'll bring out the best in them—even if their track record isn't sparkling. If they show any interest in bettering themselves, you'll get involved. It's how you often express your urge to heal and need to refine.

Emotionally speaking, however, this type of relationship can be exhausting, leaving both you and your partner or friend feeling that there's just no way to please or be pleased. So rather than choosing someone for whom or what they might become with a little polishing, hang tight until you find kindred spirits you are willing to accept just the way they are—not despite their flaws or imperfections, but because of them.

When it comes to your family members, on the other hand, you're more than willing to cast a blind eye on faults. You're a dutiful child, parent, and sibling, always willing to help—in ingenious ways.

Romantically, you're often drawn to Sagittarians, whose light-hearted spirits and witty humor pleasantly distract you. They force you to have fun and see both the forest and the trees, which is terrific for an evening but not always doable in the long run. You'll get on much better and much longer with other Virgos and with earthy Taurus, both of whom will completely understand your thoroughness and need for perfection.

Your Career and Money

Your see faults and flaws easily, Virgo, and you know how to repair them, too. That's one of the qualities that makes you perfect for healthcare. But you also notice small things that might be ruled inconsequential by others, which certainly comes in handy. Ever see *House*, the TV series that featured a rebellious healer with an uncanny eye for diagnostics? He's noticed because of his radical attention to details and his refusal to stop considering options until the "aha" moment happens. That's the perfect archetype for your sign, and the reason you're so good at ruling the sixth house, where matters of health, work, and daily schedules are handled.

Regardless of the path you choose, however, you'll need to operate freely, with only your innate personal routine to dictate how every day unfolds. You love schedules, but when it comes to work, they'd better be on your terms. Otherwise, you're outta there, with no regrets.

Financially speaking, it's all a matter of trading time for being able to do what you love, so you tend to rely less on what something is worth and more on how long you worked to have it.

Your Lighter Side

You love to be amused, educated, and enlightened at the same time, Virgo, so when you actually allow yourself some downtime, you often spend it watching documentaries—but your guilty pleasure is reality shows. Like Geminis, you enjoy Trivial Pursuit, and often engage others in a verbal battle of wits, especially if you know you're better-equipped than others to win.

Affirmation for the Year
Kindred spirits keep me emotionally grounded.

The Year Ahead for Virgo

Relationships, relationships, and relationships, Virgo. Anyone who didn't know better might think you're a Libra over the coming year—that's how focused you'll be on all your partnerships, whether they're casual, professional, or personal.

To start with, woozy Neptune, the astrological purveyor of illusion, delusion, and confusion, is still on duty in your solar seventh house of one-to-one relationships. On the positive side, this spiritual energy could mean it's finally time for you to run into your soul mate, and it will probably be quite by accident. But Neptune loves to save the helpless, so be on guard against anyone who might try to entangle you in their life by appearing vulnerable. In a perfect world, you could always use your considerable powers of empathy and unconditional understanding to help them become a better person. In reality, you might just be looking to save someone who's putting forth a defenseless front to draw you in. No, it's not nice to think of others that way, but right now, it's one of the possibilities you should be forcing yourself to consider.

Pluto's continued trek through your solar fifth house of lovers, children, and creative pursuits means you'll be willing to dig, and you'll expect nothing but complete intensity from this area of life. Your dealings with kids will be nothing short of deep, and as for your lovers—well, it's easy to see how a supposedly casual affair could turn quite serious now. If that's what you're looking for, trust your perceptive instincts to guide you toward a lover who's got a lot more than small talk about the neighbors to share.

Uranus will shake things up for you from his spot in impulsive Aries and your solar eighth house of intimate partners and joint resources. If you're involved with lawsuits, you won't believe what's about to happen. Prepare yourself for any eventuality. If you're single and you happen to fall madly and passionately in love, so much the better. Together with red-hot Mars in partner-loving Libra, Uranus will be sure to make love at first sight a definite possibility. Your mission, with romantic Neptune on duty in your solar seventh house of one-to-one relationships, is to be sure you're seeing the person clearly.

Now, let's talk about Jupiter, who always brings blessings along no matter where he appears. He'll spend the first half of the year in Cancer and your solar eleventh house of friendships, urging you to expand, extend, and overindulge yourself socially—and to go overboard for any dear one who's clearly in need of care or advice. You'll want to do all you can and be helpful, as per usual, but don't do it at your own expense. Remember, kindness can be mistaken for weakness if it's doled out without any regard for facts.

On July 16, Jupiter will set off for dramatic Leo and your solar twelfth house of secrets, urging you to retreat for a creative pursuit. If you're inclined toward art, music, or poetry, make some quality time to spend alone with You, and get back in touch with your Muse. She hasn't gone anywhere. It's you who's been busy. The secretive nature of this house also means that you may decide to do some research or go over financial accounts. Don't be surprised at anything that turns up. With red-hot Mars in Libra on duty in your solar second house of finances, surprises are definitely on the agenda until at least July 25. Some you'll be happy with and others will make you angry, but one way or the other, as 2014 comes to a close, you'll be ready to make a no-nonsense decision. Your best bet is to use the partner-oriented side of Libra to restore balance to your money matters—and don't be afraid to cut anyone off who hasn't even bothered to thank you!

What This Year's Eclipses Mean for You

This year's eclipses will focus their considerable energies on your axis of personal and shared resources and your axis of fleeting thoughts versus deeply held opinions, Virgo. Money matters and personal beliefs, then—that's where you'll be tested, and where your greatest and most sudden changes will occur.

On April 15, the first eclipse of the year will arrive, a super-charged Lunar Eclipse all done up in partner-oriented Libra. With the emotional Full Moon casting her bright light into your solar second house of personal finances, you may suddenly remember a debt, and if so, Libra's reputation for fairness will move you to get it settled. On the other hand, someone may suddenly decide to repay you—and if that's the case, chances are good you'll have forgotten all about it. The good news is that either way, your faith in yourself—and in others—will be restored. The best news is that this house deals with values, so you're on the verge of an encounter that will super-charge your self-respect.

The Solar Eclipse of April 29 will occur in Taurus and your solar ninth house of beliefs, urging you to settle down and take a firm stance on what you hold most dear. The easy part will be defending what you're familiar with, and if you choose to go that way, good for you. But if you're honest with yourself, you'll see that several deeply held beliefs really aren't relevant anymore. Cut them loose, no matter how tough it is. This house also pertains to education, so if you've ever wanted to pursue a career in a culinary or artistic field, you may get the chance to jump on board now.

On October 8, a Lunar Eclipse in impulsive, me-first Aries will create a tug of war between your solar eighth house of shared resources and your solar second house of personal finances. If someone has been taking advantage of your generosity, you'll see evidence of that now, and while it might not be pleasant, you'll at least have proof that those suspicions you've been harboring were right. Tell that to the skeptics who said you were obsessing!

On October 23, the last eclipse of the year will occur, a high-energy New Moon (Solar Eclipse) that will bring the Sun and Moon together in Scorpio and your solar third house of communications and conversations. Expect to be quite concerned with details—yes, even more than usual—and to dig relentlessly until you have all the information you need to make any decision. If you've ever been interested in CSI work or had any inklings toward becoming a detective, don't rule it out. This is the time for you to see if you've got what it takes to make a living at it.

Saturn

If you were born between September 13 and 23, your Sun will be contacted by responsible Saturn via an easy sextile. From Saturn's spot in your solar third house of communication and conversations, this fair but firm energy has been demanding that you play by the rules for almost two years now, Virgo. You've probably had to buckle down and get serious on lots of occasions, but now there'll be nowhere to hide. Don't even think about ducking out on promises or shirking your responsibilities. If you do what you said you'd do, you'll be properly rewarded. If not, you might get away with it temporarily, but you won't be happy with yourself. Saturn's presence in this house means it's time to talk turkey, and now that he's tapping you on the shoulder, there's really no way to avoid confrontations, even if you've been putting them off for years. It's time to sit down and iron things out between you and siblings or neighbors, but no matter whom you've been at odds with, you should swallow your pride and reach out now.

Since there'll be nothing even remotely resembling a "casual conversation" in your life, you should also expect to hear an awful lot of gossip—and it will be of the juiciest, most salacious kind. Yep, scandals—everywhere you turn, seems like. If you participate, you might seem like a hero now, but in the long run, your reputation will be scarred. Keep your mouth shut and wait, and eventually the right way to speak the truth will surface. In the meantime, file it all away and occupy yourself with a tough mental task.

Uranus

If you were born between September 1 and 9, Virgo, your Sun is currently being visited by startling Uranus, and he's shaking things up from his spot in your solar eighth house of intimate partnerships, joint finances, and life-and-death circumstances. Well, now! The plot has definitely thickened, hasn't it? This unconventional planet brings along the last thing on earth you'd ever expect. He revels in it. In this house and in the aspect he's making, he might bring along the news that you've won the lottery, and that your lifestyle will be changing for extremely happy reasons. Be careful, though. Remember, Uranus loves surprise endings, and he's just getting started. A windfall could arrive, but it might lead you into a reckless situation that's not to your benefit. Be sure to handle all seemingly positive sudden events with an eye toward making the best of the after-effects. On the other hand, if something you see as "negative" happens, you can console yourself with the knowledge that you are in the midst of great change. If you take charge of it now, you'll end up closer to being the person you really are.

Think, too, about the fact that Uranus loves to rebel, and he's working that radical energy from your house of intimacy. Don't engage in anything that really doesn't appeal to you simply because it goes against everything you were ever taught. Believe it or not, there might be some truth to those rumors.

Neptune

If you were born between August 27 and September 1, Virgo, your Sun is currently handling what is known as an opposition from transiting Neptune. To break it down easily, look at it like this: Neptune rules altered states. Anything that gets us out of our mundane ruts and in touch with Something Else will do. You, however, are into the material world. You're so in touch with the details of our world, in fact, that you can see flaws in the machinery that most of us miss. That makes you a terrific troubleshooter—at least, most of the time. But now, with Neptune and her pink smoke machine on duty in your solar seventh house of one-to-one relationships, you're not seeing things realistically or clearly in your closest and most personal relationships.

No, that might not be good news, especially if you've just realized how far astray you've been led by someone's lies and false promises. The good news is that if you've figured it out, you can end it—and, even better, you'll be well armed to protect yourself from it ever happening again. The tough part is that you'll be tempted to trust everyone now, in spite of and possibly even because of their negative reputation. Be careful not to fall under the spell of a deceiver because you're so invested in helping them to see just how special they are. Giving your all to someone who's using you won't help them—and it certainly won't help you, or anyone else they come into contact with in the coming years. Neptune dissolves boundaries, so you're especially vulnerable now, but if you give yourself a bit of time to listen to your intuition, you'll do just fine.

The best news is that, over the next twelve months, you stand every chance of finding the soul mate you've been searching for. Again, pay attention to your gut. If the person is attractive but something inside you still says "dangerous," know that your feelings are right. Don't take any chances.

Pluto

If you were born between September 12 and 16, your Sun will be contacted by intense Pluto this year, Virgo. This penetrating planet makes already keen wits even keener, so your ability to amaze and astound the masses with your word-wizardry will be especially lethal now. In particular, your knack for talking anybody into anything will come in handy on lots of occasions. If you add that talent to the fact that Pluto loves to dig, on any level, it's easy to see how you'll also be ready, willing, and quite able to play detective. Your mission is not to remain uninvolved—that's out of the question. But when you do choose someone or something to defend to the bitter end, be sure they're worth it, because you may not be seeing them as they really are. That's all I'm sayin'.

From his position in your solar fifth house, Pluto will turn up the passion on all your dealings with supposedly casual lovers and creative pursuits in what might be seen by others as a very controlling way. Since this is an easy trine between Pluto and your Sun, however, it's not likely that you'll have to face any real resistance. In fact, with Pluto where he is now, any threat against you will be idle. *You* hold the keys, not them—regardless of who they are. Your mission is to use this superpower you've been temporarily endowed with for good, rather than anything even remotely resembling selfish, reasons. You are quite capable of bulldozing anything now, from belief systems to social mores to the natural defenses of any mere human. Be mindful of the responsibilities—and karma—that go along with that power.

Virgo | January

Planetary Lightspots

The Full Moon in nurturing Cancer on January 15 will illuminate your axis of friends and lovers this month, Virgo. Together with several planets in sturdy Capricorn, you'll find that dear ones are more reliable than ever. In fact, if you're in need, you probably won't even have to ask. Likewise, if you sense that an old friend is bothered, you won't quit until they've told you what's up and listened to your advice.

Relationships

The New Moon on New Year's Day will plant a seed in your solar fifth house of love affairs, Virgo, urging you to give romance another shot. This time out, however, with intense Pluto on deck, you'll need to be careful that neither of you becomes obsessive about the other. If you see those signs, back off. With Neptune in your solar seventh house of one-to-one encounters, your intuition will be right on. Listen to it.

Money and Success

Charming Venus will spend the month in a fellow earth sign, Virgo, all done up in hard-working Capricorn. Around January 7 or 11, she'll arrange for you to bump into someone who can further your career goals, probably at a social gathering. Be sure to carry business cards wherever you go, and don't hesitate to do a little self-promotion.

Planetary Hotspots

Work-related disputes may occur around January 25, Virgo. If a coworker has been shirking their responsibilities or handing their work off to you, you won't take kindly to it. You probably also won't keep quiet about it for long, especially if this isn't the first time. Your best bet is to take your complaints to a supervisor. Arguing over the issue on the job won't solve anything.

Rewarding Days

7, 10, 11, 12, 15, 18, 19

Challenging Days

1, 2, 3, 4, 5, 8, 16, 25

Virgo | February

Planetary Lightspots

It's time to take responsibility for your actions, Virgo, and while it may not be easy, putting it off any longer simply won't work. On February 11 and 19, the Sun and Mercury in Aquarius will square off with serious Saturn in your solar third house of conversations and communications, and just like late last month, confrontations about work-related issues may once again be problematic. Rest assured, however, that once you've cleared the air, it could all be over by February 24.

Relationships

Is love at first sight really possible? It just might be for you on February 23 or 24, Virgo. The Sun and romantic Neptune will collide in your solar seventh house of one-to-one relationships, all done up in ultra-sensitive Pisces. This wistful duo will have some help in grounding the attraction, though, thanks to a positive sextile between loving Venus and reliable Saturn. Yep. This may be it.

Money and Success

A work-related matter may stall between February 12 and 28, Virgo, as your own planet, Mercury, makes his way retrograde through your solar sixth house. You may need to reexamine your recent efforts to see what went wrong. It's hard to believe, but even Virgos make mistakes. Don't be too hard on yourself. Fix what you can, and start over if you can't.

Planetary Hotspots

Others may seem to be asking more from you than you can deliver this month, Virgo. If you know you've already done everything humanly possible, it might be time to think about saying goodbye. Still, be sure you're not over-dramatizing the situation before you say anything you'll regret. Saturn in Scorpio will hold you to your decision, and the results will be permanent.

Rewarding Days
4, 14, 16, 20, 23, 24, 25

Challenging Days
10, 11, 18, 19, 26, 28

Virgo | March

Planetary Lightspots

On March 16, a Full Moon will cast its light into your solar first house of appearances and physical condition, Virgo, urging you to make some changes in the first impression you leave on others. That may mean you're ready to trade in your jeans for a business suit, or you may opt to focus on your daily habits with an eye toward making them more positive and productive. Work out, start walking, or put the brakes on any unhealthy behaviors.

Relationships

If you started up a casual but steamy relationship last month, Virgo, it will take off by leaps and bounds now, and by March 13, you two could be thinking about taking one major step toward making it official. Be sure you're seeing your partner clearly before you board a flight to Reno. Even if your intuition tells you this is The One, introduce them to a dear friend or family member who knows you well enough to see what you might not.

Money and Success

On March 5, Venus will enter your solar sixth house of work situations, bringing along her knack for calming troubled waters at just the right time. You were probably put through the wringer last month and have just about given up on having a peaceful workday, but hang in there and be patient. It may take a while, but time really does heal all wounds.

Planetary Hotspots

You may have one last go-round with a higher-up who seems to have you in their sights this month, Virgo, so fasten your seat belt. On March 11, Mercury will form his third square with Saturn in the past six weeks, once again inciting an on-the-job situation that started back in January. The good news is that the third time might really be the charm in this case. Expect a favorable outcome within a few days.

Rewarding Days

1, 2, 12, 13, 14, 18, 22, 23

Challenging Days

3, 10, 11, 20, 21, 29, 30

Virgo | April

Planetary Lightspots

In addition to being extremely helpful with money matters, the combined efforts of Venus, Pluto, and Jupiter from April 17 through April 20 will help settle down any simmering tensions between you and a friend you've been at odds with lately. Bring compassion with you when you sit down to chat with them, and try to see the true motivation behind their offenses.

Relationships

Romance is still very much in the air for you, Virgo, as loving Venus enters your solar seventh house of relationships on April 5 for a month-long stay. In sentimental, nostalgic Pisces, she may even lead you back for another try with someone you see as The One Who Got Away. You'll want to see only the best in others now, but don't ignore the problems that split you up to start with.

Money and Success

The Lunar Eclipse of April 15 will make financial issues challenging, Virgo. Along with the Sun and Mercury tugging on you from your solar eighth house of joint resources, getting what you've earned may not come easily. If you're after a loan or financial extension, this isn't the time to pursue it. Do your homework and wait until April 17 or 18, when Venus and Jupiter, the most benefic astrological team of all, will help you to get the nod.

Planetary Hotspots

Uranus and Pluto will once again get into a powerful, angry square on April 21, Virgo, pitting your solar fifth house against your solar eighth house of joint resources. Urgent financial expenditures on behalf of children or lovers is entirely possible, which may be quite costly. If a pattern of behavior is repeating itself and this is not the first time you are bailing them out, think. Are you really doing them a favor?

Rewarding Days

2, 5, 10, 11, 17, 18, 19, 25, 26

Challenging Days

1, 3, 8, 14, 15, 16, 21, 22

Virgo | May

Planetary Lightspots

The New Moon in Gemini on May 28 will help get the show on the road with regard to an important career matter, Virgo. It will be easy for you to chat with authority figures, and one in particular may take a liking to you. Your mission is to listen carefully to any offer you receive, and have every detail put on paper. Be sure you're not signing up for more than you can realistically do.

Relationships

Travel difficulties due to roadblocks, delays, or mechanical problems could be on the agenda for May 14, Virgo, thanks to the Full Moon in Scorpio. The good news is that the Universe often stalls us to keep us from being somewhere we shouldn't be. Keep that in mind if you're sitting in traffic or the waiting room of your local mechanic.

Money and Success

Your ruling planet, chatty Mercury, will take up residence in your solar tenth house on May 7, Virgo, and a spotlight will be trained on your wit and gift of gab. You'll be able to easily gain the confidence of higher-ups, elders, and just about any other authority figure now, but there might be a better way. Aim that keen mind of yours at tending even more carefully to the details you love, and someone above you will be quite impressed.

Planetary Hotspots

Your current partner may have a wonderful surprise planned for you on May 14 or 15, Virgo, so no matter what you have to juggle to make time for them, don't refuse any invitations. Venus, the Goddess of Love, will contact Uranus in your solar eighth house of intimacy, making spontaneous encounters quite enjoyable. This house also rules joint finances, so if you've been waiting for an answer on a loan, your answer may arrive.

Rewarding Days

3, 5, 6, 9, 12, 15, 23, 24

Challenging Days

2, 11, 14, 17, 18, 19, 28, 30

Virgo | June

Planetary Lightspots

A lighthearted Full Moon in Sagittarius will illuminate the skies on June 13, Virgo, and amp up the energy on both your home life and your professional goals. The good news is that this will bring the fortunate, optimistic influence of Sagittarius into all your dealings with family members. You may decide to travel to restore contact, or have the whole crew over for a reunion.

Relationships

Any aesthetic hobby you've been perfecting over recent years could end up becoming a part-time job later this month, Virgo, and eventually even your primary source of income. Venus in Taurus will move into your solar tenth house of career on June 23, after several weeks of inspiring you to put your creativity to work for you. Spending the month taking classes in your chosen field will certainly help.

Money and Success

Fiery Mars is still on duty in your solar second house, Virgo, an impulsive energy that hasn't done wonders for your checkbook over the past six months. He'll move on next month, but not without trying to pry that hard-earned cash out of your hands one more time. If you're shopping around June 24 or 25, take a chaperone along.

Planetary Hotspots

Mercury's retrograde trek from June 7 on will be a bit befuddling, Virgo. He'll retrace his steps through Cancer and back up into Gemini on June 17, where he'll stay for another month. In the meantime, you may need to rethink goals you've set for your family, especially if they weren't practical to begin with. After June 17, an offer from an old boss to return to work will be tempting, but don't act on it just yet.

Rewarding Days

4, 5, 6, 8, 17, 18, 28, 29

Challenging Days

7, 11, 12, 14, 19, 20, 24, 25

Virgo | July

Planetary Lightspots

After three long weeks in retrograde motion, Mercury, your ruling planet, will finally turn direct on July 1, just dying to get the right information to the right people after being responsible for muddling things up. In your case, the facts of the matter will finally become apparent now, especially with regard to career matters and encounters with respected authority figures. You'll probably find that someone who seemed to be giving you a hard time was really on your side all along.

Relationships

On July 19 and 24, Mercury and Venus in nurturing Cancer will take turns moving into easy trines with Neptune, the Queen of Compassion. These planets will link your solar seventh house of one-to-one relationships with your solar eleventh house of friendships, Virgo. If you haven't yet introduced your sweetheart to The Gang, you're probably already aware that they want to meet. So what's the holdup? You chose them all. They must have something in common!

Money and Success

Up until July 18, Venus will hold court in your solar tenth house of authority figures, all done up in witty Gemini. This easygoing energy will prompt you to do whatever it takes to make your boss's job easier, and you'll no doubt receive kudos for your efforts. Look to July 13 for grateful hugs, and to July 22 for written or spoken appreciation.

Planetary Hotspots

You're not fond of waiting, Virgo, especially when it's for a result you already mentioned wouldn't be accurate. So on July 8, 19, and 24, when the power of a group holds you back from making your point, you may be quite frustrated. The good news is that if you can hold back until July 24, Mercury will join forces with serious Saturn to inform the world that you were right after all.

Rewarding Days
6, 7, 8, 13, 19, 23, 24

Challenging Days
3, 4, 5, 18, 21, 22, 27, 28

Virgo | August

Planetary Lightspots

The New Moon on August 25 in your sign and your solar first house of personality and physical appearance means not only that your look is due for a change, Virgo, but that you're ready to get the show on the road. If you want a makeover, go for it. Shopping for a new wardrobe would be great, too, but if you're looking for something deeper, don't shy away from plastic surgery. No one will know unless you tell them.

Relationships

This month, Virgo, lots of planetary energies will be flowing easily from your solar fourth house of home to your solar eighth house of intimate partners and on into your solar twelfth house of secret moments. Put them all together and it's easy to see how you might fall madly in lust. Fortunately, you're far more practical than most of us, so rather than going along blindly, you'll think about the motivation behind your attraction, and even if you don't like the answer, you'll react accordingly.

Money and Success

You might not see this coming, Virgo, but right around August 1 and possibly again around August 26, loving Venus might decide to call on you to support someone you love, and whether or not you have the rainy-day funds put aside will be the deciding factor. If you do, be careful not to spend it all unless it's really a last resort. Call on a dear old friend or elder to advise you.

Planetary Hotspots

You're not usually fond of spending time alone, Virgo, unless, of course, you're working on a project you just can't trust in anyone else's hands. That may be the case now, so when Mercury and intensely private Pluto get together, you may not be willing to mingle. That's okay. If you're busy, carry on. They'll all be there when you're done.

Rewarding Days
6, 8, 9, 18, 26, 27, 28, 29

Challenging Days
1, 2, 3, 7, 15, 25

Virgo | September

Planetary Lightspots

One of the longest-standing of all astrological debates involves whether or not your sign is ruled by Mercury or the "new" comet/asteroid Chiron. The good news is that you're probably ruled by both, as will be evidenced by the influence of Chiron, the healer, in your life this month. Look to September 7 and 17 for proof.

Relationships

You're quite fond of fixing things, Virgo, and that often means you take on a quest to make the people in your life better than they are when you find them. That's all well and good if they're cooperative and want to be fixed, but right around the end of the month, those you're donating your skills to might not be willing to be helped.

Money and Success

The New Moon on September 24 will cast its bright light across your money axis, Virgo, urging you to start up that new business you've been talking about for years. If that's a possibility now, you'll receive all the help you need from the Universe. If you've been a bit remiss in your duties, you may need to put in another six months or so until you've been deemed celestially worthy to receive these boons.

Planetary Hotspots

The hottest spot this month will be the trine on September 25 between extravagant Jupiter and spontaneous, eccentric Uranus, bringing together your solar twelfth house of Privacy, Please with your solar eighth house of intimate moments. Yes, "hot" is definitely the word to be heard, and every fiber of your being will respond to that impulse. Your mission is to be sure you're devoting all that energy to The Right One.

Rewarding Days

2, 3, 5, 10, 14, 15, 20, 21, 25

Challenging Days

6, 7, 8, 12, 13, 17, 28, 29

Virgo | October

Planetary Lightspots

With Mars in Sagittarius and your solar fourth house of home until October 25, no matter what's going on with family members, your first line of defense will be making light of the situation. Any way you can insert a bit more levity and a lot more philosophical insight will help, but laughter, as you well know, is the best medicine.

Relationships

It's all going to be about you this month, Virgo—but not that you'd notice. Loving Venus, the Sun, and your ruling planet, Mercury, will take turns making their presence known in your solar eighth house of intimate partners. Oddly enough, both our archenemies and the dearest of the dears are included in that house's jurisdiction, so the stronger you feel about someone, the more they'll be included in your month—for better or worse.

Money and Success

With loving Venus, Mercury, and the Sun on duty in balance-loving Libra and your solar second house of personal finances, you'd think money matters would go along fine, without anyone's input, right? Wrong. Libra isn't balanced, it's seeking balance, and this sign tends to end up in unfair situations or face to face with situations that seem to be out of control, without a hope for compromise. Your mission is to put that energy to work, and bear up in the process.

Planetary Hotspots

Once fiery Mars sets off for your solar fifth house on October 26, Virgo, there really won't be much you can do to keep your admirers at bay—and why would you want to, anyway? The worst possible scenario will be that you'll have far too many first dates and no long-term relationships. If you're smart, however, you'll take the best from what they all offer and spin it into gold.

Rewarding Days
5, 6, 14, 15, 22, 23, 26, 27, 28

Challenging Days
3, 4, 7, 10, 11, 16, 17, 18

Virgo | November

Planetary Lightspots

The Sun, Mercury, and Venus will take turns in your solar third house of communications this month, Virgo, all of them inspiring you to speak your mind clearly—which, of course, depends on you and the mental and emotional state you bring to all your conversations. If someone close to you senses that you're not quite on your game around November 9 or 13, don't be mad. They care, or they wouldn't have said a word.

Relationships

Just when you thought it wouldn't ever be safe to have a long-distance relationship again, Virgo, the Full Moon on November 6 will convince you that your far-off pen pal really is genuinely interested in getting to know you better—or getting to know you again. If you make contact with an old sweetheart from college or even high school, give yourself a few days to chill out before you decide to marry them.

Money and Success

Up until Mercury leaves fair-minded Libra and your solar second house of personal money matters behind, Virgo, you'll probably be fine with negotiating any recent financial disputes. Once November 8 arrives, however, Mercury will enter Scorpio and be in the mood to dig for facts, so anyone who hasn't already come clean will find the next few weeks of your intense scrutiny quite difficult. How sad for them.

Planetary Hotspots

Once Mercury, the Sun, and Venus enter Scorpio and your solar eleventh house of friendships and group affiliations, Virgo, you'll probably find more than one situation you thought was comfortably on hold suddenly way out of control. Don't get in the middle, no matter how convinced you are that you're the only one who can help. You have bigger fish to fry.

Rewarding Days

1, 2, 3, 16, 17, 21

Challenging Days

8, 9, 10, 12, 13, 18, 22, 25, 26

Virgo | December

Planetary Lightspots

You're usually quite infatuated with details, Virgo, and while every other sign is grateful to you, every now and then you need to get away from the computer and/or calculator. Fortunately, now is the time for you to make a break. The Universe, in its wisdom, has arranged to make it easy for a lovely long-distance trip for you or yours to go off without a hitch.

Relationships

You'd never agree to a "sugar-daddy" relationship, Virgo, but if you just so happen to be quite involved with an elder who's well off and wants to help you—well, as long as you're putting in your time, who's to say? Be sure that any arrangement between you and your ward is well documented, to protect both of you.

Money and Success

Success is measured in many ways, Virgo, but usually, fortunate Jupiter weighs into the mix. Lucky for you, he'll be paying homage to several planets in your solar fourth house of home and domestic situations this month, so when and if you need a visit from either a guardian angel or Santa Claus to help you take care of business, rest assured that Jupiter will have them in place. Lucky you!

Planetary Hotspots

Saturn isn't your ruling planet, Virgo, but since he's such an earthy, practical energy, you tend to respond to his moods—big time. So over the next two and a half years, as he makes his way through your solar fourth house of home, family, and domestic matters, you may become quite obsessed with security, physical foundations, and the surety of your domestic situation. The fun starts on December 23, but after that, all bets are off.

Rewarding Days
1, 2, 4, 10, 12, 14, 16, 20

Challenging Days
6, 8, 15, 19, 23, 24, 25, 26

Virgo Action Table

These dates reflect the best—but not the only—times for success and ease in these activities, according to your Sun sign.

	JAN	FEB	MAR	APR	MAY	JUN	JUL	AUG	SEP	OCT	NOV	DEC
Move						12					22	
Start a class				24–26	6							
Join a club					24	27						
Ask for a raise							7, 13		24	21	1	4
Look for work	7, 11				12, 15			10			6	
Get pro advice			1, 13			8, 18			25	16		14
Get a loan				2, 25				8				
See a doctor		11										20
Start a diet					9				3, 21			
End relationship						12						
Buy clothes									2, 10			
Get a makeover			16					15, 23, 25	5			
New romance	30	14, 23	1	5, 11, 17					14, 21	27		
Vacation					28							

Libra

The Balance
September 22 to October 22

Element: Air

Quality: Cardinal

Polarity: Yang/masculine

Planetary Ruler: Venus

Meditation: I balance conflicting desires

Gemstone: Opal

Power Stones: Tourmaline, kunzite, blue lace agate

Key Phrase: I balance

Glyph: Scales of justice, setting sun

Anatomy: Kidneys, lower back, appendix

Colors: Blue, pink

Animals: Brightly plumed birds

Myths/Legends: Venus, Cinderella, Hera

House: Seventh

Opposite Sign: Aries

Flower: Rose

Keyword: Harmony

The Libra Personality

Your Strengths and Challenges

Your mission in life is to restore balance, Libra, and your ruling planet, Venus, has blessed you with all the qualities you need to pull that off beautifully. Her gifts of charm, poise, keen social skills, and the ability to put anyone at ease in your company make you someone everyone loves to have around. You tend to have a wide circle of acquaintances, but one-to-one relationships are your specialty, so while friends are important, they always take a back seat to your primary partner, and you'll do anything to keep them pleased and happy.

You learned at an early age how to make others like you and to make peace and create harmony. Those aren't easy tasks, so you often keep your true feelings to yourself, even if it means taking someone's side when you completely disagree with them. As you get older and have more life experience under your belt, however, you're more likely to agree to disagree, politely change the subject, and find common ground.

Now, about that reputation for indecision, a trait others find both endearing and endlessly irritating. Yes, it is tough for you to make choices, especially if both options are appealing, but once you do make up your mind, that's that. Give yourself the time you need to reach a verdict, but don't get stuck weighing the options forever or considering the preferences of others more important than your own. Remember, you can be fair without giving up your individuality.

Your Relationships

Your symbol is the scales, Libra, and you certainly do have a knack for balance, but you don't come by it easily. Sun signs describe the qualities we're learning to perfect this time around, so if your mission is balance, it stands to reason that you'll be drawn toward situations and relationships that are anything but. That's how you hone your skills, but it can be exhausting. Never mind the fact that you're automatically the person everyone turns to for mediating, negotiating, and smoothing out differences between warring factions, which puts you smack dab in the middle of conflicts and confrontations, both of which you avoid like the plague. You also feel the need to keep things on an even keel in social situations, so while you might seem to be a lighthearted social butterfly, even when you're at play, you're really on duty. If anyone in the group doesn't seem comfortable, you'll go out of your way to introduce them around and make them feel accepted.

One-to-one relationships, however, are your specialty, and once you're attached, you devote every ounce of your being toward keeping your beloved happy. That can mean a bit of sacrifice every now and then, but you usually manage to sweetly inspire the same level of dedication in your partner, if not more. All that Venusian charm makes you the perfect companion, so coaxing others to do things your way is a piece of cake—hence your reputation for being "the iron hand in the velvet glove."

Sagittarians are great fun and make terrific playmates, but you're often romantically drawn to your opposite sign, fiery Aries, or to attentive, romantic Leo. Earthy, comfort-loving Taurus can also steal your heart, but Cancer and Capricorn can be tough matches.

Your Career and Money

You're a born people person, Libra, so you make a terrific social director, but you may also choose to use those skills for counseling, where your understanding nature and ability to connect with others are huge assets. Your skill in mediation could draw you into couples counseling, or even something as exciting as hostage negotiation. No matter where you work, if you're content, others will enjoy your company, appreciate your willingness to help, and consider you family. If your work surroundings are offensive in any way, however, you may tough it out for a day, but first thing in the morning, you'll call in and quit—nicely, of course. Because you're so partner-oriented, you often end up happiest when you're working as part of a team, many times even alongside your significant other. This arrangement certainly can bring out the best in you both, but combining business and pleasure can also take the fun out of your relationship. Remember to take time apart. It can be just as important as time together.

Your Lighter Side

You are truly Venus's child, Libra, so you adore beautiful surroundings, pleasing sights and sounds, and spending time around others who are polite and charming. You love art and music, but you don't enjoy either as much when you're alone—in fact, you don't like to do anything alone. Sharing pleasant aesthetic experiences with someone special by your side is your idea of Nirvana.

Affirmation for the Year
Relationships are important, but I value my independence.

The Year Ahead for Libra

What a year, Libra! Your sign and your solar first house of personality and appearance will play host to Mars until July 25, an unusually long visit. This assertive planet will inspire you to step up, take charge, and put your foot down in your own defense, possibly for the first time in a long time. You're as partner-oriented as a sign could possibly be, so this sudden urge to call your own shots may be a bit unsettling—at first, anyway. After all, you're never happier than when you have someone by your side, so making a few concessions comes naturally to you. Why rock the boat? Well, if you're involved in an unhealthy or harmful relationship just because you don't like to be alone, that's a great reason to start rocking. Forget about keeping the peace at your own expense. Mars simply won't stand for that now. Never mind what They like to do, eat, and watch on television. What do *you* like? This red-hot planet will make that abundantly clear to you during his seven-month trek, and once you have your top ten list in hand, he'll push you hard to get out there and pursue it.

Mars will have some help, too. Startling Uranus is currently on duty in your solar seventh house of one-to-one relationships, urging you to spend your time only with companions who accept you as you and allow you to express yourself freely. If you need to end a relationship, especially if you're feeling repressed, unappreciated, or stifled, you'll do it now. You'll probably have someone new waiting in the wings, and they may temporarily distract you, but don't get comfortable just yet. Uranus's influence means all your current partnerships are subject to sudden change, and with this planet in cahoots with Mars—the ancient God of War, you'll remember—you will have some uncertainty in your personal life, and a fair amount of drama, too. Don't shy away from confrontations. Get yourself free. Something better is en route.

Speaking of something better, let's talk about Jupiter, who'll make his way through nurturing Cancer and your solar tenth house of career matters and authority figures straight through July 16. This benevolent planet will bring you blessings in all your encounters with higher-ups and elders. Because of the emotional nature of Cancer, you may also spend a fair amount of time learning from dearly loved mentors and meeting new friends who'll take you quite lovingly under their wing. If you have the chance to do the same for a child, student, or apprentice, you'll jump on it. Your unselfish efforts won't go unnoticed, either. Jupiter will see to it that someone benevolent in a position of authority over you is watching, and quite impressed. That promotion you've been hoping for could be right around the corner.

After July 16, Jupiter will set up shop in your solar eleventh house of group affiliations and friendships, all done up in theatrical Leo. This show-stealing energy will undoubtedly put you on center stage for the coming year, and you will love every exciting, romantic moment—especially since one of your costars could become your new leading man or leading lady.

Frugal Saturn is at the end of his two-and-a-half-year trek through your solar second house, where money matters are handled, so things haven't been easy for you here. In fact, you've probably had to tighten your belt and stick to a rather restrictive budget. The good news is that you've gotten good it. When this transit ends on December 23, you'll breathe a little easier, but you won't forget the lesson: live within your means. Saturn's mission here is to get you to be realistic about what really matters and what you truly value. Get those priorities in order and build your life around them.

Neptune will remain on duty in your solar sixth house of work and health throughout 2014, bringing compassion and empathy to your dealings with coworkers and higher-ups alike. These lovely gifts will help you to make a difference in someone's world, but be sure it's the right someone. It will be easy for you to be taken advantage of now. If you aren't happy with the type of work you're doing, a more spiritual path may call, which is an excellent use of this energy. Still, be sure you can support yourself on this new venture before you leave your current position. If health-related matters are vague or confusing, do not pass Go before you get a second opinion. Get a third, too, if you're still not satisfied. You know your body better than anyone else. Listen to it.

Pluto will continue on his way through your solar fourth house of emotions, home, and family matters, so power struggles may arise and domestic situations will be tense at times. The best use of this intense planet's energy is to purge. Get rid of what's irreparably broken in your home and find a way to let go of grudges.

What This Year's Eclipses Mean for You

The year 2014 will host four eclipses, Libra, two solar and two lunar. Solar Eclipses bring together the Sun and Moon in a highly charged New Moon. They meet up in the same sign and degree and herald new beginnings. Lunar Eclipses are equally potent Full Moons—an opposition between the Sun and Moon. They specialize in activating tugs of war in our lives, showing us the results of our actions and forcing us to find a way to either compromise or let go entirely.

The first eclipse of the year will arrive on April 15, a Lunar Eclipse in your very own sign and your solar first house of personality and appearance. You'll be given a chance to change something about the way you present yourself to others, so if you're unhappy with your attitude, your physical self, or your emotional reactions to others, this is an excellent time to shift gears. Get yourself on a diet, quit a bad habit, or begin a more healthy daily regime. Since one-to-one relationships are your sign's primary focus, you may be craving these changes because you're not fond of what you've been attracting lately, and if that's the case, good for you! Our outer selves most definitely reflect what we think we deserve, so any alterations you make now will eventually show up in better, more positive relationships.

The second eclipse will be solar, and will occur in steady, solid Taurus on April 29 and your solar eighth house of joint finances. If someone close to you hasn't been contributing to your domestic situation, you won't stand for it any longer. You'll present them with a realistic look at what it costs to keep your lifestyle intact, and insist they take responsibility for their part. If times are good, you'll be more than willing to give your partner a pat on the back for the hard work and effort they've put into making your teamwork a profitable venture. If you need to take out a loan or repay one, this is a great time to do it. You may also be dealing with inheritances or the sudden need to cut back, but not to worry. Taurus planets always see to it that we have what we need.

On October 8, a second Lunar Eclipse will occur, and you may feel as if events and circumstances from early April have returned. This time, however, the Moon will be in fiery, impulsive Aries and your solar seventh house of one-to-one relationships, and all that hard work you've been putting into creating a new you might just pay off. One way or the other, keep in mind that Aries is assertive and aggressive, and not afraid to display anger. Stay away from potentially volatile situations, and don't be afraid to put a sudden end to any and all negative relationships.

The last eclipse of the year will be solar, activating your solar second house of personal finances. This lunation will occur in Scorpio, a sign that insists we let go of anything useless or broken. This is a great time to do some serious housecleaning and get rid of clutter, even if you're sentimentally tied to it. Close credit accounts that are draining you, and find better interest rates for savings or investments.

Saturn

If your birthday is between October 14 and 24, Libra, your Sun will be contacted by serious Saturn this year, from his current position in your solar second house of personal finances, values, and possessions. Since this aspect is a semisextile, you may feel as if your attitude in this area of life is just now beginning to change, but don't doubt that those changes won't stick. Saturn doesn't kid around, and when he's touching your Sun, you won't be willing to, either. In particular, you will want the facts and nothing but the facts in all money matters or disputes over possessions, and that's your best course of action right now. Don't let anyone guilt you into doing something you're not comfortable with or intimidate you into letting go of what you know you deserve. If that means saying goodbye to someone who's a little too good at spending your money, so be it. You need to share financial responsibility fairly and prevent yourself from being drained by anyone who isn't willing to shoulder their part of the burden. You may also become involved in lawsuits or court cases to defend what you hold dear, but so much the better. The point of any Saturn transit is to test our foundations, find the flaws, and repair them so that we're better prepared to face the future. In particular, your mission now is to be realistic about what you really need and what you've honestly earned. If you're willing to let go of anything that's controlling your lifestyle and values in a negative way, you'll come out of this far stronger than you were, and much more secure. If that means switching to a lower-paying job you love because it better reflects your personal values, go for it. It may be tough at first, but in the long run you'll be better off. You're planting the seeds of a lifelong career now, and the more diligently you tend to that, the hardier your prospects for success will be.

Uranus

If you were born between October 1 and 11, your Sun will be opposed by startling Uranus this year, Libra. Oppositions tend to act out in our relationships, and since you value nothing more than partnerships, this could be quite the unsettling time for you. Uranus just loves last-minute changes and sudden turnarounds, so don't be surprised if at least one someone near and dear to you does something that absolutely knocks your socks off—or if you beat them to it and raise some eyebrows yourself. If you've been feeling repressed or held back by a partner, professionally or personally, you'll rebel, in no uncertain terms. No one will be able to tell you what to do now, and the harder they try, the more you'll fight for your rights. Again, relationships that restrict your personal freedom or threaten your independence may end, and you may be tempted to replace them immediately with a partnership that's different from any you have ever known. Love at first sight is definitely a possibility—at least once, by the way—but don't head for the chapel just yet. Those who enter our lives under the influence of Uranus aren't usually there to stay. They're messengers, sent along to help us get ourselves free. If your Uranian "representative" sticks around, however, that's good news. It means you've found a way to join forces and yet allow each other to be individuals—and those are the relationships that often last the longest.

Neptune

If your birthday is between September 26 and October 2, your Sun will be contacted by Neptune this year, from her spot in your solar sixth house of health and work. Now, Neptune rules intuition and psychic abilities, but she's been known to be in the neighborhood when we're forced to deal with something we can't quite put our finger on. So over the coming year, your work situation may be unsettling, although you may not be able to say why. If coworkers or higher-ups seem to have hidden agendas, you may be right, but before you stalk out the door, be sure those agendas aren't innocent. It's easy to fall prey to illusion now, as well as to delusion and confusion. Still, it's best to be sure. Document anything that doesn't seem right to you, especially if shady circumstances could make you look bad in the long run.

Healthwise, if you have strange, unexplained symptoms, don't ignore them, and be sure you consult with a reputable professional for answers.

It's also a good idea to have someone else with you to ask questions during doctor visits. Your mission is to bring your beliefs into your daily life. Pursuing a lifestyle more appropriate to or a job more in keeping with those beliefs may be challenging, but it's necessary to your mental, physical, and spiritual health.

Pluto

If you were born between October 3 and 8, Libra, your Sun will be touched directly by intense Pluto this year. The aspect involved is a square, an irritating relationship between two planets that insists we take action to make ourselves more comfortable—even if we're quite uncomfortable in the process. The Sun in our charts is the place where we store our identity—basically, it's how we project ourselves, based on how we see ourselves. When Pluto comes along, we get a glimmer of what we're really made of, deep down—and often of what we're capable of. Critical or urgent situations may arise in your personal life, demanding to be dealt with, or you may be asked to help a dear one with equally pressing concerns. Regardless of which it is, you'll be a formidable enemy and a determined ally. Pluto is relentless, and while he's visiting your Sun, you will be, too. You'll refuse to take no for an answer, a definite asset as long as you don't take it too far and resort to bulldozing or manipulating to get your way. You'll also need to watch out for a tendency to become obsessed with someone or something. Pluto forces us to stop focusing on anything surface or shallow and start investigating who we really are. This is a terrific time to begin therapy, especially if it's to cleanse yourself of the past. If you need to do any research, you'll be absolutely tireless. The good news is that any Pluto transit is like being temporarily endowed with super-powers. Your perceptive abilities will be especially keen. Your mission now is to remain as objective as possible until you have all the facts.

Libra | January

Planetary Lightspots

The New Moon on January 30 will plant a seed in your solar ninth house, Libra, and suddenly, you'll have a serious urge to go back to school, take a long trip, or find some other way to break your routine. You're after adventure now, but as per usual, you won't want to go without your sweetheart. If you're somehow single at the moment, expect to find your next flame where and when you'd least expect to.

Relationships

The Sun, Mercury, Pluto, and Venus will take turns firming things up at home this month, Libra, since all four will hold court in your solar fourth house. They're all wearing no-nonsense Capricorn at the moment, however, so you may need to set down some non-negotiable ground rules to straighten things out. Be firm, and don't buckle. You can do it!

Money and Success

On January 7, chatty Mercury will join forces with your ruling planet, Venus, who just so happens to be in charge of the planetary purse strings. There will be lots of conversation about money and business dealings, and if you're thinking of investing in a home, this wouldn't be a bad time to do the negotiating. The charming presence of Venus will help you attract what you're after. Nice!

Planetary Hotspots

The Full Moon on January 15 will occur in nurturing, sympathetic Cancer and your solar tenth house of elders and authority figures, Libra, and you may need to divide your time between helping them out and tending to your normal domestic duties. If you can, get everyone involved in errands or shopping trips. Make a family outing of it and you'll be able to keep everyone happy.

Rewarding Days
10, 11, 12, 17, 21, 23, 24

Challenging Days
1, 2, 3, 5, 7, 8, 16, 25, 26

Libra | February

Planetary Lightspots

Your solar sixth house of work and health issues will play host to Mercury retrograde from February 6 through February 12, Libra. You may have to deal with a nagging health matter, or someone who has been a thorn in your side at work could find yet another way to irritate you. No, you're not fond of confrontation, but there's something to be said for clearing the air. Buck up.

Relationships

As of February 12, Mercury will have backed up into your solar fifth house of lovers, fun times, and dealings with kids. From then until February 28, you'll have plenty of opportunities to make up for time you weren't able to spend with loved ones recently. Last-minute schedule changes may be the reason you'll finally have a bit of free time, but no one will mind the spontaneity.

Money and Success

You are probably getting tired of Saturn's presence after almost two years in your solar second house of money matters, Libra. This notoriously frugal planet never was fond of frivolities, and you may not have had much to spend on them, anyway. But right around February 24, Saturn will be softened by the touch of your ruling planet, loving Venus, so you may be able to raid the cookie jar for dinner and a movie.

Planetary Hotspots

If you've been thinking about a job change, Libra, you might cross paths with someone around February 23 who'll be able to help. Pay special attention to all your encounters with like-minded others who share your beliefs. One of them may be looking for a partner or employee who isn't just phoning it in. Just don't be taken in by a smooth line with nothing to back it up. Be sure the job pays what you need to live.

Rewarding Days

4, 5, 14, 18, 20, 23, 24

Challenging Days

6, 10, 11, 12, 19, 25, 26

Libra | March

Planetary Lightspots

The Sun, Mercury, and Neptune will keep you busy this month, Libra, from their spot in your solar sixth house of work, but don't overlook your health. If you're feeling stressed, this is a great time to investigate yoga, meditation, or holistic medicine. Be sure to find a reputable practitioner.

Relationships

Prepare for romance, Libra—big time. Your ruling planet, Venus, the Lady of Love herself, will set off for your solar fifth house of lovers on March 5, and the parade will begin. With Venus in unconventional Aquarius, of course, you can expect your admirers to be a bit "different"—at least, compared to the type of person you're ordinarily drawn to. Rebels and eccentrics can be fun, but don't get comfy just yet.

Money and Success

Mercury will remain on duty in your solar fifth house until March 17—a creative guy in a very creative spot. In inventive Aquarius, he'll inspire you to think outside the box, so if a radical idea suddenly occurs to you, don't dismiss it without trying it out. You might be on the verge of finding a whole new source of income—one that you'll really love. Nothing ventured, nothing gained.

Planetary Hotspots

It's time to follow your bliss, Libra—straight to the bank. Now, you usually pursue just about everything with a partner, and that will definitely work to your advantage at this time. On March 20, the Sun will enter Aries and your solar seventh house of relationships, and you may find that your fiery, impulsive sweetheart has some ideas that will help you further your work-related goals, especially if you're trying to turn a hobby into a vocation.

Rewarding Days

12, 13, 14, 18, 22, 27, 28

Challenging Days

1, 10, 11, 23, 24, 29, 30

Libra | April

Planetary Lightspots

You're usually the very soul of cooperation, Libra, and will do just about anything to keep the peace. This month, however, with assertive Mars on duty in your sign and all those planets in Aries provoking him into action, you'll be far more likely to Just Say No, even if you know others won't be pleased. Well, good for you! Even Librans get to blow off some steam every now and then. It's your turn.

Relationships

Fasten your seat belt, Libra, because your love life will be pretty darn unpredictable this month. On April 2 and 14, the Sun and Mercury will take turns contacting startling Uranus in your solar seventh house of one-to-one relationships, and then, on April 15, a Lunar Eclipse will occur, also in your sign. Without warning, you might just decide you've had it with your current partner. Don't hesitate. A bad relationship is much worse than no relationship.

Money and Success

The Solar Eclipse on April 29 will plant a supercharged seed of change in Taurus, a sign that's often referred to as a money magnet. With this lunation also occurring in your solar eighth house of joint finances, opportunities to invest could come along quite suddenly. Check them out carefully and make sure everything is completely aboveboard.

Planetary Hotspots

Six planets and a Lunar Eclipse, all in change-oriented cardinal signs, will poke, prod, and shake things up around the angles of your solar chart this month, Libra, so without a doubt, change is on the horizon. The fast-acting nature of all these energies means you may not have much time to prepare, but chances are good you'll have seen it all coming for some time. Your sudden reactions will surprise others, but those closest to you will respect and support your decisions.

Rewarding Days
10, 11, 17, 18, 19, 25, 26, 29, 30

Challenging Days
1, 3, 8, 14, 15, 16, 21, 22, 23

Libra | May

Planetary Lightspots

Curious Mercury in Gemini will team up with the New Moon in that same sign this month, Libra, and right around May 29, you may actually make good on your threat to return to school. You might also decide it's time for an adventure, and your partner will most likely be not only ready and willing but also impatient. Have some fun, learn something new, or explore a far-off place you've always wanted to visit.

Relationships

Bright and early on May 2, loving Venus, your ruling planet, will set off for impulsive Aries and your solar seventh house of one-to-one relationships. If you're not already seeing someone, an ardent new admirer will storm onto the scene and be absolutely impossible to ignore—and why would you want to? Well, if they seem a bit too focused on where you go, what you do, and with whom, especially around May 14, back off.

Money and Success

Once again, your best bet financially may be to form a partnership, Libra, but before you go into business with a fiery new friend, be sure they're everything they say they are. Do your homework and check out their background. Talk to others who've known them longer. If you still feel confident you can trust them, look to May 28 to sign the paperwork.

Planetary Hotspots

You're not fond of drama, Libra, but at times it seems to follow you around. That may be the case again this month, as Venus in passionate, impulsive Aries storms through your solar seventh house of one-to-one relationships. A power struggle over a menial issue could arise on May 14 when she squares off with controlling Pluto. Don't let anyone push you around.

Rewarding Days

3, 5, 6, 9, 12, 15, 23, 24

Challenging Days

2, 10, 11, 14, 16, 18, 27, 28

Libra | June

Planetary Lightspots

Once Venus takes off for your solar ninth house on June 23, Libra, you may see a return on recent investments you've made in classes or tutoring to amp up your resumé. And when the New Moon on June 27 occurs in your solar tenth house of career matters, the show will be on the road. Ready or not, here comes success.

Relationships

A casual relationship could turn quite serious this month, Libra, and with Venus in touch-loving Taurus and your solar eighth house of intimate matters, your friends will begin to wonder where you've been. Now, love is definitely grand, but don't forget about friendships—which tend, statistically, to last a lot longer.

Money and Success

The Full Moon in lucky Sagittarius on June 13 will put you in touch with someone prosperous and successful who can help point you in the right direction, Libra. With this lighthearted energy putting its all into your solar third house of conversations, you'll also be in the mood for some serious fun. Dismiss your partner for the evening and head out with old friends. Absence really does make the heart grow fonder.

Planetary Hotspots

Sparks will fly on June 7, Libra, as the emotional Moon collides with both shocking Uranus and assertive Mars in your own sign and your solar first house of personality. Communicative Mercury will begin his three-week retrograde period in your solar tenth house of authority figures that same day, so an age-old irritating issue could surface, demanding to be solved. You like to talk things over and find compromises, but this time out, you may not be quite so accommodating.

Rewarding Days

3, 4, 6, 8, 12, 18, 28, 29

Challenging Days

7, 11, 13, 14, 19, 24, 25

Libra | July

Planetary Lightspots

After three long weeks of moving retrograde, Mercury will finally turn direct on July 1, Libra, and long-distance news you've been waiting for will finally arrive, most likely by July 7. If you've been toying with the idea of making reservations for a cruise or some other group-oriented trek, this would be a great time to do it. Look to July 13 and 14 for all your careful planning to pay off.

Relationships

Reunions with far-off loved ones will be easy to arrange this month, Libra, so stop wishing you could reach through the phone and touch them and make it happen. You'll have plenty of energy and determination, thanks to yet another month of energetic Mars in your own sign. Put him to work for you before he takes off on July 25.

Money and Success

You're quite susceptible to Venus's moods, Libra, since she's your patron planet, so when she arranges for you to meet a new admirer with a terrific accent around July 7, you'll be quite willing to take a chance. Even if they're not local, don't worry about geography being a problem. People move all the time to be closer to the one they love. This may be one of those times.

Planetary Hotspots

The Full Moon on July 12 will energize your solar axis of home and domestic matters versus professional dealings, Libra, and you'll feel torn now between taking care of your loved ones and working to ensure their happiness in the future. Fortunately, if anyone can juggle responsibilities, it's you, so if you're smart about your time, you'll be able to pull it off. Just don't forget about your own needs!

Rewarding Days

6, 7, 13, 23, 29, 30

Challenging Days

3, 4, 8, 19, 20, 22, 24, 28

Libra | August

Planetary Lightspots

Your social schedule will be quite busy this month, Libra, thanks to Mercury, Jupiter, the Sun, and your ruling planet, charming Venus. This pack will move through dramatic Leo, the sign that most loves the applause of a crowd, and no matter where you go, you can count on being the star of the show. Just don't do anything now that you don't want the world to hear about—because they most certainly will.

Relationships

The Full Moon of August 10 will activate your solar fifth house of love affairs, Libra, and at least one new admirer who's absolutely determined to get your attention will begin to make themselves known—in a very big way. If you're already attached and want to stay that way, don't be led astray by romantic displays. If you're single, however, you're in for some fun—and some seriously lavish evenings out, too.

Money and Success

When Venus is in Leo, entertainment is everything, Libra. She'll enter that sign on August 12, urging you to pull out all the stops to turn a simple party into the event of the season. As sociable as you are, you're already guaranteed an A-list of guests, but remember—the best things in life may not be totally free, but if you shop around, you can find the real deal.

Planetary Hotspots

Mars and Saturn will collide in intense Scorpio on August 25, a little while after the New Moon arrives. Now, New Moons mark beginnings, but Mars and Saturn often inspire taking steps to say goodbye, so you'll be faced with a bit of a dilemma. The good news is that since nature does, indeed, detest voids, once you've cleared the decks, all things will become possible.

Rewarding Days

7, 8, 14, 15, 21, 23, 25

Challenging Days

1, 9, 17, 18, 24, 26, 27, 29

Libra | September

Planetary Lightspots

The New Moon in your sign on September 24 will bring the Sun and Moon together in your solar first house, Libra, urging you to make some changes in your look and personal presentation. Your love of restoring balance may mean you're ready to get back on track physically, and if you start now, you'll be determined to finish. Diets, quitting bad habits, or starting good habits are all favored.

Relationships

What you crave most is a solid, reliable partner, Libra—someone you can trust with your deepest, darkest secrets who'll always have your back. Well, if you've been good, that wish may come true this month. Around September 14, you'll see evidence that you're just as important to them as they are to you, and by September 21, you two may be making big plans—of the most permanent kind.

Money and Success

The fun starts on September 2, Libra, when chatty Mercury sets off for your own talkative, sociable sign and your solar first house of personality. Up until he takes off for Scorpio on September 27, this outgoing energy will inspire you to meet, greet, and mingle with new, interesting people, several of whom may be able to advise you on a current business situation.

Planetary Hotspots

You've waited a full year for this, Libra, but the wait is almost over. Your ruling planet, loving Venus, will enter your sign and your solar first house on September 29, and all those qualities you're already famous for—charm, tact, fairness, and cooperation—will be running on high. You may be asked to mediate a battle, probably among family members, but it won't be a problem.

Rewarding Days
3, 4, 10, 11, 14, 24, 25, 29

Challenging Days
8, 9, 12, 13, 21, 22

Libra | October

Planetary Lightspots

Mercury will retrograde back into your sign on October 10, Libra, urging you to take another look at how your personality and appearance have affected your relationships. Is there something about yourself you'd like to change? Last month's New Moon probably got the show on the road, but you'll be extra motivated now to keep at work on the project. Time for a new wardrobe?

Relationships

Venus will face off with shocking Uranus on October 11, Libra, from her spot in your sign. Now, Uranus is the celestial King of Unpredictability, so one never knows what might happen, but it's a given that you won't let anyone tell you what to do, when to do it, or who to do it with. Yes, you're about to turn into quite the rebel. Enjoy it!

Money and Success

Restoring balance is your job, Libra, and you're good at it. That's not to say that learning this trade hasn't taken its toll on you, but you'll be glad you have this talent on October 8, when a family member may ask you to intervene on their behalf to settle up a financial situation, once and for all. Go in with a smile, insist that everyone be civil, tactful, and fair, and don't let them leave the room until they are.

Planetary Hotspots

The Lunar Eclipse on October 8 will occur in your solar seventh house of relationships, Libra. This lunation will ask that you bring closure or at least permanence to your primary partnerships, so both business and personal matters will demand your attention. Fairness to others won't be an issue. Try to be just as good to yourself.

Rewarding Days

5, 13, 14, 15, 26, 27, 28

Challenging Days

3, 4, 6, 7, 10, 16, 23, 24

Libra | November

Planetary Lightspots

When Venus and Jupiter form an energetic square, the Goddess of Love pushes the God of Excess into action. That's what will happen on November 9, and while someone's extravagance might mean a fun evening out creates quite the memory, don't invest too much into it. This, too, may pass. Protect your heart—but feel free to enjoy the ride!

Relationships

The Full Moon on November 6 will occur in your solar eighth house of intimate matters, Libra, and since it will be all done up in sensual, touch-loving Taurus, it's not hard to imagine how you might go about enjoying it. Your mission is to not let your libido run away with your head. No one's saying you can't enjoy some sexy fun, but don't book a flight to Vegas just yet.

Money and Success

A business deal that seemed to be wrapped up and ready to go could come up against some roadblocks on November 12, Libra, thanks to cautious Saturn, who'll get together with Venus in your solar second house of money matters to issue a warning. Do yourself a favor. If you're signing anything official around that time, be sure it's been carefully looked over by an impartial third party.

Planetary Hotspots

You'll need to give someone your final answer around November 25, Libra. You're usually not much for issuing ultimatums, but at this time, after weeks and possibly even months of trying to deal with someone's jealousy or resentment, chances are good that you'll have just about had it. Don't beat yourself up about it. Even Librans get to let off some steam every now and then.

Rewarding Days

1, 2, 3, 11, 20, 21, 28

Challenging Days

8, 9, 10, 13, 17, 18, 22, 25

Libra | December

Planetary Lightspots

The Full Moon on December 6 will accentuate Gemini, a fellow air sign you've always been fond of. Add to the mix the fact that it will also turn the celestial spotlight on in your solar fifth house of fun times with kids, recreation, and hobbies, and it's not hard to imagine you with a great big smile on your face. Take the kids out for pizza and a movie—and while you're at it, throw in some ice cream.

Relationships

Venus and Mercury in fun-loving Sagittarius and your solar third house of communications will meet up with generous Jupiter on December 4 and 8, Libra, urging you to go overboard to make someone's special day even better. You have a knack for arranging events that turn into cherished memories. Use it now. They'll never forget it.

Money and Success

Saturn is the head of the department of career matters, Libra, and he's about to switch signs, for the first time in two and half years. He'll enter your solar third house of conversation and communications on December 23, all done up in outgoing Sagittarius. Making beneficial new contacts will come easily, and your natural charm will make lasting friends of many of them.

Planetary Hotspots

Once again, rebellious Uranus will square off with controlling Pluto on December 15, Libra, a battle that's only half over but still raging. This Clash of the Titans will put your solar fourth house of family matters at odds with your solar seventh house of relationships, and someone from either side may insist that you make a choice. You're not in the mood to be told what to do, but don't rule out the possibility that they may simply be worried about your recent choices.

Rewarding Days
2, 4, 5, 12, 14, 19, 23

Challenging Days
1, 8, 15, 20, 21, 24, 25

Libra Action Table

These dates reflect the best—but not the only—times for success and ease in these activities, according to your Sun sign.

	JAN	FEB	MAR	APR	MAY	JUN	JUL	AUG	SEP	OCT	NOV	DEC
Move	7, 11											21
Start a class					28		16					
Join a club	15						26	2, 8, 18				4
Ask for a raise		24	1								1	1
Look for work				25		27					11	
Get pro advice						8, 18	24		21			
Get a loan								15			6	
See a doctor								23				
Start a diet		24								23		
End relationship	2, 16		29	8, 16, 23				26	9, 13	8		
Buy clothes									24	27		
Get a makeover									29			
New romance		14	30					10				
Vacation				12								

Scorpio

The Scorpion
October 22 to November 21

♏

Element: Water

Quality: Fixed

Polarity: Yin/feminine

Planetary Ruler: Pluto (Mars)

Meditation: I can surrender
my feelings

Gemstone: Topaz

Power Stones: Obsidian,
amber, citrine, garnet, pearl

Key Phrase: I create

Glyph: Scorpion's tail

Anatomy: Reproductive system

Colors: Burgundy, black

Animals: Reptiles, scorpions,
birds of prey

Myths/Legends: The Phoenix,
Hades and Persephone, Shiva

House: Eighth

Opposite Sign: Taurus

Flower: Chrysanthemum

Keyword: Intensity

The Scorpio Personality

Your Strengths and Challenges

Your ruling planet is Pluto, Scorpio, the mythical Lord of the Underworld—which certainly does explain your fondness for digging, on all levels. His jurisdiction over your sign also makes you magnetic, personally powerful, impossible to ignore, and, yes, quite secretive at times.

Those gifts make you a born researcher, analyst, and detective, with an amazing ability to notice and interpret clues that most of us miss. It might be an ordinary gesture, a subtle glance, a nod, or a flinch. Doesn't matter. Any tiny element of body language that catches your eye is enough to get your water-sign antenna twitching, and the more interested you are in your subject, the more determined you are to get to the bottom of things. It might take days, months, or decades, but you won't quit and you won't waver. You wrote the book on perseverance, willpower, and tenacity.

Those qualities are terrific assets when it comes to achieving your goals, but when you're bored, they can turn inward. That's when you find yourself lying in bed awake, fixating on something trivial. So, are you obsessive? You bet. That's why it's so important for you to find positive, appropriate channels for your particular brand of relentless, enduring energy. The more you use those natural abilities productively during your waking hours, the less likely you'll be consumed with someone or something that's really not worth your time.

Your Relationships

You're the human equivalent of a lie detector, Scorpio, and you take your equipment along on every encounter. So for someone to get to know you—the real you, that only a select few see—they have to pass your test. If something about a new friend or admirer doesn't seem quite right, you're out of there. That goes double for someone who asks too many personal questions too soon. Trusting others is a slow process for you, but if and when you do feel safe enough to open up, you'll tell all, right down to your deepest, darkest secrets.

Now, let's talk about sex. Every sign rules a part of the human body, and you probably aren't surprised to hear that yours rules the genitals. So, along with your innate craving for emotional intensity and deep connections, it only makes sense that you folks are highly sexual creatures—and that you tend to have significant others who grin a lot. When you fall for someone, it's usually because (a) they're incredibly sexy, and (b) you can't seem to solve the mystery of how they tick. The more fascinated you are in both departments, the more you'll keep coming back for more. The good news is that the vibes you put out when you're interested are magnetic, potent, and just about irresistible, so there usually isn't any shortage of intimacy in your life. One of your very best matches is Taurus, the most sensual sign in the zodiac—for obvious reasons. Not only does Taurus love to touch, but they're also just as stubborn as you are, and best of all, once they're committed, Taurus stays put. Virgos can be fun, since their eye for detail rivals your own, but Leos and Geminis aren't a match made in heaven for you.

Your Career and Money

You're a water sign, Scorpio, so if you're going to devote your life to a profession, you absolutely must be emotionally drawn to it. Once you've found your particular niche, however, your fixed nature kicks in. You become focused, determined, and next to impossible to call off. Even if it seems obvious that a project won't work and the mission should be aborted, you won't quit until you've done everything in your power to finish. If there's a component of secrecy or a mystery of some kind involved, such as research, detective work, or analyzing clues of any kind, you'll even keep at it in your spare time. This makes you an excellent, devoted employee who easily impresses authority figures. You understand the concept of process, of how things work—and that includes other people. With that x-ray vision, along with your incredible diligence, you are inevitably put in charge. After all, who understands the work like you do? Once you become the authority figure, you make it clear that you expect nothing less than 110 percent commitment from those under your supervision—and one less-than-pleased glance from you is enough to ensure that you'll have it.

Your Lighter Side

It's tough for you to relax, Scorpio, and even harder to stop doing what you do best and most naturally—investigating. So when you're unwinding, you often spend time alone, watching mysteries, solving puzzles, and poking around the Internet. Once you've been enticed out of the house, you let your keen wit, almost slapstick sense of humor, and blunt honesty have free rein with a select group of friends.

Affirmation for the Year

Facing change with a take-charge attitude serves me well.

The Year Ahead for Scorpio

This will be a year you'll probably regard as pleasant overall, Scorpio, despite a few challenges. Fortunately, all but one of the outer planets will remain in signs that are supportive to yours, so while there are definitely some big changes in store, with the help of these powerful cosmic allies, you can easily be the architect.

To start with, your ruling planet, Pluto, will form a supportive sextile with your sign from his position in Capricorn, while serious Saturn, the ruler of Capricorn, will continue to operate from Pluto's favorite sign—yours. These two planets ordinarily represent very different urges. Saturn builds up and Pluto tears down. Rather than creating a tug of war inside you, however, their easy relationship (called "mutual reception") this year will allow you to end negative situations and come up with practical, realistic plans for the future. This applies to any and all life departments, but your closest relationships will likely be where their energies will show up first. You won't be satisfied with shallow or casual relationships, so anyone who isn't pulling their own weight and assuming their share of responsibilities will need to go. The good news is that you won't have any regrets. In fact, you might wonder what took you so long.

Neptune will continue on her trek through ultra-sensitive Pisces, bringing intuition and divine inspiration to your solar fifth house of lovers, fun times, and leisure-time pursuits. If you're artistic, you'll be especially creative. Your dealings with youngsters will take on an almost spiritual quality, allowing you to become friend, teacher, and mentor rolled into one. Casual love affairs may come and go as you search for a true soul mate. There may be several false alarms along the way, but they'll be learning experiences. Never mind what you want in a relationship. What *don't* you want? Figure that out and you'll be able to spot the right one far more easily.

Uranus's continued presence in your solar sixth house of work will also make finding the right job very important, and personal freedom may become quite the issue. Any work situation that makes you feel stifled or restricted will become intolerable, and the erratic nature of this planet could mean you'll change jobs more than once. Rather than allowing yourself to become unsettled by these sudden changes, think of this as an opportunity to explore your options. Try out any occupation you've ever thought of pursuing, no matter how odd your choices seem to others. There's a good chance you'll eventually settle on something unusual, so let your imagination be your guide. Forget about applying for what you've already done. What would you like to do, ideally, for the rest of your life?

Now, let's talk about Jupiter, who'll spend half the year in Cancer and your solar ninth house of long-distance friends and far-off places, a place where he operates quite freely. This outgoing, benevolent planet will inspire you to broaden your horizons through travel and exploring new experiences—anything that will give you a wider perspective. Don't forget that Jupiter also rules higher education, however, making this a terrific time to go back to school, even if it's just for a few night classes to pad your resume. Taking online classes wouldn't be a bad idea, either, since you'd be able to work from home at your leisure. Your belief system may change, too, and incorporating these beliefs into your daily life will become a priority.

On July 16, lucky, prosperous Jupiter will head off into dramatic Leo and your solar tenth house of authority figures and career matters, which could mean you'll be given a promotion at your current place of work. More likely, however, since Uranus has been urging you to experiment with interesting new ways to earn your daily bread, you'll run into at least one someone who's already made it in an unusual occupation you've recently become drawn toward. Jupiter will see to it that these individuals are supportive, helpful, and willing to teach you whatever you need to know. Take advantage of this gift. Your quest to find the right life path could be coming to a happy end.

And then there's passionate Mars, who'll spend the first seven months of the year in Libra and your solar twelfth house of secrets. Libra just loves to be involved in relationships, but the hidden nature of this house may entice you toward an exciting but forbidden encounter. If you're currently attached and happy about it, think before you give in and break the rules. If you're unhappy, do the right thing and break it off before you look elsewhere. If you're single, be on guard against anyone who's unavailable, especially if they give you a sob story about being "misunderstood" by their significant other. You're pretty good at sniffing out deceit immediately, so you won't get into trouble if you trust your antennae—and not your libido.

What This Year's Eclipses Mean for You

There will be four eclipses in 2014, Scorpio. The first of two Lunar Eclipses will occur via a highly charged Full Moon on April 15, all done up in partner-oriented Libra and your solar twelfth house of secrets. Oh my... certainly does sound like someone's about to become involved in a rather clandestine relationship, doesn't it? If you're happily attached, take this as a warning: eclipses bring sudden change into our lives, so if you're not looking to change your relationship status, don't fool around, no matter how sexy a new admirer happens to be. If you're single or still looking, however, rest assured that opportunities to meet someone you really connect with on a very deep level will definitely come your way.

On April 29, a Solar Eclipse will arrive, bringing the Sun and Moon together in your solar seventh house of one-to-one relationships. Since both will be wearing stubborn Taurus, if you're still mulling over whether or not to make a drastic change in your love life, you should mull a little longer. Taurus rivals even your sign when it comes to determination, but Taurus tends to hold on, while your first impulse is often to throw out the baby with the bath water. Your mission is to find the balance point. Sort out the positive and productive relationships in your life from those that are weighing you down and taking advantage of you.

The second Lunar Eclipse of the year will occur on October 8, pitting the Moon in fiery, impulsive Aries against the Sun in partner-oriented Libra. If you've been hiding something, the bright light of this Full Moon will probably expose it. Prepare yourself, especially if that secret involves a clandestine relationship with a coworker. On the other hand, the efforts you've been putting into a particularly tough project will finally be noticed, and you may be put in charge of overseeing its completion.

On October 23, the last eclipse of year will arrive, bringing the Sun and Moon together in your own sign and your solar first house of personality and appearance. This is a powerful call for change, and while you might decide to give yourself a drastic physical makeover, this eclipse's influence won't just occur on a superficial level. You'll turn inward to examine how the way you initially present yourself to others affects your relationships. This time of introspection won't be easy, but if anyone is up to the task, it's you. Just don't spend too much time alone, and try to keep a lid on the brooding. If you find you're becoming obsessive or depressed, call a trusted friend and talk it out.

Saturn

If you were born between November 13 and 23, Scorpio, your Sun will be contacted by Saturn this year, the strictest and most cautious of all the planets. But Saturn is in your very own sign and blending with your Sun via a conjunction, so rather than erecting roadblocks to stall you, this no-nonsense energy will act as a very valuable ally, providing you with a built-in safety net, no matter where you are or who's challenging you. Go ahead and speak your truth, and do it righteously. If you know you're acting with honesty and integrity, you really can't fail. That goes double if you have a tough work project to tackle. You'll be absolutely unstoppable, and the more your heart is invested, the more formidable you'll be. Does that mean you'll always eventually get what you go after this year? Maybe. If you're willing to put your all into it, it's tough to believe you could possibly fail. If you ignore your responsibilities, however, be warned that Saturn will be especially tough on you. Remember, Saturn rules authority figures, and when he's visiting our Sun, he brings the subject of just who's in charge into our lives. On a positive note, you may end up being put in a position of authority now, and if that happens, rest assured that you've most certainly earned it. Saturn doesn't pass out treats like Jupiter does. The blessings we receive under Saturn transits are our just desserts. Enjoy yours!

Uranus

If you were born between November 1 and 10, your Sun will receive a startling and possibly unsettling visit from Uranus in Aries this year. But since virtually all of the outer planets except this one will play supportive roles in your life in 2014, even if Uranus decides to upset the applecart from his spot in your solar sixth house of work-related matters, you'll undoubtedly end up on your feet. That doesn't mean there won't be moments when you'll want to throw up your hands in frustration, especially if your current employment doesn't allow you the freedom to make your own schedule and call your own shots. Uranus brings along the last thing we'd ever expect, usually via quite the "interesting" human representative, so dealings with coworkers could be tumultuous, to say the least. You may see sides of them you'd never have expected, and their behavior will seem erratic, unpredictable, and even unstable at times. If you feel the need to put an end to the madness, before you pack up your desk, think about it. Letting someone drive you away from a happy job situation will make you crazy, so if you're content, plant your feet on the ground and stay put. If, on the other hand, you're secretly dying for a reason to walk out that door...well, then, go for it. With benevolent, generous Jupiter due to set up shop in your solar tenth house of career ventures as of July 16, it might just be the perfect time for a change.

Healthwise, you need to watch out for stress—the Aries planets' illness of choice—and avoid these situations at all costs. You have so much going for you now. Why take chances with your well-being? Be sure you get some exercise now. It doesn't have to be strenuous, but it should tire you out enough to sleep.

Neptune

If you were born between October 27 and 31, your Sun will enjoy a special blessing this year, Scorpio—an easy trine from dreamy, romantic Neptune. Now, Neptune rules water, and Pisces, the water sign she's in, is her favorite conduit. You're also a water sign, and since you're a master at perception and Neptune heightens intuition, your antennae will undoubtedly be firing on all six cylinders. Neptune has taken up residence in your solar fifth house of love affairs, dealings with children, and creative pursuits, so you can expect to be ultra-sensitive to the needs of your kids and your casual playmates, who'll subtly manage to keep your attention. But if you can carve out a few hours alone, your ability to bring divine inspiration to all your creations is really where you should be focusing your efforts. If you write, paint, or make music, devote yourself to your craft now. Uranus brings moments of genius, but Neptune inspires us to create masterpieces. You're now capable of producing something that will touch our hearts and open our eyes. Use this energy wisely.

Pluto

If you were born between November 3 and 7, Scorpio, your Sun will be contacted by your ruling planet this year—intense, focused Pluto. The good news is that he'll be creating an energizing sextile with your

Sun, so if and when dramatic change comes along, you'll be up for it. If anyone gets along with Pluto, it's you, so while many of us tend to come undone when this powerful planet is in the neighborhood, you cope quite well with his visits. In fact, since this is an energy you're so familiar with, you often sense what's coming—and what's leaving—well in advance. One of Pluto's gifts is perception, so this innate ability will be running on high—and heaven help anyone who thinks they can get pull one on you. You'll sit them down, explain that you know exactly what they're up to, and then let them in on why they're going to fail. All that, combined with that penetrating stare you tend to wear when you're flushing out prey, will render them defenseless—as per usual. The good news is that the sextile's energy is active and productive, so rather than it creating problems, you'll probably nip quite a few right in the bud. You'll gain respect, even from those who'd seen you as an adversary. Your sign wrote the book on keeping your enemies closer than your friends, but if you play your cards right, you'll be able to flip them. You probably already have a collection of lifelong friends you really weren't fond of when you first met them. Prepare to add a few names to that list.

Scorpio | January

Planetary Lightspots

You're always pretty darn intense, Scorpio, but you do tend to be able to keep your mouth closed—most of the time, anyway. So on January 1, when a New Moon joins forces with your ruling planet, all-or-nothing Pluto, what tumbles from your lips will amaze you. If disputes arise over your verbal display later in the month, tell them to handle it—or not.

Relationships

Between January 2 and 9, a pack of planets in respectable, inflexible Capricorn and your solar third house of conversations could make it quite difficult to communicate with anyone who's less than willing to see things your way, Scorpio. The good news is that the more convinced you are that you're right, the less willing you'll be to give an inch.

Money and Success

Neighbors and siblings may provide you with an excellent idea on how to make a career out of your most deeply held beliefs this month, Scorpio. So just this once, when they start telling you what you "ought" to do, listen up. If you don't tune them out, you might be on the receiving end of some wonderfully astute financial and professional advice.

Planetary Hotspots

On January 16, loving Venus in Capricorn will get into a square with passionate Mars, and when these two ancient lovers lock horns, the result is often "If You Loved Me, You Would" syndrome. Don't fall prey to this not-so-positive energy. Guilt, remorse, and worry are the best you'll glean from the experience. This is no time for games.

Rewarding Days

10, 11, 14, 17, 21, 24

Challenging Days

1, 2, 3, 5, 7, 8, 16, 25

Scorpio | February

Planetary Lightspots

Although this month's only Full Moon will activate your solar tenth house of higher-ups and career matters on Valentine's Day, Scorpio, you might not necessarily have to work overtime to enjoy it. In fact, if you've had a crush on an authority figure for some time now, this might be the perfect time to test the waters—that is, of course, if they don't beat you to it.

Relationships

With Saturn on duty in your sign, Scorpio, you've become known in some circles as an honorary principal of sorts—someone who can always be relied on to take charge of disorganized situations. That's all well and good, but you'll want to have some actual fun this month, and on February 11 and 19, you may feel a bit invaded. Might it be time to rethink this recent commitment?

Money and Success

Thank the Universe for Venus in Capricorn, a practical, earthy energy that never fails to drag us back to reality when on the verge of plunging ourselves into bankruptcy. She'll be on duty all month, so while Jupiter in your solar ninth house will be doing his best to convince you to travel and to go first class, Venus will agree, but will insist on economy—literally. The good news is that by the time the date arrives, you'll be glad you used common sense to plan it.

Planetary Hotspots

Confrontations aren't your specialty, Scorpio. You usually retire to your room to sit in the dark for hours, if not days, stewing and plotting the imminent demise of your opponent. You might have those same urges this month, but around February 11, 19, and 26, three explosive squares will shove you right back out into The Enemy's face. Careful. This is powerful stuff.

Rewarding Days
4, 5, 9, 14, 16, 20, 23, 24

Challenging Days
10, 11, 15, 18, 19, 25, 26

Scorpio | March

Planetary Lightspots

Two New Moons will give you a chance to start over this month, Scorpio, in two very different areas of life—but the results may be the same. On March 1, this lunation will occur in Pisces and your solar fifth house of lovers and recreation. If you've been lingering a bit too late after happy hour with the gang, it's time to change that. On March 30, the New Moon in feisty Aries will set up shop in your solar sixth house of health habits, urging you to change a few more that aren't working out so well.

Relationships

With serious Saturn on duty in your solar first house of personality and appearance for the past two years, Scorpio, you probably haven't had much time for good, old-fashioned romance. On March 1 and 13, however, the Sun in your solar fifth house will find a way to put a spring back into your step. Your mission is to keep penciling fun times in to your day planner—and to resolve to show up at least once!

Money and Success

As of March 5, Venus will set off for your solar fourth house of home, Scorpio, all done up in spontaneous Aquarius. If you and yours have occasionally entertained thoughts of moving, now will be the time for you to make your move. On March 18, a place you can afford more easily could become available. On March 29, you'll need to decide between what you want and what you can realistically manage.

Planetary Hotspots

Venus, the Goddess of Love, will get into an easy trine with her ancient lover, Mars, the God of War, on March 29. To many, love and war aren't concepts that go together easily, but if anyone understands the importance of having a seasoned soldier by their side, it's you. Someone who shares your feelings will be along shortly. If you have to argue with them before you give in and admit you're interested, that's fine.

Rewarding Days
1, 12, 13, 17, 21, 22, 27, 28

Challenging Days
10, 11, 19, 20, 29, 30, 31

Scorpio | April

Planetary Lightspots

The Lunar Eclipse in Libra on April 15 will give you plenty of incentives to make your surroundings beautiful, Scorpio. Whatever you modify within your own home, you'll do with an eye toward creating not just a comfortable place but also a safe one. Home security will also be an issue around April 20. Be sure not to leave the key in an obvious place if you're away.

Relationships

On April 5, loving Venus will set off for your solar fifth house, where love affairs and good times are often had. She'll be all done up in dreamy, romantic Pisces, and set to meet up with Neptune on April 11, so whether you're single or not, someone with what you'll think of as movie-star charm could be right around the corner. Pisces planets aren't notoriously realistic, however, so take your time and get to know the person well.

Money and Success

If you're madly in love, Scorpio, there'll be absolutely no way to convince you to be careful with your money. Having fun with your beloved will take precedence over just about anything else, and you'll spare no expense to do it up, as often as possible, as lavishly as possible. Easy, there. No one's saying you can't have some good times, but please don't mortgage the house to do it.

Planetary Hotspots

Money-related arguments on the job are a distinct possibility this month, Scorpio, especially around April 3 and 14. It won't be easy to remain objective, but try to put your personal feelings aside, especially if you're not directly affected by any losses. Around April 16, a rather explosive encounter will reveal all.

Rewarding Days

2, 5, 6, 17, 18, 24, 25, 26, 29

Challenging Days

1, 3, 13, 14, 16, 21, 22, 23

Scorpio | May

Planetary Lightspots

The Sun and Mercury in your solar seventh house of one-to-one relationships will keep you steady on the course this month, Scorpio. Even if problems come up, you'll know exactly who to see, what to ask for, and what to expect. That goes double for May 11, when your financial sixth sense will be especially keen.

Relationships

Talking things over with your sweetheart will be especially easy up until May 7, Scorpio, thanks to the efforts of chatty Mercury, who'll be on duty in your solar seventh house. No, you may not be able to resolve absolutely everything, but right around May 18, you'll probably think you have—and it will feel pretty darn good.

Money and Success

If you've recently come into a bit of a windfall, Scorpio, your mission during May will be to hold on to it—as much as possible, anyway. On May 17 and 18, that may be tough, however, so prepare yourself. Venus and Jupiter, the heavens' "feel good" energies, will come together in an irresistible square, and overdoing it will come naturally. Take a Capricorn friend along to advise and assist.

Planetary Hotspots

Mercury will oppose Saturn on May 2, and since Saturn just so happens to be rigidly holding court in your sign, an argument could come up involving a financial agreement. If you don't get it all worked out right then and there, look to May 10 for the same issue to boil up again. Do yourself a favor. As soon as you can, get all your papers together and sit down together with a neutral third party.

Rewarding Days

3, 5, 6, 9, 12, 15, 23, 24

Challenging Days

1, 2, 10, 11, 16, 17, 18, 28

Scorpio | June

Planetary Lightspots

On June 18, loving Venus and outgoing, expansive Jupiter will form an easy sextile, Scorpio, linking your solar seventh house of relationships with your solar ninth house of long-distance people and places. The energies these two create when they're in cahoots are all good, so if you miss someone, stop wondering about them and call.

Relationships

When it comes to you and one-to-one relationships, Scorpio, no matter what category they fall into, they stand a far better chance of lasting if they're emotionally intense. So this month, when solid Venus in Taurus makes contact with both spiritual Neptune on June 4 and your own sexy patron planet, Pluto, on June 8—well, it's easy to see how lust at first sight might just turn into finding your soul mate.

Money and Success

There simply is no better time for you to shop, invest, or apply for a loan than on June 8, Scorpio. All your money-related matters will go along so swimmingly, in fact, that you might even begin to worry about it. Relax. The other shoe isn't about to drop. Every now and then, the Universe passes out presents, and you've been good. That's all.

Planetary Hotspots

June 7, 14, and 25 are potentially volatile days, Scorpio, and while you tend to avoid direct confrontations, you may inadvertently be pulled into someone else's drama. If and when that happens, your mission will be to stay calm—especially since no one else will be able to manage it. Fortunately, you shine in situations that raise your adrenaline level.

Rewarding Days

3, 4, 6, 8, 9, 18, 28, 29

Challenging Days

7, 11, 12, 14, 19, 25, 26

Scorpio | July

Planetary Lightspots

The Sun, Venus, and Mercury will all spend some time this month in your solar ninth house, Scorpio, amping up the urge to learn, grow, or expand your horizons. They're all in home-loving Cancer, however, so taking classes and researching potential vacation venues might be best for now, especially if you can do it with a kid or a cat on your lap.

Relationships

Venus in fickle, lighthearted Gemini will keep you busy in the department of intimacy right up until she moves on around July 18, Scorpio. Up until then, however, sexy little you will experience a veritable buffet of tasty human delights. Your mission is to pick your favorite by July 13 or so.

Money and Success

Your solar eighth house of joint resources will play host to Venus, the Goddess of Love and Money, until July 18, Scorpio. If you're smart, you'll take advantage of this charming, intelligent energy while she's in the neighborhood. On July 13 or 14, she might even let you in on a little-known maneuver that will aide and abet your financial mission.

Planetary Hotspots

Talk about hot, Scorpio! On July 19, the Sun and Mars, aka "the red planet," will form a square, an equally fiery aspect that can only be described as irritating. When either of these planets feels that way, explosive situations are possible, but when they're locked into this ticking time-bomb relationship, there's really no way you won't experience some fireworks. Don't get so rattled that you lose control of domestic situations.

Rewarding Days

6, 7, 13, 14, 18, 23, 25

Challenging Days

4, 5, 8, 19, 22, 24, 27, 28

Scorpio | August

Planetary Lightspots

You tend to do slow boils when you're angry, Scorpio, but every now and then, something tweaks you just the right way and you blow. That may well be the case on August 25, when red-hot Mars provokes Saturn into giving up control—from his powerful spot in your sign and your solar first house of personality, by the way. If people came with warning labels, you'd be wearing one right now. Be merciful, anyway.

Relationships

With Mars on duty in your sign and your solar first house, you've been pretty darn hard to ignore lately, Scorpio. The good news is that the quiet power you've been oozing from every pore has finally caught the attention of someone just as fond of total commitment. You probably know exactly who they are, but don't ruin the surprise. Bet they confess by August 15.

Money and Success

You should think twice before agreeing to relocate for work this month, Scorpio, especially if the offer arrives around August 1. There may be more to this position than you've been told, and some of it might not strike you as savory. If it sounds like a get-rich-quick scheme, trust your gut. You might be right. Do your homework thoroughly.

Planetary Hotspots

You've never been afraid to say no or goodbye, Scorpio, and it has often mystified you how others seem to have so much trouble with it. So this month, when Mercury and Venus square off with no-nonsense Saturn, if you need to end a relationship situation, you'll say so. This doesn't mean you don't care, only that you have nothing left to give—which is really saying something.

Rewarding Days
7, 8, 14, 15, 20, 21, 25

Challenging Days
1, 2, 9, 18, 26, 27, 29

Scorpio | September

Planetary Lightspots

The New Moon on September 24 will occur in balance-loving Libra and your solar twelfth house, Scorpio, urging you to take a few days away from the maddening crowds to think over a brand-new course of action. If you've been having doubts about your partner's fidelity, however, having an honest heart-to-heart might be more productive. No matter what you're trying to understand, if you invest some of your energy into metaphysical or spiritual activities, you'll find your answers.

Relationships

A Full Moon will light up the skies on September 8, Scorpio, and bring its high-energy emotions into your fifth solar house. Your compassion for kids and even the most casual partner will be running on high, and you'll finally begin to see just how tough things have been for them lately. Getting them through the current situation is terrific, but helping them set up a plan to stop the pattern would be better.

Money and Success

If a group financial venture is offered to you between September 5 and 29, Scorpio, you owe it to yourself to at least investigate it. Venus will bring her magnetic money-making abilities to your solar eleventh house of groups during this time, so pooling both money and effort with a like-minded group could be quite profitable. At the very least, you'll learn something.

Planetary Hotspots

You may feel a bit confused and befuddled around September 21, Scorpio, but you probably won't mind much. Impulsive Mars will team up with Neptune, who just loves to dissolve reality, making it all too tempting to overindulge. This team isn't into self-restraint, so telling you to take it easy is futile. Just be sure to hand over the keys and get yourself a taxi.

Rewarding Days
2, 3, 5, 10, 14, 24, 25

Challenging Days
6, 7, 9, 12, 13, 20, 21

Scorpio | October

Planetary Lightspots

The Solar Eclipse on October 23 in your sign will light a fire under you, Scorpio, encouraging you to stop stalling and get busy making all those changes you've been talking about. With charming, attractive Venus on board, you really don't need to worry about being lonely, either. It's time to clear the decks. Make a clean break, and don't look back.

Relationships

Up until October 23, Venus will spend her time tiptoeing through your solar twelfth house of Privacy, Please, urging you to spend some quality time alone with someone you trust implicitly. It might be that you need to talk, or maybe you'll just want to sit next to them. Either way, charm your way into a hug, because you probably need one. You're dealing with a lot of intense energy now.

Money and Success

With optimistic Mars in extravagant Sagittarius on duty in your solar second house, you've probably not been a font of willpower lately, Scorpio. The urge to once again wreak havoc on your checkbook or plastic will arise on October 5, for what will probably seem like a very good reason. Hold on, though. When was the last time you checked your balances?

Planetary Hotspots

October 23 through October 26 will be challenging, Scorpio, for several reasons. A Solar Eclipse in your sign, along with Mercury's direct station, could draw you inward for a bit to lick your wounds, but you won't have long. On October 26, when Mars storms off into hard-working Capricorn, you'll need to bring you're A-game to work. Nothing less will do, so grin and bear it.

Rewarding Days
5, 13, 14, 15, 27, 28, 29

Challenging Days
3, 4, 7, 8, 11, 16, 23, 25, 26

Scorpio | November

Planetary Lightspots

Mercury will spend November 8 through November 27 in your sign, Scorpio, bringing all his detective-like abilities to your every encounter. Heaven help anyone you suspect of anything at all over those three weeks, because they won't stand a chance of hiding it from you. Warn them not to bother lying.

Relationships

Your antennae will be especially keen this month, Scorpio, with all those planets in your perceptive sign, and Pluto, your ruling planet, on duty in your solar third house of thoughts. You'll be equal parts detective and analyst at all times, and while you do so love to solve mysteries and puzzles, by the New Moon on November 22, you'll probably be pretty darn drained. Take a break from your current investigation on November 26.

Money and Success

Just when you were getting caught up on the bills from all those impulsive spending sprees, Venus, the Sun, and Mercury will tempt you once again to go overboard, Scorpio. Well, it is almost the holiday season, so you certainly have good reason for being a bit extravagant, but don't spend the entire coming year paying for it. Try to be generous but reasonable.

Planetary Hotspots

Talk about a big finish, Scorpio. That's what's due on November 22, as the Sun and Moon leave your sign behind for a meeting via the New Moon in Sagittarius. That same day, thoughtful Mercury and excessive Jupiter will square off, a team that just loves to exaggerate. Before you dismiss anyone forever from your presence, be sure you have the facts straight.

Rewarding Days

1, 2, 3, 8, 10, 11, 17

Challenging Days

6, 9, 12, 13, 18, 19, 22, 26

Scorpio | December

Planetary Lightspots

You really can't help but enjoy yourself this month, Scorpio. Mercury, Venus, and the Sun in Sagittarius simply won't allow any of us to escape. These fun-loving fire energies will join forces with optimistic, excessive Jupiter, however, so be warned: you may be prone to letting go and forgetting about your responsibilities for a few hours. Oh, go ahead. Get wild!

Relationships

Someone a bit older or younger than you may catch your eye after December 10, Scorpio, and regardless of that and any other differences, you'll be madly attracted. If what you have in common is substantial, don't do the math. You're not getting married, after all—at least, not yet. Around December 20, you might be thinking along those lines, though.

Money and Success

You'll have a no-nonsense attitude this month toward your personal finances, Scorpio, possibly because you'll have to buckle down after what you did to your credit cards over the past few weeks. Fortunately, with Venus in frugal Capricorn, cutting back to the bare necessities isn't a problem. Your mission is to get everyone to pay their share of the expenses.

Planetary Hotspots

After two and half years of keeping you up at night, wondering if you've done the right thing, serious Saturn will leave your sign behind, Scorpio. As of December 23, this stern, uncompromising planet will have moved on to Sagittarius, and you'll be free. It might take you a while to get used to not feeling overburdened and overwhelmed, but you'll get used to it. Take a deep breath and smile. You passed the test.

Rewarding Days

2, 3, 4, 5, 12, 14, 19, 21

Challenging Days

1, 8, 15, 16, 20, 24, 25, 26

Scorpio Action Table

These dates reflect the best—but not the only—times for success and ease in these activities, according to your Sun sign.

	JAN	FEB	MAR	APR	MAY	JUN	JUL	AUG	SEP	OCT	NOV	DEC
Move	30											
Start a class												
Join a club						18		25	5			
Ask for a raise			16				16	8		14	16	23
Look for work							26					4
Get pro advice	1, 7, 11		30									
Get a loan										14		
See a doctor										5		
Start a diet												
End relationship			29	29	2, 10						12	
Buy clothes												
Get a makeover		24						15	27			
New romance		14	1	17, 30		18, 29				26–28	6	
Vacation	15					27						

Sagittarius

The Archer
November 21 to December 21

Element: Fire

Quality: Mutable

Polarity: Yang/masculine

Planetary Ruler: Jupiter

Meditation: I can take time to explore my soul

Gemstone: Turquoise

Power Stones: Lapis lazuli, azurite, sodalite

Key Phrase: I understand

Glyph: Archer's arrow

Anatomy: Hips, thighs, sciatic nerve

Colors: Royal blue, purple

Animals: Fleet-footed animals

Myths/Legends: Athena, Chiron

House: Ninth

Opposite Sign: Gemini

Flower: Narcissus

Keyword: Optimism

The Sagittarius Personality

Your Strengths and Challenges

To understand you, Sagittarius, one need only look at your symbol, the centaur. Half beast and half human, you have a great kinship with the animal kingdom, but are constantly looking up, up, and away toward greener pastures, untried experiences, and new friends to add to your substantial and varied collection. Of course, operating those four hooves while searching the heavens with bow and arrow for your next exciting target isn't an easy job, so you do tend to be a bit on the clumsy side. Fortunately, you know how to laugh at your own mistakes, and you hold no grudges when someone else joins in.

You have an insatiable quest for knowledge—in fact, many Sagittarians are lifelong students. Once you have learned a skill or field, however, you are more than happy to share what you know, and because of that, you make an excellent teacher. Your style is to explain what you know through humor and shared experience, so others enjoy listening and walk away both entertained and educated. Your ruling planet is benevolent, lucky Jupiter, by the way, the heavens' answer to Santa Claus, so you carry his traits and qualities with you, including generosity, abundance, and expansion. And speaking of expansion, you are quite familiar with the concept of excess, believing that "much," "many," and "more" are far better than having just a taste of anything. That extravagance may extend every now and then to overindulging yourself, but since you are happy to share with others to enhance the experience, no one will ever tell you to stop going overboard!

Your Relationships

When it comes to surrounding yourself with people you love, Sagittarius, your motto has always been "The more, the merrier." You have a wide circle of interesting, funny friends, most likely from all over the world, and you just love listening to their accents and hearing about their experiences. Your love of new vistas makes you an excellent traveling companion, and you are only too happy to go anywhere and everywhere with equally ardent friends. In friendships and in one-to-one relationships—once you give in, let go of your precious freedom, and sign up for the long haul—you are loyal, trustworthy, and willing to do anything and everything to make your companions happy, from making them laugh at misfortune to buying them whatever their hearts desire. Obviously, your fortunate partner will enjoy the very best it is possible for you to give, which, along with your generous spirit, amazing sense of humor, and perpetual optimism, will keep them by your side forever—as long as they don't bore you! You can tolerate just about anything from a partner but tedium, which has ended more than one Sagittarian's relationship. Fortunately, you are more than open to taking them along to meet your friends, whether far or near, and actually prefer it when your sweetheart is part of your closest inner circle. You often have rather odd, long-distance relationships with your family members and tend to think of friends as your "true" family—and those friends often include four-legged, furry critters, whom you consider your children. You lavish love and attention on anyone and anything you are fond of, and are well loved by just about everyone lucky enough to know you.

Your Career and Money

Whatever professional path you decide to follow in life, Sagittarius, you will follow it with energy and passion, as your fiery disposition dictates. You make an excellent teacher, but tend to teach wherever you go, anyway, whether or not it is your actual job. Many Sagittarians are also comedians and performers, putting Jupiter's gift of laughter to work for them. "Work," however, is not something you are fond of, and you are easily bored. So whatever you choose to do with your life, it absolutely must reflect your beliefs and offer you the daily personal freedom you need to keep your curious soul amused.

Now, as to dealing with money—well, let's just say it's not your strong suit. You see money as tokens, exchangeable for amusement, entertainment, and gifts for your lucky loved ones. Telling you to keep a rein on your finances and not overextend is futile, but fortunately, the older you get, the more that lesson will sink in. In the meantime, try not to spend more than you earn!

Your Lighter Side

You have an odd but endless sense of humor, Sagittarius, and your innate optimism and love of new experiences enable you to laugh at whatever the Universe tosses your way. In fact, you love laughter more than anything—other than animals, of course. You often play the clown for others, and are never, ever without a happy, grateful audience. You need travel to keep your mind fresh and your soul at peace, and love nothing more than to hang your hat in interesting new places.

Affirmation for the Year
Broaden your horizons—but stoke the home fires first!

The Year Ahead for Sagittarius

From January through July, Jupiter will spend his time in sensitive Cancer, passing out gifts from his spot in your solar eighth house of loans and shared resources. Someone in authority, quite possibly a family member, will be only too happy to provide help. Your mission will be to accept graciously and repay the debt as soon as possible. If you are asked for help, you will do what you can, but if the loan is substantial, do it with the guidance of an advisor. This house is also the realm of Pluto, who rules all major passages, including death. If someone or something you love is taken from you now, face your loss with the optimism and understanding that only Jupiter provides. Jupiter's benevolence ensures that anything that leaves your life now is actually a blessing, which you will eventually see.

In July, Jupiter will enter home turf: your solar ninth house of long-distance travel, education, and new experiences. Whatever burdens or sorrows you have will dissolve, and a higher understanding about what has happened will become clear to you. You would do well now to travel, the restorative nature of which is well known for all, most especially for you. Sign up for classes this summer, especially if you have been longing to return to school for some time now. You will learn much, since you will be open to all new opinions, especially if they are presented by someone who entertains as well as teaches you. This would also be a fine time to take your show on the road and take a stab at teaching yourself. You have a lot to share, and now is definitely the time to do just that.

Regardless of whom you spend your private time with over the coming year, Sagittarius, you will likely need quite a bit of time to yourself during 2014. In any case, you will be quite choosy about confidants, and quite cautious as well. Serious Saturn, the most careful planet of all, will spend most of the year in your solar twelfth house of secrets and Privacy, Please, urging you to hang a sign on your doorknob and not allow anyone entry who hasn't been tried, tested, and proved to be true. Trust your intuition above all else, and share your most secret thoughts only with those who pass your careful inspection. Other than that, you would be wise to keep your own counsel. Saturn provides us with discretion for a reason.

In late December, Saturn will enter your sign, and if you were born between November 22 and 25, you will find your responsibilities and duties increasing by leaps and bounds. You will also be put in the position of assuming the helm, either at work or with regard to a current situation that has been left unmanaged for far too long. Fortunately, you will be more than up to the task, and will be able to offer an honest and aboveboard guiding hand to bring past troubles to an end. Remember, however, that Saturn rules lead, so if you feel especially heavy, physically as well as emotionally, you would do well to look to the future and know that this, too, shall pass. You have been given the celestial honor of controlling a very important decision, most likely involving not just your own future but that of others. Be sure to take it seriously and act as your conscience dictates. What you do now will affect you for the next two and a half years. Be sure it is done well and thoroughly. This planet will not settle for anything less!

Now, startling, eccentric Uranus has been traveling through your solar fifth house of lovers, children, and leisure-time pursuits for several years, so you have already gotten used to the unpredictable with regard to those areas of life. Fortunately, Uranus has been wearing Aries for the duration, a fellow fire sign whose tactics you are quite familiar and comfortable with. Change is the name of the game now, but since you are far more open to it than many signs, you will accept it, adapt to it, and be only too happy to assimilate it into your life. In fact, you will probably enjoy the variety and last-minute changes Uranus brings along. Keep an open mind with regard to new lovers, if you are single. You will undoubtedly be surprised at just how "different" these new admirers are, and it will amuse you to no end! Think of this as a celestial buffet, and resolve to try all new experiences and learn from them, however briefly this erratic planet's representatives linger in your life. And speaking of erratic, your luck will be a bit on the unpredictable side during the year, thanks to Uranus's love of surprise endings. Remember, this house also rules speculation and gambling, so great losses are just as likely as great wins.

The lovely lady Neptune may be a tad more problematic for you as she continues on her long journey through Pisces and your solar fourth house of home, family matters, and emotional security. On a physical level, this could mean you will need to watch for problems with water in your home, but it may simply create the urge to live by water, for its soothing qualities. That could mean moving to a site near a pond or lake or taking your show on the road to live by the ocean. You can also conjure water into your life by giving yourself a spiritual or metaphysical foundation, either of which will be something your soul craves now. Neptune brings us the need for connection with The One. However you find it, and whatever form you give it, it is time for you to restore that connection. You will also find that your compassion and empathy now extend to all creatures, human or otherwise, and you may become quite a guardian angel in the process. The good news is that since you are Jupiter's child, whatever you give out will return to you tenfold. Neptune also passes out disappointments where she travels, however, since she raises our expectations so high that others are often unable to fill the bill. Be careful not to see your loved ones only through rose-colored glasses.

Pluto will spend his time in your solar second house of personal finances, demanding, as relentlessly as only Pluto can, that you tend carefully to your monetary picture, with an eye toward cleaning up the past and preparing for the future. This may mean you will need to repay loans, deal with old tax issues, or settle an unpleasant inheritance situation. Regardless, know that it is you who wields the power now. Pass it out carefully, wisely, and fairly, and both you and others will have what you need. Pluto's presence in Capricorn insists that you are unbiased and unemotional in these dealings, and if you discover that is not possible, you should consult with a trusted advisor who you are positive can give you the advice and guidance you need. Remember, Pluto is the planet of regeneration and often brings total destruction before rebirth. If you have to let go of someone or something important to you, do it willingly. This planet needs your full cooperation to clean the slates and activate new beginnings, and whether or not you go along with whatever is financially inevitable now doesn't matter. It will happen, and you know that. You can only surrender, look to the future, and keep that positive, optimistic outlook your sign is so famous for.

What This Year's Eclipses Mean for You

Two pairs of eclipses will occur in 2014, Sagittarius, so life will most definitely not be boring. The first one, a Lunar Eclipse in Libra on April 15, will focus its spotlight on your solar eleventh house of friendships and group affiliations, and may help hand you the reins with regard to leading your current circle of peers. The second will arrive on April 29, a Solar Eclipse in earthy Taurus and your solar sixth house of work. This quality-conscious sign loves to make money, so a new opportunity to earn your daily bread by doing something you love may be offered. Don't look any gift horse in the mouth. A new work situation could be in the works and involve the bonus, raise, or promotion you've been aiming for. If it doesn't happen right away, be patient. Your talents are appreciated. This eclipse will also call attention to your health habits, urging you to do the right thing for your body. End an unhealthy habit or start a new physical regime.

The second pair of eclipses will occur on October 8 and 23. The first, a Lunar Eclipse, will activate your solar fifth house of love affairs, recreational pursuits, and children. Since it's basically a high-energy Full Moon in action-oriented, impulsive Aries, you may suddenly decide to have a child, adopt a pet, or take a current affair one last step toward exclusivity. If you're single, this fiery pair may also bring you a new lover—someone who is finally fiery and interesting enough to keep you occupied, entertained, and happy!

The Solar Eclipse celestially scheduled for October 23 will be in secretive Scorpio as well as your solar twelfth house of secrets. This may mean someone confides something to you in clandestine fashion—and you really should resolve not to let the cat out of the bag, in that case—but it may also mark the start of a period of introspection, during which you will examine yourself, your life, and what you want to do with the time remaining to you. It is perfectly all right to retreat for a while, to enjoy your own company and think things over. Your friends will certainly not forget you!

Saturn

Your ruling planet, Jupiter, is quite different from Saturn, so you often have trouble with this planet's visits. Saturn is frugal, pessimistic, and cautious, qualities that are often quite foreign to your outgoing, eager, and optimistic nature, Sagittarius. This year, however, Saturn will stay hidden in your solar twelfth house of secrets and subconscious desires, urging you to step back and take stock of what you really want from life. The call of this planet will be especially demanding during late October, when it will combine talents with the Lunar Eclipse to shed light on a situation you may have been trying to bury or ignore. The good news is that since Saturn is already patient and will be in perceptive, thorough Scorpio, if you need time to work out an intensely private situation, you will have it. Before you make any drastic changes, however, allow yourself enough time to prepare—and that goes double if you are considering a major, life-altering decision. You may find that your life becomes substantially quieter than it has been, but that will change for most of you right around Christmas. If you were born between November 22 and 25, however, then on December 23, when Saturn enters your own sign and your solar first house of personality, you will come out of your shell, but only to take charge of a situation that requires much effort and perseverance. Rest assured that if you face facts, pay your dues, and act with integrity, you will undoubtedly earn what you deserve.

Uranus

If you were born between November 29 and December 10, you will have quite the amazing year, Sagittarius. While serious Saturn will urge you to retire inward, especially during the summer months, unpredictable Uranus will insist that you mingle, exchange ideas, and come out of your shell immediately! You will have to find a happy medium between these two, but regardless of what you plan, Uranus will be sure to disrupt it—and suddenly, too—from his position in your solar fifth house of lovers, children, and recreational pursuits. Fortunately, this shocking planet is all done up in fiery Aries, a kindred fire sign you are quite fond of, so no matter what drastic, immediate changes he brings along, you will be most happy for the distraction. In fact, whatever happens at this time may be just what the doctor ordered to drag you out of any ruts you have gotten yourself into. Don't bother trying to prepare for this planet's influence. No matter what you do, you will most certainly be startled in this area of life, and it will do you good to be awakened. If you were born before November 29, you will spend the year assimilating recent changes with regard to love affairs, dealings with children, and new hobbies, and you really should throw yourself in wholeheartedly and enjoy those new beginnings. This is a planet that change-loving you can live with. Have fun with it!

Neptune

If you were born between November 25 and December 1, you will feel the siren's call of this dreamy, woozy, and highly spiritual planet more than others of your sign during 2014. Neptune will contact your Sun from your solar fourth house of home, family, and domestic matters, urging you to make your nest a place of refuge, safety, and spiritual comfort. She may also inspire you to adopt someone or something, to take someone less fortunate under your wing to help and protect. That is all well and good if it has four legs, feathers, or fins, but before you open your home to another person, be sure to consult with your intuition, and be absolutely positive the person is worth it. Otherwise, you may be the victim of someone who is out to take advantage of your generous spirit, who will also take you for an unpleasant financial ride. If you were born on November 28, 29, or 30, you will feel this more urgently during May, June, and July, when Neptune will stop in her tracks to station, demanding that you pay less attention to your outer, materialistic needs and bypass anything that is not necessary to the evolution of your inner self. Remember, too, that this planet can also create a great deal of confusion if everything you say or do is not clear to others. Be sure to make your goals and motivation known, and don't hesitate to have heart-to-heart chats often with those who share your home.

Pluto

Pluto is an all-or-nothing type of planet and is often in the neighborhood when major life changes occur. This year, Pluto in strict Capricorn will pass through your solar second house of personal finances and resources, Sagittarius, urging you to take care of unfinished business, especially in relation to money matters and possessions. On a deeper level, however, Pluto will be silently at work from behind the scenes to subtly change what you value—and what you are willing to sacrifice to have it. You may find that you are able to get by on a lot less than what you have, in which case, although it is not in your nature to do so, you should put something aside for a rainy day. Since Pluto will be at war with shocking Uranus in your solar fifth house of children and lovers, you may also be called on to extend an unexpected loan or cosign for a loved one—or you may need one yourself. Either way, enter into the negotiation with clear eyes, and if you don't feel that you can trust your own judgment, don't hesitate to call on a professional you trust for their expert opinions. One way or the other, who and what you hold dear will be put to the test this year, most especially if you were born between December 1 and 5.

Sagittarius | January

Planetary Lightspots

If there's one sign that never fails to delight you, Sagittarius, it's unpredictable Aquarius. As the month progresses and Mercury and the Sun settle into that sign and your solar third house of conversations and dealings with siblings and neighbors, you'll have all kinds of stimulating conversations and exciting interactions. This is a great time to learn more about your computer, too.

Relationships

All those planets in no-nonsense Capricorn and your solar second house of personal resources will be hard at work during the early part of the month, Sagittarius—which means you will be, too. However, with your ruling planet, Jupiter, in emotional Cancer, your attention may also be required by family. What to do? Tend to your work responsibilities, but when you do get home, leave the job behind and spoil your dear ones rotten.

Money and Success

Your year will start with a lot of activity in your solar second house of finances, Sagittarius. The New Moon on January 1 will inspire you to take a look at how you handle your money. The thing is, since Pluto will add his intensity to the mix, you may also be at the beginning of a power struggle over money, possessions, or other resources. Hire a trusted professional if you need advice.

Planetary Hotspots

Fiery Mars in Libra and your solar eleventh house of friendships may bring along disputes within your current peer group, Sagittarius, especially around January 2, 8, or 16. If money is the issue, know what you're getting into before you take sides. On January 11, you'd do well to sit down with an elder or authority figure and ask for advice.

Rewarding Days
10, 11, 12, 17, 24, 29, 30

Challenging Days
7, 15, 16, 25, 26

Sagittarius | February

Planetary Lightspots

Valentine's Day looks like it's going to be quite romantic for you, Sagittarius—even if you have to fly your date in from another state, coast, or country. A Full Moon in Leo and your solar ninth house of long-distance friends and lovers will amp up your emotional determination to be together, and an easy trine between the Sun and Mars will help your plans go smoothly.

Relationships

Someone you've been seeing casually (and possibly secretly, too) could cause a bit of turbulence to enter your world around February 11, 19, or 26, Sagittarius, so if you're not already too deeply involved, it might be best to back away slowly. If you're happily attached, an easy Venus-Saturn sextile may convince you to sign up long term on February 24.

Money and Success

Venus will spend the month in your solar second house of personal finances, Sagittarius, all done up in practical, responsible Capricorn. This is a great time to settle money matters, including loans and debts that need to be paid off for the sake of your credit. The good news is that with charming Venus here, you'll be well equipped to negotiate.

Planetary Hotspots

With Mercury retrograde from February 6 through February 28, Sagittarius, you may find it necessary to rethink some recent decisions regarding a family member who hasn't quite been themselves lately. Sit down and have a chat with them, and don't leave until you get to the root of the issue. There may be something they've been hiding that really needs to come out—now.

Rewarding Days

9, 14, 15, 16, 20, 24, 25

Challenging Days

10, 11, 19, 23, 26, 27

Sagittarius | March

Planetary Lightspots

The New Moon in your solar fifth house of recreational pursuits, lovers, and dealings with kids will occur on March 30, Sagittarius, all done up in impulsive Aries, a kindred fire sign. This fast-acting energy will bring a quality of excitement into your life. You'll thrive on adrenaline now, and want to have adventures with the family or with your current flame. Bungee jumping, anyone?

Relationships

With loving Venus off for a month in unpredictable Aquarius, if you're still unattached, Sagittarius, you can expect a veritable parade of admirers now, many of whom will be introduced to you by siblings, neighbors, or casual acquaintances. You could also run across someone you feel immediately drawn to while you're out doing errands. Love in the produce aisle? Maybe.

Money and Success

If you've ever thought of patenting an idea, Sagittarius, this is a great time to investigate the process. Venus, the purveyor of the heavens' purse strings, will enter inventive Aquarius and your solar third house of thoughts on March 5, and will stay put all month. Your famous sense of humor will be running on high, too, and with charming Venus on board, no one will take what you say the wrong way—just this once.

Planetary Hotspots

The Full Moon on March 16 will occur in precise, meticulous Virgo, which isn't an energy you're famous for enjoying, Sagittarius. Fortunately, whatever details this lunation reveals with regard to career matters or authority figures will come in handy, and you'll be glad to hear them. If you're bucking for a raise, bonus, or promotion, better cross those t's and dot those i's.

Rewarding Days
1, 12, 13, 14, 18, 30

Challenging Days
10, 11, 17, 22, 28, 29

Sagittarius | April

Planetary Lightspots

Your sign craves adventure, Sagittarius, and if there's anything you really can't tolerate, it's boredom. Well, not to worry, because that won't be an issue this month. The Sun and Mercury in Aries will see to it that surprises abound, thanks to their contacts with unpredictable Uranus on April 2 and 14. Expect surprising communications, and don't set anything on your schedule in stone.

Relationships

With loving Venus in compassionate Pisces and your solar fourth house of home and family matters, Sagittarius, you can expect your family and/or domestic partners to be just a tad needy now, probably due to a tough string of recent events. Take time to hear them out and let them know you understand. Share your own experiences to help them see there's always a bright side.

Money and Success

If you're shopping for a home loan, Sagittarius, make the appointment for April 17, 18, or 25, when several planets will conspire to make the process smooth. If you're already nestled in comfortably, you may decide that a few days in the sun by a pool would be the perfect antidote to the stress and tension of recent weeks. If you can afford it, why not? Get yourself an April tan, and show it off.

Planetary Hotspots

Two eclipses will occur this month, Sagittarius, the first on April 15 in your solar eleventh house of friendships. At this time, you could be put in the position of mediating an ongoing issue between two dear friends, or new information regarding someone in your current circle of friends could entirely change your mind about them—for better or worse.

Rewarding Days
10, 11, 17, 18, 25, 26, 30

Challenging Days
1, 2, 3, 8, 16, 20, 21, 22, 23

Sagittarius | May

Planetary Lightspots

Contrary to popular opinion, Sagittarius, opposite signs often do quite well together, and no example proves that more easily than your relationship with Gemini. You're both inquisitive, curious signs that can't stand being bored, and you also share a love of activity. So when Mercury enters that sign and your solar seventh house of one-to-one relationships on May 7, your social schedule will fill up fast. Hire a secretary—or at least get a new day planner. You'll need it.

Relationships

Chatty Mercury will enter Gemini on May 7, Sagittarius, and will immediately get to work in your solar seventh house of relationships. Along with loving Venus in red-hot Aries as of May 2—in your solar fifth house of lovers—you can expect at least one exciting new individual to enter your life. Gemini and Aries planets don't always hang around permanently, however, so make sure you two have what it takes to stay together yet maintain your personal freedom.

Money and Success

It doesn't take much to talk you into going overboard, Sagittarius. So on May 18, when Venus squares off with your ruling planet, extravagant Jupiter, you might be tempted to overspend, especially if you've just started seeing someone and you're out to impress them. There's nothing wrong with spoiling someone, but don't go into debt to do it.

Planetary Hotspots

The Full Moon on May 14 in Scorpio and your solar twelfth house of secrets will shine a bright light into this ordinarily very private place, Sagittarius. This could mean you're ready to reveal some information you've been mulling over, or you might inadvertently become involved in a scandal of sorts, especially since loving Venus will square off with sexy Pluto that same day. Behave yourself, now...

Rewarding Days
3, 5, 6, 7, 12, 13, 15, 28

Challenging Days
2, 10, 11, 14, 17, 18

Sagittarius | June

Planetary Lightspots

The Full Moon this month will arrive on June 13, occurring in your very own sign and your solar first house of personality and appearance, Sagittarius. This high-energy meeting of the Sun and Moon will activate your axis of relationships, and there'll be plenty of opportunities to do what you love best with your significant other: travel, take classes, and tackle your top ten list of new experiences. Have some fun!

Relationships

You'll be quite focused on others this month, Sagittarius, especially if they have what it takes to keep you amused, even when things aren't going as you'd planned. On the other hand, your ability to show others the silver linings may also be called on. But with the Sun and Mercury in your solar seventh house of one-to-one relationships, you'll definitely be meeting an exciting new cast of characters.

Money and Success

Up until June 23, Venus will stay on duty in Taurus, the sign that's best known for being a money magnet. This charming energy will make her way through your solar sixth house of work-related matters, so an opportunity to change jobs for better financial rewards could certainly arrive. This is also your house of health, and since Venus does love her creature comforts, you should try not to spoil yourself too much. No one's saying you can't party, but be sensible.

Planetary Hotspots

Make sure you have your ducks in a row on June 7, because it will be far too easy to get into a dispute over inheritances, loans, or old debts. Mercury will turn retrograde in your solar eighth house of joint resources that day, just as the emotional Moon collides with both assertive Mars and unpredictable Uranus. This isn't a great time to settle up. You'll be a little too rebellious, which could affect your judgment.

Rewarding Days

4, 6, 8, 17, 18, 19, 28, 29

Challenging Days

7, 12, 13, 14, 24, 25, 26

Sagittarius | July

Planetary Lightspots

After three long weeks in retrograde motion, thoughtful Mercury will finally turn direct on July 1, Sagittarius, and since he'll be in your solar seventh house of one-to-one relationships at the time, a State of the Relationship meeting could be in order. There may be a lot that's been left unsaid between you and your primary partner or best friend, but you can work it out now if you're honest and not out to retaliate.

Relationships

By July 18, the Sun, Mercury, and Venus will all have passed into your solar eighth house of intimate partners, and they'll be wearing sympathetic, nurturing Cancer. This attentive, caring pack of planets will inspire you to take a personal interest in the care and welfare of the people you're closest to, which certainly includes your current love. Extend yourself to them whenever possible. You may not be able to heal them, but listening and holding them close will certainly help.

Money and Success

Some startling financial surprises could be on tap for July 7, Sagittarius, when Venus gets together with unpredictable Uranus. The good news is that their connection will be via a stimulating, positive sextile, so any changes that occur stand every chance of turning out well. This wouldn't be a bad time to talk turkey with a prospective financial partner, either.

Planetary Hotspots

A connection between Venus and Mars on July 13 will make life quite pleasant for you, Sagittarius. These two famous ancient lovers will come together in an easy trine, linking the energies of your solar seventh house of relationships with those of your solar eleventh house of friendships. If you've been seeing someone who hasn't yet met The Gang, this would be a perfect time to introduce them.

Rewarding Days
6, 7, 12, 13, 29, 30, 31

Challenging Days
4, 5, 18, 19, 21, 22, 24, 28

Sagittarius | August

Planetary Lightspots

Mercury, the Sun, and Venus will all spend time in Leo this month, where your own generous planet, Jupiter, is currently on duty. This dramatic group of players will ensure that your solar ninth house takes center stage in your life, and since that's where issues of politics, religion, and higher education are dealt with, there's a good chance that you'll want to make a bit of a splash in one of those departments. Whether you decide to teach or preach, you'll definitely not be ignored.

Relationships

Since a pack of planets in Leo will spend most of the month in your solar ninth house of far-off places, you may suddenly remember how much you loved one of the places you've visited over the years—mostly because you had a wonderfully romantic time there. Remember that our memories are often selective, and be sure you're seeing things clearly before you spontaneously rent that U-Haul.

Money and Success

The restlessness you'll be feeling this month could work out well for you, Sagittarius. Several planets in your solar ninth house of higher education might even talk you into going back to school or doing some teaching yourself. You need to be on stage now, and even if it's just to talk about your world-travel experiences with a group of friends, your audience can't help but be appreciative.

Planetary Hotspots

The New Moon in Virgo on August 25 will occur in your solar tenth house of career matters and authority figures, Sagittarius, which could mean you're due to be offered the reins on the job. If you've spent a lot of time making sure the higher-ups can see just what you're capable of, they may make you an offer. If it involves long-distance relocation, so much the better.

Rewarding Days

2, 3, 6, 8, 12, 15, 21, 25

Challenging Days

1, 18, 23, 24, 26, 27, 29

Sagittarius | September

Planetary Lightspots

Mercury will enter sociable Libra on September 2, Sagittarius, setting up shop in your solar eleventh house of friendships until September 27. This chatty, witty, charming guy will turn up the volume on your already sought-after company, and your social schedule will be quite full. If you simply can't keep up with the offers and invitations, it might be time to set some priorities.

Relationships

Venus, the Goddess of Love, will set off for precise, detail-oriented Virgo on September 5, a sign you've never really been able to get along with easily. If your partner seems to be a bit too picky about how you dress or eat, or your health habits, don't throw up your hands and write it off. There may be something to their suggestions. Listen up. Anyone who truly loves you will have only your best interests at heart.

Money and Success

You have a guardian angel on duty, Sagittarius, who is determined to put you in touch with someone who'll be able to guide you toward the life path that best reflects your beliefs. Whether they show up in human form or not, their influence will be most noticeable around September 21. Your mission is to not overlook even the tiniest hint that you have been astrologically lured to the right place at the right time.

Planetary Hotspots

The Full Moon on September 8 will activate your axis of home and domestic issues versus career and professional matters, Sagittarius, urging you to choose—and to choose your family over your work. That may not be easy for you to do, however, especially if you've just made a major career change and you're out to impress your new boss. The good news is that you can easily share your feelings with them now if you take the time to explain.

Rewarding Days

3, 4, 10, 14, 20, 21, 25

Challenging Day

8, 9, 13, 22, 23, 27, 28

Sagittarius | October

Planetary Lightspots

An easy, cooperative trine between impetuous Uranus in Aries and fiery Mars in your own sign and your solar first house of personality and appearance will occur on October 5, Sagittarius, and while you've never shied away from taking chances, you'll be even more optimistically reckless now. No one's saying you can't have some fun, but do be sure you're not risking your physical safety for a quick thrill.

Relationships

There's going to be a Lunar Eclipse on October 8, Sagittarius, and while all eclipses are unpredictable, this one will draw startling Uranus into the mix as well. It's going to occur in your solar fifth house of lovers, creative associates, and dealings with kids, so someone from at least one of those groups may have something up their sleeve that will absolutely knock your socks off. Your mission is to stay open to positive but possibly unsettling circumstances.

Money and Success

Startling announcements regarding money matters may be along on October 11, Sagittarius, as Venus, the Goddess of Love and Money, faces off with erratic, unpredictable Uranus. Your rainy-day fund may need to be tapped into now. If it's to take care of a friend's financial woes, be sure you'll be paid back. The nature of this pairing is often quite iffy.

Planetary Hotspots

On October 14, an easy but stimulating sextile between Venus and your ruling planet, travel-loving Jupiter, will occur. If you've been day-dreaming about a far-off place, Sagittarius, you'll want to return there now—especially if it's to cast your eyes on a certain someone you're quite fascinated with. This is a great time to break routine and get out of your rut—no matter what the real reasons.

Rewarding Days

4, 5, 6, 13, 14, 15, 26, 27

Challenging Days

1, 2, 7, 11, 12, 16, 23, 24

Sagittarius | November

Planetary Lightspots

With responsible Saturn still on duty in intense Scorpio and your solar twelfth house of secrets, Sagittarius, you're at the end of a two-and-a-half-year period of keeping mostly everything to yourself. But this month, the Sun, Venus, and Mercury will make their way into that dimly lit place. Do you feel as if your conscience is bothering you and you need to come clean? Well, then, go for it. It's time.

Relationships

You're extravagant Jupiter's child, Sagittarius, and highly susceptible to his moods. So on November 9, when he forms an active square with Venus, who revels in nothing but the best, you might be tempted to buy a gift or invest in an adventure for someone you're quite smitten with. The good news is that if you wait until November 12, you'll be able to save some serious money.

Money and Success

Don't even try to participate in any financial dealings that aren't entirely aboveboard in every way this month. Venus, Mercury, and the Sun are in your solar twelfth house of secrets, but on November 9, an argument with someone you've been very close to may mean they'll be telling tales. As soon as November 12, their stories could reach the ears of someone who's playing a big part in your professional life. If you don't want anything unsavory to come out, don't get involved.

Planetary Hotspots

You probably have some goodbyes to say, but may not be all that eager to have those conversations. If you have been putting off the inevitable with regard to a relationship that just isn't working, you won't be able to stand it anymore as of November 12, when Venus and Saturn compare notes and pronounce their judgment. Any endings or beginnings that day will occur quite suddenly, so fasten your seat belt.

Rewarding Days

1, 2, 3, 11, 15, 16, 21, 27, 28

Challenging Days

8, 9, 12, 13, 22, 23, 25

Sagittarius | December

Planetary Lightspots

Mercury, Venus, and the Sun will all be in your solar first house of personality and appearance until December 10, Sagittarius, and they'll be wearing your sign as well. These three will bring out the wise, humorous, and philosophical sides of your nature, and whichever is called for at the moment will be what you'll naturally exhibit. Don't ask so many questions or spend so much time expressing your opinions that you forget to have some good, old-fashioned fun.

Relationships

The Full Moon on December 6 will set up shop in chatty, witty Gemini, and will activate your solar relationship axis, Sagittarius. Your personal presentation, especially the first impression you make, will suddenly be quite important to you now, and the reason will probably be a certain someone you've been thinking about approaching. Regardless of the reason, any positive physical change will benefit you. If it's to attract a new sweetheart, so much the better.

Money and Success

You've always been a bit of a gambler, Sagittarius, and while that's no way to make a living, every now and then a sign as lucky as yours has every right to invest in a scratch ticket. Your good fortune in all areas of life will be emphasized on December 4, 5, 8, and 14, so give it a shot. This does *not* mean, however, that you should take off to Vegas with the mortgage money.

Planetary Hotspots

Prepare yourself, because as of December 23, serious, practical, responsible Saturn will set up shop in your own sign and your solar first house of personality, urging you to Get It Together. The good news is that over the next two and a half years, whatever you've honestly earned will come your way, and that certainly does include career kudos.

Rewarding Days
3, 4, 5, 8, 12, 13, 14

Challenging Days
1, 15, 19, 20, 23, 24, 25

Sagittarius Action Table

These dates reflect the best—but not the only—times for success and ease in these activities, according to your Sun sign.

	JAN	FEB	MAR	APR	MAY	JUN	JUL	AUG	SEP	OCT	NOV	DEC
Move			1	5								
Start a class	15						26		25			
Join a club	30								24			
Ask for a raise			28			18	12	21				1, 10
Look for work								21, 25			6	
Get pro advice	7, 11			2, 25		8						
Get a loan					6							
See a doctor									14, 21			
Start a diet										26		23
End relationship											9, 13	
Buy clothes									29			
Get a makeover											22	
New romance												6
Vacation					24				25	5, 14, 15		4, 12

Capricorn

The Goat
December 21 to January 20

♑

Element: Earth

Quality: Cardinal

Polarity: Yin/feminine

Planetary Ruler: Saturn

Meditation: I know the strength of my soul

Gemstone: Garnet

Power Stones: Peridot, onyx diamond, quartz, black obsidian

Key Phrase: I use

Glyph: Head of goat

Anatomy: Skeleton, knees, skin

Colors: Black, forest green

Animals: Goats, thick-shelled animals

Myths/Legends: Chronos, Vesta, Pan

House: Tenth

Opposite Sign: Cancer

Flower: Carnation

Keyword: Ambitious

The Capricorn Personality

Your Strengths and Challenges

Practical? Ambitious? Yes, indeed you are, Capricorn, and proud of it, too! You love it when a plan comes together—and most of yours do. Typically, at an early age, you choose a life path and, from that point on, aim all your energy in that direction. You do your homework, pay your dues, and soak up as much experience as possible. When you decide you're ready, you go after your goal, step by step, carefully laying the foundation for long-term success. Once you actually achieve your aims, you hold on to them quite easily—which only makes sense. At that point, you've already done so much preparation that you know exactly what to expect and how to handle it all, including the "what-ifs." That makes you an expert troubleshooter with a knack for solving problems before they arise. That makes sense, too. Your ruling planet is serious Saturn, who loves nothing more than preparation. His gift is your ability to plan for the future, whether you pursue a career path, devote yourself to raising a family, or, like many of you, juggle both. You won't sign up until you know what you're getting into, but once you're in, you're in for the long haul.

When a plan doesn't come together, however, you often blame yourself, even if you had nothing to do with the outcome. You can be quite hard on yourself, so resolve to give yourself a break every now and then, and try not to take the failures of others personally. You can only do so much.

Your Relationships

Your sign has a reputation for being cool and ultra-cautious in all relationships, Capricorn, which isn't entirely earned. True, you only become involved once you know someone is really worth it, and until that point, you usually hold them at arm's length, giving just enough of yourself to keep them around and holding back enough to stay safe. But you don't act that way because you don't care. In fact, you often care too much for others, and assume their debts and other responsibilities. After one too many bad experiences, you learned to "interview" all prospective companions in either department the same way you'd interview a prospective employee. It sounds calculating, but it's really a form of self-defense. Life has shown you that kindness and empathy are often seen as weaknesses, and you can't afford to be weak. You always have

232 Llewellyn's 2014 Sun Sign Book

at least one someone depending on you, and you're painfully aware of your obligations. The good news is that eventually you'll come to demand self-reliance in your partner. It may take years of trial and error to find the right fit, but once that happens, you'll invest yourself in the relationship with the same no-nonsense attitude and all-out commitment you show in every other area of life. Anyone who truly knows and loves you will say you're a devoted spouse and a treasured friend. Your mission is to learn to value yourself the way they do.

The other earth signs, Taurus and Virgo, can make great friends and terrific professional partners, but when it comes to romance, you often find yourself drawn to Scorpio, whose business sense and overall shrewdness appeal to you. But oddly enough, Sagittarians are often your perfect match. They're smart but playful, and able to bring out your lighter, more carefree side and keep you laughing.

Your Career and Money

You don't shy away from hard work—in fact, you thrive on it. You set goals on a regular basis and don't get distracted. You were raised with a strong work ethic and never, ever shirk your responsibilities, either on the job or in financial matters. You are on a constant mission to climb the ladder of success, and you know that reputation is everything, so you keep your credit clean and your name untarnished. This makes you an employer's dream and, along with your natural respect for and affinity with those in positions of authority, often helps you rise quickly in the ranks, well before others who have put in a lot more time and energy. But then, you are the honorary principal wherever you go, thanks to your ruling planet, Saturn, the celestial authority figure. Remember, this is the Lord of Karma, the guy who keeps records and decides exactly what's owed to each of us, for better or worse. That's exactly the attitude you have when you're holding the reins, and you are most often regarded as firm but fair.

Your Lighter Side

What's fun for you? Well, you love to build things from the ground up, so a tree house for the kids is quite enjoyable, but the beginning of any new project, even if it's work-oriented, is always exciting. When you actually cut loose (and, contrary to popular opinion, you most certainly do), you're out for a much-needed vacation from responsibility, and your choice of companions often reflects it.

Affirmation for the Year
Reaching out to others will bring me success and prosperity.

The Year Ahead for Capricorn

It's time to clear the decks, Capricorn, to let go of negative influences in your life and pave the way for new growth. These changes will take place primarily due to your own initiative, especially if you take advantage of the many gifts the Universe is offering.

To start with, generous, lucky Jupiter will spend the first seven months of the year in your solar seventh house of one-to-one relationships, putting you in touch with prosperous people who'll be happy to share the secrets of their success. Since Jupiter will be in nurturing Cancer, one of those new contacts may end up taking you under their wing as a protégé or private student. Along with their personal stories, their counsel will inspire you, subtly pushing you toward becoming everything you want to be and having everything you crave. With Jupiter, however, the danger always lies in becoming overconfident or reckless. Your ability to trust others will be far more accessible, and while you will meet lots of new people who are trustworthy and reliable, you may also find disappointing reasons to rein in your enthusiasm about a new friend every now and then. Either way, you'll know quickly whether you've made a good decision or not. Your mission now is to extend unconditionally to those who've earned it and pull back from those who haven't.

On July 16, Jupiter will enter fiery, fixed Leo and your solar eighth house of intimate partners and joint resources. If you've been with someone for a while, the intensity of this house may mean you decide it's time to take your relationship to a whole new level. Romantically speaking, this could be the beginning of a passionate, exciting new affair. Financially, it might mark the start of a partnership. The nature of this sign is not in accord with your own, however, so adjustments that aren't easy could be on tap. You may need to take drastic and rather dramatic measures to ensure your financial security, including selling a substantial interest in your business to a partner. Personally speaking, the romantic side of Leo will be fun, but you should make your intentions clear as soon as you realize what they are. If you're serious, talk about the possibility of working together toward a future. If you're not, make sure that's crystal clear.

Your ruling planet, Saturn, will continue along his path in your solar eleventh house of friendships and future aspirations until December 23, Capricorn. From his spot in Scorpio, forming an exciting but stabilizing sextile by sign, you can expect him to prompt you toward either discovering or rediscovering a friend or group affiliation. If you parted badly with someone years ago, this would be a terrific time to mend fences—as long as you forgive but don't forget. The same goes for groups you've left behind. If you opt to reconcile and allow reentry into your life, before you do, be sure the same old problems won't eventually cause you to end the relationship a second time. You are quite fond of your patterns and routines, but just because a person or situation is familiar doesn't mean they're a positive influence in your life.

Startling Uranus will work his way through impulsive Aries and your solar fourth house of domestic situations, joining forces with the eclipses on April 15 and October 23 to bring about equally startling changes in your home life. Your best bet is to prepare for all unforeseen circumstances, no matter how bizarre they sound to others. Your perceptive abilities will be running on high. Even if what's keeping you awake at night seems trivial to others, invest in a solution and you'll sleep better for it. If wiring up your home with the help of a security company will do the trick, go right ahead. Uranus in this house makes us feel anxious and apprehensive, so do whatever you can to take the edge off that physical and emotional stress.

Woozy Neptune will remain on duty in your solar third house of thoughts and communications, and you will probably be feeling quite nostalgic and sentimental, even though those aren't usually emotions you allow yourself to indulge in. The good news is that this mystical, magical planet will endow you with a heightened psychic awareness and a sensitivity to your environment. So no matter what you're involved with, if it doesn't "feel" right, you won't let yourself go on with the charade for another day. That goes for relationships, business deals, and family matters as well.

With intense, powerful Pluto on duty for yet another year in your sign and your solar first house of personality and appearance, you can expect to be even more formidable than usual once you've set your mind on a particular path. You absolutely will not allow yourself to be dragged away from pursuing the path you know you were born to follow. At the same time, you will want to steer clear completely of anything that even remotely smacks of control or repression. Do not allow yourself to be manipulated, but be sure you are not obsessing over minor details.

Fiery Mars will spend the first seven months of the year in your solar tenth house of career, professional matters, and reputation, gaining you some attention in this most public area of life. Rewards for time served and appreciation for past efforts will likely be coming up, but even if you know one last push might be all it takes to gain what you want, be careful not to alienate an authority figure whose recommendations you'll need in the process.

What This Year's Eclipses Mean for You

The year 2014 will play host to four eclipses, Capricorn. Two will activate your axis of family and career matters, and two will go to work on your solar fifth house of creativity and lovers and your solar eleventh house of friendships. The first, a Lunar Eclipse on April 15 in partner-oriented Libra, will activate your solar tenth house of profession and public reputation. You may suddenly feel the urge to strike out on your own and start your own business, and if you do, you'll want to do it with a partner. In fact, you'll want to do just about everything professionally with one other person. Keeping the relationship on an even keel could be challenging, especially since you may end up being romantically drawn to one another. If you do start a business from a hobby, start off at home.

On April 29, a Solar Eclipse in Taurus will plant a seed in your solar fifth house of lovers, and someone new might just sweep you off your feet. If you suddenly see the truth about a sweetheart, your fling might also fizzle out. Either way, it's important now to sort out your feelings for the primary people in your life. Are they worth the time you've invested, or should you begin the process of separating from them permanently? As with all transits of the emotional Moon, the only solution is to listen to your gut.

The second Lunar Eclipse of the year will arrive on October 8, in impulsive Aries and your solar fourth house of home and family. If you have been restless in your domestic life, resisting change now will be futile. Sudden or urgent circumstances could mean a drastic change, such as offering to share your home with a loved one, but you might also ask someone to hit the road, especially if they have not been carrying their share of the weight. Don't hesitate to lay down the law. You need to make your boundaries clear. Plant your feet, and resolve to stick by what you say, even if children or family members aren't particularly happy about it.

On October 23, a Solar Eclipse in Scorpio will come your way. This intense combination is a serious push, especially in fixed energies. Both the Sun and Moon will insist on tossing out the trash and starting over. From their position in your solar eleventh house of goals for the future, these two will work hard to convince you to take up with a new peer group that's more in tune with your aspirations, especially career-wise. Just be sure not to dismiss any friends simply because they're not "useful" to you at the moment.

Saturn

Your ruling planet, Saturn, is an energy you're quite familiar with, Capricorn. You understand the concept of rules, the need for structure and discipline, and the inevitably of eventually reaping what you sow—for better or worse. Those of you born between January 7 and 20 will enjoy the best this year, thanks to an easy sextile between the energies of transiting Saturn and your natal Sun. This aspect will likely be quite positive and helpful, adding stability and a comfortable predictability to all relationships. From his spot in your solar eleventh house of group affiliations and friendships, Saturn will arrange for you to have the support and advice of stable, concerned friends who've already been where you are right now. You'll find that both new friends and lifelong dear ones will have your back, even under stressful circumstances. Establishing yourself as a team player in the eyes of higher-ups will also go along quite well.

And speaking of authority figures, if you need help, be sure to ask for it. The Universe is ready, willing, and able to provide you with mentors, counselors, investors, and coaches at every turn. Be open to them when they arrive.

Since Saturn will be in potent, determined Scorpio and working together with Pluto in your own ambitious sign, it's also easy to see how many of the life goals you've set for yourself may finally become reality. There may be a period of testing, but if you've done your homework, you'll find yourself surrounded by all the trappings of success, materially and personally.

Uranus

If you were born between December 30 and January 8, Capricorn, you are in for an "interesting" year. Unpredictable Uranus will form an action-oriented square with your Sun, urging you to become someone completely and entirely new. From his spot in your solar fourth house of home, emotions, and domestic matters, he'll also make you restless for personal freedom, so much so that you may suddenly decide to strike out on your own for the first time, or to become single again after a long period of cohabitation. Your mission now is to use your practical energy to make drastic changes without tossing the baby out with the bathwater.

If you need to move, relocate long distance, or change your current lifestyle entirely, you may not have time to come up with a plan before you make your move, so you'll have to be on your toes and prepared for anything, no matter how unlikely the possibility. Remember, however, that sudden opportunities to better the circumstances of your home life are also possible now. You're a born troubleshooter. Use that knack to plan for the unexpected. Be sure insurance policies are current and home-security devices are functional.

Neptune

If you were born between December 25 and 29, the lovely lady Neptune will visit with your Sun this year, Capricorn, from her spot in your solar third house of thoughts and communications. Now, Neptune is currently all done up in her favorite sign, Pisces, so she's operating even more subtly and invisibly than usual. She'll touch your Sun via an easy sextile, so her gifts of psychic ability and ultra-sensitivity to your environment will be quite obvious in your life, and if you pay attention, you'll be able to make the most of them. You are usually quite cautious, and while there is no reason to change that now, you may find that siblings and neighbors provide you with a reason to trust them, no matter what happened last time. You will want to open yourself up to others in all your encounters, so don't be surprised if you hear more than one secretive, scandalous story—but don't tell! Resist the urge to gossip. Record your "aha" moments in a journal, and your dreams as well.

No matter what else you do now, listen to the voice of your intuition. If something or someone seems too good to be true, you may be right.

Pluto

If you were born between January 1 and 5, Pluto will directly contact your Sun this year, Capricorn. This intensely focused, determined planet is in your sign and your solar first house of personality and appearance, pouring all his energy into amping up the volume on your natural drive for security, success, and stability. You may be nearly at the end of a climb to the top career-wise, and if success comes your way now, you can rest assured it's because you've really earned it. Much like your ruling planet, Saturn, any transiting planet in Capricorn spends its time teaching realistic lessons about life, testing us to see if we've been paying attention, and finally passing out grades. If you've worked hard and paid your dues, your "A" will arrive through both personal and professional accomplishments. If not, you'll get a reality check, and it won't be subtle. In this sign, and because this visit will occur via a conjunction, the most potent of all planetary relationships, Pluto is an especially strict taskmaster, demanding nothing short of complete and total devotion to achieving concrete goals. No matter what happens along the way, it's important to remember that you're in the process of transformation, and that a new life is at the end of the road.

Pluto insists on major change. It's time to take control, give up what's no longer useful or productive in your life, and start over. Eventually, just as forest fires create prime conditions for new life, you'll be able to look back at this period with acceptance and understanding.

Capricorn | January

Planetary Lightspots

Bright and early on New Year's Day, Capricorn, you'll enjoy the energy of a New Moon in your sign and your solar first house. This is a very public place, since it's where personality and appearance originate, and when New Moons arrive, they plant seeds. If you're in the mood to change your physical self, that's all well and good. The reasons for this outward change probably run a bit deep.

Relationships

Venus will make her way through your sign this month, Capricorn, bringing all the magnetism and charisma this planet is famous for into your solar first house. Needless to say, anyone who shakes your hand will get quite the jolt, and if you're feeling a connection, too—well, anything is possible. You'll take your time, but around January 11, you might decide to trust them.

Money and Success

You're usually pretty darn frugal, Capricorn, so as the month progresses and the Sun and Mercury take up position in your solar second house of resources in erratic Aquarius, you might be spending with a bit more abandon than usual. If you've thought this through and you're sure both you and your family or partner can benefit, seal the deal on January 11.

Planetary Hotspots

Everyone knows how to manipulate, Capricorn, as you're well aware. So when an authority figure begins laying the groundwork for what you'll be able to tell will be a serious guilt trip, you'll have a decision to make. Should you defer to experience—something you're quite respectful of—or opt not to adopt their guidelines and assert yourself? Count on aggressive Mars to help you out with that one on January 16.

Rewarding Days
1, 7, 10, 11, 12, 15, 21

Challenging Days
2, 3, 4, 5, 16, 17, 24, 25

Capricorn | February

Planetary Lightspots

If there's anything you can't tolerate, Capricorn, it's when a plan refuses to come together—especially since any plan you're part of is so well thought out. So once Mercury turns retrograde on February 6 in your solar third house of short trips, conversations, and communications, it's going to be up to you to troubleshoot. Before you leave the house, be sure you've got the directions—and a cell phone that's charged.

Relationships

With Venus, the Goddess of Love and Money, currently on duty in your sign and solar first house of personality and appearance, Capricorn, life has probably been pretty good. This magnetic planet never fails to attract admirers from this position, and with extravagant Jupiter in your solar seventh house of one-to-one encounters, you may be enjoying quite the buffet right about now. One of them will stick out, however, and on February 24, Saturn will help you narrow down the list.

Money and Success

Your practical, frugal side will receive a boost this month from Venus, who rules finances and will spend the month in your own responsible sign. You're quite the wheeler dealer when you want to be, so this magnetic planet's influence certainly can't hurt if you're pitching a deal or looking for business investments.

Planetary Hotspots

Startling Uranus has been locked into a testy square with intense Pluto for years now, Capricorn, so this unpredictable planet is on his toes and his energy is quite potent. On February 26, he'll square off with another planet, mighty Jupiter, a kindred planetary spirit who's just as fond of personal freedom. If you're feeling repressed, especially in your relationship, remember, there are fifty ways to leave your lover.

Rewarding Days

2, 18, 20, 22, 23, 24, 25

Challenging Days

10, 11, 19, 26, 27

Capricorn | March

Planetary Lightspots

Your business skills are famous, Capricorn, so when Mars stops in his tracks on March 1 to turn retrograde in your solar tenth house of career matters, you'll instinctively know it's time to put a certain deal on hold. That may mean passing on a position you're interested in for the moment, and you might wonder if you shouldn't just go for it, regardless of your gut feelings. Don't. You know what you're doing.

Relationships

Venus will leave your sign behind on March 5, Capricorn, opting for something a little more unpredictable—Aquarius. If you've just begun seeing someone and all has been well, one or two snags may come up over the coming month, mostly related to freedom, independence, and how close is too close. Fortunately, you're pretty darned self-sufficient yourself, so you'll be able to work something out.

Money and Success

Mercury and Venus in Aquarius and your solar second house of money matters could make finances a bit unsettling this month, Capricorn, but not to worry. If anyone knows how to set money aside for a rainy day, it's you, so even if you have to tap into that fun now, your ruling planet, Saturn, will make sure you have what you need by March 13. Be sure to get it all in writing.

Planetary Hotspots

An issue of control could come up within the group of friends you associate with around March 11 or 29, Capricorn, and you'll be able to tell that this is one dispute that won't go away. If it involves you directly, it might be time to take charge and force a confrontation. If you're an innocent bystander, think before you take a side and set a precedent.

Rewarding Days
1, 12, 13, 14, 18, 27, 28

Challenging Days
9, 10, 11, 22, 29

Capricorn | April

Planetary Lightspots

The Lunar Eclipse on April 15 will activate your axis of domestic matters and professional responsibilities, Capricorn, and since you're so devoted to both, it could be a testy time. Once again, you'll feel torn between home and career, and an ultimatum may be issued. Since you are who you are, you'll probably opt for career, which, in your mind, will benefit your family in the long run.

Relationships

The Sun and Mercury will spend most of the month in Aries and your solar fourth house of home and family matters, Capricorn—and remember, Aries is quite the passionate sign. Now, passion can be delightful, but it can also lead to anger. But even if you're walking a bit of a tightrope domestically for a few weeks, the perks will make it all worthwhile.

Money and Success

With your ruling planet, Saturn, on duty in intense Scorpio at the same time Pluto is in Capricorn, two major astrological concepts—doing business and gaining power—have come together. In your case, this certainly could mean professional success has come easily lately, but impulsive Mars could make your life more stressful around April 8, 16, or 23. Sit tight and don't overreact.

Planetary Hotspots

Kids may take up more time than usual later in the month, Capricorn, as the Sun and Mercury set off for Taurus. If they seem needier than usual, consider that all this might be a play for your attention. Even if you can spend only one day a week with them, put it into your schedule and don't ever cancel. You can nip future problems in the bud by getting to know them as people, not just children.

Rewarding Days
2, 16, 17, 18, 19, 20, 25, 26

Challenging Days
1, 3, 7, 8, 14, 16, 21, 22, 23

Capricorn | May

Planetary Lightspots

The Full Moon on May 14 will link your solar eleventh house of group affiliations with your solar fifth house of hobbies, Capricorn, and—lo and behold—the break you've been waiting for to turn a hobby into income may finally arrive. Your mission is to market yourself to the very best of your abilities around this time. Shake every hand, kiss the babies, and smile.

Relationships

The Sun and Mercury will take turns passing through earthy, sensual Taurus and your solar fifth house, Capricorn, turning up your craving for creature comforts, physical pleasure, and leisure-time activities. Now, you're not famous for taking vacations, but if you haven't earned one, nobody has—and now's the time. Oh, go ahead. Indulge. And go first class while you're at it.

Money and Success

Your ruling planet, Saturn, will do his part to help you achieve your financial goals this month, Capricorn, and as long as you pay attention to the signs along the way, it will be tough for you to fail. Mingling will come easily, especially since you've become quite a commanding presence among your current social circle lately. You're on a quest. Talk to absolutely anyone who might be able to guide you.

Planetary Hotspots

Venus is the most charming of all the planets, Capricorn, and Pluto is the shrewdest, and he just so happens to be in your sign. Put them together and you have the King and Queen of Getting Your Way on the same page. So when they square off on May 14, you'll probably tap right into their energies and suddenly see exactly what to do and say to ... well, to turn situations around to your advantage, let's say.

Rewarding Days

3, 6, 9, 12, 15, 23, 24

Challenging Days

2, 10, 11, 14, 17, 18, 29

Capricorn | June

Planetary Lightspots

An easy trine between Venus and Pluto on June 8 will bring together your solar fifth house of love affairs with your solar first house of personality and first impressions, Capricorn. These two will combine talents to get you noticed—and you may not even have to say a word. You've certainly been learning to carry yourself differently lately. Someone is about to make a note of it.

Relationships

If you're not attached, Capricorn, someone just as driven, successful, and ambitious as yourself could be en route shortly. Venus is in her earthiest, most sensual outfit in Taurus, and she's making her seductive way through your solar fifth house of lovers. The best part is that she'll contact lucky Jupiter on June 18, who's on duty in your solar seventh house of relationships. Yes, indeedy. Be on the lookout for someone tall, good-looking, and financially comfy. That one's yours.

Money and Success

If you've been looking at a new form of income, Capricorn, especially if it involves a pet project or beloved hobby, you'd do well to take your idea to a successful, experienced pro around June 18. Whether you need a financial investment or just some tips on how to get the ball rolling, you can count on the Universe to open all kinds of doors.

Planetary Hotspots

We're all going to have trouble navigating the events of June 7, Capricorn. Mercury will stop to turn retrograde just as the emotional Moon gets into it with aggressive Mars and shocking Uranus. In your case, however, since all this will occur in action-oriented cardinal signs like your own, it's going to take all that famous resilience and patience to keep things on an even keel—but our money's on you.

Rewarding Days
3, 4, 6, 8, 17, 18, 28, 29

Challenging Days
7, 11, 12, 13, 14, 19, 24, 25

Capricorn | July

Planetary Lightspots

After all the time you've put into learning your trade and establishing a good professional reputation, Capricorn, you may decide now that it's time to take the show on the road and strike out on your own. The good news is that Jupiter will help take the sting out of the process once he enters your solar eighth house of joint finances on July 16, making it ever so much easier to get a loan or mortgage on a business property.

Relationships

Believe it or not, even your stoic little self can be thrown off by negative energy, Capricorn. So if there's any way to avoid being around controlling or manipulative people this month, it will be worth the effort to stay away. That goes double for July 4, 22, and 28, when the Sun, Mercury, and Venus will all fall into tugs of war with Pluto. News on the work front will make your day on July 13.

Money and Success

The New Moon on July 26 will set up shop in your solar eighth house, Capricorn, making joint finances and shared resources a priority for the next two weeks. No one needs to remind you to tend to your books and be sure they're in order, but if you haven't been handling them yourself, you might want to be safe rather than sorry. Look them over.

Planetary Hotspots

You may have been talking over a home purchase with your significant other or domestic partner of late, Capricorn, but this really isn't the best time to do it. Several planets in home-oriented Cancer will tug on your heartstrings, but in the back of your mind, you'll know there's something not quite right with the offer. Don't give in to keep the peace.

Rewarding Days

8, 12, 13, 18, 20, 22, 24

Challenging Days

3, 4, 19, 21, 26, 27, 28

Capricorn | August

Planetary Lightspots

It's time for a break, Capricorn, and not just a long weekend, either. The Sun, Mercury, and Venus will join forces with fun-loving Jupiter in playful Leo this month—and if this isn't the astrological formula for fun, nothing is. You may need to put out a couple of bucks to make a dream trip a reality, but you're guaranteed to feel like a brand-new person when you get back.

Relationships

A relationship that's gotten rather serious lately could turn quite passionate this month, Capricorn—and even, well, romantic. No, you're not usually much for that kind of sappy stuff, but several planets in Leo, who live for love, will inspire you to relax, let go, and allow your passionate, sensitive side to emerge. Your lucky partner will think they've died and gone to heaven!

Money and Success

The Full Moon on August 10 will shine its spotlight on your axis of financial matters, Capricorn, and since the emotional Moon in inventive Aquarius will be the star of the show, you're due to come up with a business plan that's anything but conservative. This is a great time to do a test run on possible investors, if for no other reason than to get their input and advice.

Planetary Hotspots

The new Moon this month will occur on August 25, Capricorn, and, along with fleet-footed Mercury, will inspire you to get out of town. You're not usually prone to spontaneous decisions, but if you think about it, you'll realize that you've been mulling this over in the back of your mind for some time. So why not? A little R&R will boost your productivity when you return.

Rewarding Days
10, 11, 15, 20, 21, 23, 25

Challenging Days
1, 2, 8, 18, 26, 29

Capricorn | September

Planetary Lightspots

It will be fairly easy for you to get your way this month, Capricorn. With magnetic Pluto on duty in your sign and your solar first house of personality, you've been impossible to refuse for a while now, but with the Sun and charming Venus in your earth-sign cousin, Virgo, you'll be positively oozing persuasion. Don't turn this stuff in the direction of anyone defenseless. It wouldn't be right.

Relationships

Once Venus takes off for Virgo, a fellow earth sign, on September 5, you'll find that just about everyone is finally on the same page as you. They'll take pride in their work, tend meticulously to details, and unhesitatingly cancel an evening out to straighten out their nest. One of those like-minded individuals could cross your path now, and if you're smart, you won't be too busy exchanging financial tips to get their number.

Money and Success

Picture a well-dressed businessperson strolling across a conference room, hand extended, ready to introduce themselves to the high rollers in the room. That's you this month, Capricorn, so gird your loins, make sure your business cards have no typos, and use your breath freshener. If you want it—whatever "it" is—with a little effort, you can have it now.

Planetary Hotspots

No matter what you're aiming to convince a higher-up about, you really can't go wrong around September 21, Capricorn—but then, you've probably already figured that out. In fact, with your ruling planet in perceptive Pluto's sign, you've likely been laying the groundwork for some time. Well, good for you. As you well know, nothing much is usually achieved by accident.

Rewarding Days

3, 4, 10, 14, 20, 21, 24, 25

Challenging Days

5, 8, 9, 13, 17, 22, 29

Capricorn | October

Planetary Lightspots

If you've been angry about something for the past month but not yet ready to let it out, Capricorn, you may find yourself a lot more willing to clear the air around October 5. Fiery Mars in your solar twelfth house of secrets has been stewing and suffering in silence, only allowing you to express your frustration when you're alone. On October 5, however, startling Uranus—who never did care what the neighbors think—will prompt him to seize the moment and speak. Go get 'em!

Relationships

The air may be turning colder, Capricorn, but with the Sun and Venus moving into sexy Scorpio on October 23, by the time Halloween rolls around, you'll probably be warm as toast. Oh, and that same day, by the way, a Solar Eclipse in that same position will plant a very sexy seed in your solar eleventh house of groups. Yep. You've been wondering if there might be more than friendship between you. Soon, you'll know.

Money and Success

With so much going on in your solar tenth house of career matters, Capricorn, you've probably not had much else on your mind but work. The good news is that the Sun, Mercury, and Venus are on duty, doing their best to get you connected with prospective business partners, mentors, and elders who admire and respect your ambition.

Planetary Hotspots

Changing conditions in your home life, thanks to startling Uranus in your solar fourth house of domestic matters, have kept family issues on edge for some time now, Capricorn, and you've had to monitor at least one sudden dispute. There may be a couple more of those on tap this month, but you won't be quite as emotionally involved as before. That will work to your advantage—and theirs, too.

Rewarding Days
5, 6, 13, 14, 15, 26, 27, 28

Challenging Days
3, 4, 7, 11, 16, 17, 22, 23

Capricorn | November

Planetary Lightspots

The Sun, Mercury, Venus, and Saturn all have plans for your solar eleventh house of friendships and group affiliations, Capricorn. This intense, relentless pack of Scorpionic energies will simply not rest until you've reached out to the one particular person in your crowd whom you've been eyeing from afar. And why should you wait, anyway? Who could possibly resist you, especially now?

Relationships

On November 6, a bright light will activate your axis of friends and lovers, Capricorn, involving the emotional Moon in sensual Taurus and the Sun in sexy Scorpio. This lovely, passionate Full Moon won't allow you to spend any more time alone than is absolutely necessary—unless, of course, you're spending those private hours with an intimate partner. In that case, all bets are off. Carry on.

Money and Success

There's an awful lot going on in your solar eleventh house at the moment, Capricorn, and since that's where the issue of goals for the future are handled, whether you know it or not, some very subtle events are occurring that will affect you in the long run. If you're not happy with the behavior or attitude of some current associates, it might be time to step away from the crowd.

Planetary Hotspots

You're under the gun right now, Capricorn, in many ways. You feel a duty to take care of your own needs, but self-imposed guilt may have you thinking you're only being selfish. Fortunately, with me-first Mars on duty in your sign and your solar first house of personality, you really won't have much of a choice. Defend your own rights as vigorously as you defend those of others. Why should you be less deserving?

Rewarding Days

1, 2, 3, 6, 7, 16, 17, 21

Challenging Days

8, 9, 10, 12, 13, 18, 22, 26

Capricorn | December

Planetary Lightspots

You're going to be forced to let loose and enjoy yourself this month, Capricorn. Resistance is futile, since the culprits are several planets in Sagittarius, full of the holiday spirit. After all the conflicts you've had to moderate, both at home and on the job, if you give in and cooperate, by the end of the month you'll feel rejuvenated.

Relationships

A New Moon on December 21 in your sign and your solar first house of appearance will urge you to make some changes, Capricorn, and as per usual, you'll take the hint very seriously. You've never been known for being excessive, so while it's a good idea to cut back on any extravagant habits, don't take this energy too far. Even Capricorns need to cut loose and have some fun every now and then. Don't feel bad about it.

Money and Success

Once again, on December 15, shocking Uranus will prod Pluto into action via a square from your solar fourth house of home and domestic matters. Now, these two often bring up urgent situations, and your sign definitely considers financial issues to be priorities, so one of those family-based emergencies could be that a family member is in desperate need of a loan. You'll want to help, and if you can, you should, but don't endanger your own stability to do it.

Planetary Hotspots

Your ruling planet, Saturn, will end his two-and-a-half-year trek through Scorpio on December 23, Capricorn, opting for something a little lighter—outgoing, expansive Sagittarius. Now, Saturn isn't fond of expansion or optimism, as you've no doubt learned over the years, but every now and then it's good to let go of the reins, sit back, and gloat quietly over what you've earned. It's your turn to do that now.

Rewarding Days
4, 5, 11, 12, 14, 19, 20, 21

Challenging Days
1, 7, 8, 15, 16, 22, 24, 25

Capricorn Action Table

These dates reflect the best–but not the only–times for success and ease in these activities, according to your Sun sign.

	JAN	FEB	MAR	APR	MAY	JUN	JUL	AUG	SEP	OCT	NOV	DEC
Move			30		2							
Start a class								5, 21, 25	14, 21			
Join a club			13	2	24		25	15				
Ask for a raise		24			19				2	14		
Look for work							7, 13					6
Get pro advice	1		14	17								1
Get a loan						8		18		14		
See a doctor				11			13					
Start a diet					28							
End relationship		26					12					
Buy clothes	7					4						
Get a makeover	11									26		21
New romance	15			26, 30	3, 6, 9	27	18				6	
Vacation						18			5			

Aquarius

The Water Bearer
January 20 to February 19

Element: Air

Quality: Fixed

Polarity: Yang/masculine

Planetary Ruler: Uranus

Meditation: I am a wellspring
of creativity

Gemstone: Amethyst

Power Stones: Aquamarine,
black pearl, chrysocolla

Key Phrase: I know

Glyph: Currents of energy

Anatomy: Ankles,
circulatory system

Colors: Iridescent blues, violet

Animals: Exotic birds

Myths/Legends: Ninhursag,
John the Baptist, Deucalion

House: Eleventh

Opposite Sign: Leo

Flower: Orchid

Keyword: Unconventional

The Aquarius Personality

Your Strengths and Challenges

You are a keen observer with a knack for considering unusual alternatives, Aquarius, two qualities that have combined to earn your sign its well-deserved reputation for producing geniuses. "Think outside the box"—which, of course, is where true genius first makes itself known—is your motto. You also know, however, that in order to think outside that box, you've got to become an expert on what's in there. As a result, you have always been a keen and avid observer, both of interesting individuals and of the human condition in general.

You watch current trends, but instinctively know where and when those traditions will no longer be applicable to what's really going on with humanity today. You watch a coworker and immediately understand why they are not suited to their work. Either way, you never hesitate to share your findings, and you're definitely not shy about expressing your opinions.

All this makes perfect sense. Your ruling planet is Uranus, the rebellious, radical rule breaker, so whenever you challenge the status quo—especially if you're absolutely sure you have a better idea—you're at your best. "Question authority" is your favorite slogan, as long as you're not the authority being questioned. In that case, the fixed nature of your airy, cerebral sign will work tirelessly to convince any who disagree with you that by not allowing themselves to consider all possibilities, they are limiting possibilities and falling into ruts, which you consider a death sentence.

Your Relationships

You, Aquarius, are quite aware of how unique each of us truly is—just like snowflakes. You, however, go way, way, way out of your way to make others notice exactly how different your breed of snowflake really is, so when it comes to friends and lovers, "unusual" and "different" are qualities that interest you. That may mean your new flame or BFF came complete with odd piercings, obvious multicolored tattoos, and/or purple hair on the left side of their head, but even if they're wearing pinstripes and sensible shoes, there absolutely has to be something rebellious in their nature. If you're honest about it, you'll admit that's a big part of why you chose them. They're nonconformists, just like you, so you often feel more comfortable around these kindred spirits than you do around your own biological tribe. The good news is that you tend to find "family" wherever you are, and all are welcome. You love socializing with new people from a wide variety of backgrounds. It keeps your spirit alive. Your unbiased views toward race, creed, and sexuality make you an exciting, open-minded companion, able to remain completely objective about the lifestyles of others—and determined to live your own life exactly as you see fit. Obviously, no one with an ounce of prejudice will gain access to your world, platonically, romantically, or any other kind of way! One whiff of a judgmental attitude is enough to chase you off, and you won't be back. For that reason, fiery, opinionated Sagittarians are often a good match for you, with curious Geminis a close second. Either of these signs will keep your interest, which is quite a feat. Librans are also fun, attentive, and just as sociable as you, but are usually not quite as interested in group activities, a possible problem over the long run.

Your Career and Money

If it's a vocation that most people haven't ever heard of, Aquarius, your interest in it will be piqued. If the schedule is guaranteed to be erratic and the work itself appeals to the rebel in you, you'll sign up. The deal breaker? The potential for boredom, which you have a very low tolerance for. In your mind, it's like this: if you've got to spend most of your waking hours doing one particular thing, it better be interesting, and it better be flexible, because life changes all the time. Period.

Once you've found that very special little niche, however, you'll be more than willing to put in the time to finish up a project. You're one of the three fixed signs, remember, all of which are notoriously stubborn, albeit in different ways. In your case, once you get an idea in your head, you really can't let it go, so shutting the computer and getting some sleep doesn't come easy. With or without a computer, however, any occupation that raises an eyebrow, like every other aspect of your life, will do just fine.

Your Lighter Side

You love the group dynamic almost as much as you love change, Aquarius, so when you discover what you deem to be a worthy cause, you set out to share the message, whatever it takes and quite relentlessly. You'll march, protest, man the phones, and plaster bumper stickers on the back of your vehicle. Social networking, e-dating, and tweeting are your guilty pleasures, and anyone who tries to separate you from your phone, computer, and iPad better be ready for a fight.

Affirmation for the Year
Balancing home and career is challenging but rewarding.

The Year Ahead for Aquarius

Thanks to the influence of your own unpredictable ruling planet, Uranus, you're quite adept at handling sudden change, Aquarius, so when life throws you curve balls, you tend to bounce back much faster and more easily than most of us. That quality will come in handy during 2014, which looks to be a year of sudden shifts for you, domestically and professionally. The good news is that no matter what comes along, you'll have Uranus by your side from his position in Aries in a positive, energetic sextile to help you make lemonade from what might initially just seem like lemons. The best news is that Uranus will be on duty in your solar third house of thoughts and communications. Another gift Uranus has given you is the ability to consider possibilities that most of us would never even think of, much less put into action. No matter how radical these solutions seem to be to others, you will know your insights are accurate. You'll have more than one "aha" moment, but these passing thoughts will be fleeting. Be sure to record them so you won't forget.

There's more good news on tap, too, thanks to the helpful influence of Jupiter, who'll spend up until July 16 in your solar sixth house of work and health-related matters. Jupiter loves freedom almost as much as Uranus, and brings about fortunate encounters with those who are willing to help. So if serious Saturn in your solar tenth house of career matters puts too much pressure on you, just as you're at the end of your rope, Jupiter will step in and save the day by putting you in touch with higher-ups who know what you're capable of, possibly through an introduction from a coworker. Investigate any new job before you sign up, however, and be sure you're not overextending yourself by committing to something you're not quite capable of or taking on more than you can handle. Remember, too, to look before you leap. If you don't have another job on tap, temporarily sitting tight might be best. In the meantime, investigate all work-related possibilities with an eye toward finding the perfect fit. You need to make your own schedule and call your own shots, and you can find that now, as long as you take only calculated risks. That doesn't mean you should turn down any unconventional occupation, only that being sure it's a step up should be your priority.

Jupiter's passage into fiery Leo on July 16 will bring this generous, lucky planet into your solar seventh house of one-to-one relationships, prolonging your ability to be in the right place at the right time to have fortunate and possibly "coincidental" encounters. Of course, you're used to running across new friends, lovers, and even business contacts under unusual circumstances. That's nothing new, but from July 16 of this year until August 15 of 2015, you can expect a veritable parade of interesting, successful, and creative new people in your life. If you're single, at least one of them may actually keep you interested long enough to become romantically involved, and as per Leo's love of passion and infatuation, it will most definitely be a very romantic relationship. Watch out for anyone who seems too good to be true, however. You could be right about them. If you're already involved, your relationship with your current partner will become your focus, and you may decide to get married, move in together, or have a child. Keep in mind, though, the freedom-loving side of Jupiter we talked about earlier. If you're not satisfied with the situation, this may be the time you choose to get yourself free, and you really shouldn't hesitate. With Jupiter on duty in this house, you definitely won't be short on company.

Speaking of new companions, expect some of them to arrive with an accent, especially during April, when an eclipse will combine talents with passionate, restless Mars, who'll be in the middle of a long transit through your solar ninth house of new experiences, travel, and long-distance friends and lovers. Up until July 25, Mars will bring a cast of characters into your life who aren't from your neck of the woods. Some could be quite positive, but you'll have to watch out for a tendency to be too optimistic and impulsively put yourself into dangerous situations with people you really don't know. Be on guard against Internet relationships, and don't fall for a smooth line that's backed up by shady real-life references. If you're feeling intellectually restless, consider going back to school or going into teaching yourself. And since this house is also where we form opinions about The Big Picture, expect to be quite assertive about your views on large issues, such as religion or politics. Remember, you get more bees with honey than with vinegar!

Since Uranus and Jupiter will have already put you in the mood to do something for work that reflects your personal beliefs, however, you may have the opportunity to become an activist of some sort, and the more closely attached you are personally to the issue, the more fervently involved you'll become.

We've already talked about Saturn and Uranus, so let's turn for a moment to Neptune and Pluto, who'll be on either side of your Sun sign during the year. Compassionate, intuitive Neptune will be on duty in ultra-sensitive Pisces and your solar second house of finances, yet another indication that the way you make your money needs to be in concert with your personal beliefs. Listen to the whispers of this invisible energy, even if your current reality doesn't seem to allow you that luxury. Pluto will be holding court in Capricorn and your solar twelfth house of subconscious desires, also urging you to be true to yourself. You may have flashbacks of times past when you made what you now think of as bad decisions or frivolous choices, but their purpose is to steer you away from repeating old patterns.

This is an incredibly important year for you, Aquarius. Changes are due in the major sectors of your life: home, career, and relationships. You will have to do some juggling to set things right, but if anyone is qualified, it's you—and you'll probably enjoy every minute of it!

What This Year's Eclipses Mean for You

There will be four eclipses this year, Aquarius, two solar and two lunar. The first will occur on April 15, a Lunar Eclipse in partner-oriented Libra and your solar ninth house of education, travel, and dealings with others who are quite a distance from you. Together with your sign's affinity for computers and group affiliations, this Full Moon may inspire you to become involved in social networking, but be very careful of online romance. Eclipses are erratic energies, and while positive opportunities to reach out and electronically mingle are certainly possible, you may also draw someone into your life who'll have a disruptive effect on it.

On April 29, a Solar Eclipse in Taurus will arrive, a super-charged New Moon that could put your solar fourth house of home at odds with your solar tenth house of career matters. Together with ultra-responsible Saturn, an emotional tug of war could ensue, forcing you to make changes in one or both areas of life to accommodate the needs of the other. If family members are upset because you're spending so much time at work, or if they express concern about the physical or emotional stress your current work puts you under, listen up. They may be right.

On October 8, a second Lunar Eclipse will occur, this time in impulsive Aries and your solar third house of communication and conversations. Together with your ruling planet, startling Uranus, also currently on duty there, you can definitely count on raising some eyebrows, not just because of what you say—which will be just as startling to you as it is to others—but also because of what you'll be willing to do. Aries loves adrenaline, and you're a big fan of it yourself, so you'll need to channel this energy carefully. Avoid confrontations that aren't necessary, and don't put yourself in situations where you're vulnerable.

The second Solar Eclipse of the year will arrive on October 23 in Scorpio and your solar tenth house of profession and reputation. This super-charged New Moon, just like the first one on April 29, will push you to balance career responsibilities with the inevitable needs of your domestic situation. Your mission will be to use that brilliant, inventive mind of yours to think outside the box. If anyone can come up with an innovative way to make both your home life and your chosen path work well together, it's you. You might want to consider starting your own business, working freelance, or putting in an office at home.

Saturn

If you were born between February 9 and 19, your Sun will experience a square from responsible, conservative Saturn this year. There's no denying that this is ordinarily quite a stressful time for most of us, but it may be especially tough for someone as freedom-oriented as you. Added responsibilities within your personal relationships are possible, especially with parents and elders. But since Saturn will be operating from his position in your solar tenth house of career matters and dealings with authority, increased job duties may also come your way and be a bit overwhelming at times, causing you to question whether it's really worth it to keep doing what you're doing at the expense of your mental and emotional health. You may feel like an emotional pressure cooker that's ready to blow at any moment. The good news is that your ruling planet, Uranus, will be ready, willing, and able to help you get yourself free from any situations that are stagnating, personally or professionally. Saturn's job is to show us what's not working, or where we're ill-prepared or unrealistic. But with Saturn in cahoots with Uranus, this could well be a time of quite positive, long-term change. Your mission is to take charge of your life, to assume responsibility for your own happiness, and to make needed changes in your life path.

Uranus

If you were born between January 28 and February 5, Aquarius, you are currently experiencing a very pleasant visit from Uranus, the planet of enlightenment, genius, and independence. Now, Uranus is your planetary ruler, so you are already quite in tune with his unpredictable, freedom-oriented energies. In fact, you enjoy change and have always fought for your rights without batting an eyelash. But now, in an easy, stimulating sextile to your Sun this year, Uranus will inspire you to become even more determined to let your true self show. Of course, the decisions we make while on this quest for personal freedom often seem quite far from conventional, and our behavior often seems quite odd to others—which, of course, you just love. What will make this period even more fun is the fact that Uranus will be operating from his spot in impulsive Aries and your solar third house of communication and conversations. You'll amaze not just the masses with what tumbles out of your mouth, but yourself, too, so anyone who asks for your opinion had obviously better be ready to hear it. New interests will hit you out of the blue, and you'll probably be attached to your computer. But since this is also a house concerned with transportation, you might just decide to trade up—and it won't be for a sensible vehicle. Before you drive off into the sunset with your trusty laptop on the seat beside you, however, make sure your license is valid!

Neptune

If you were born between January 23 and 27, your Sun will be contacted by dreamy, romantic Neptune from your solar second house of values. Now, what you value, Aquarius, can be anything from money, possessions, and material resources to qualities you admire in yourself and in others, but with Neptune invisibly at work helping you to open up to new belief systems and eroding past priorities, what was previously important to you may begin to fade off into the sunset. Not to worry, however. This transit is subtle but extremely potent, and since you received such a strong dose of reality from Saturn last year, you may just be grateful for the relief, and ready to set down a whole new personal top ten list.

Changing what's important to you could also mean you're not quite as willing to trade hours of your life for "things," so a job change could also be on the horizon. Even if you end up cutting back on material possessions or luxuries, you won't mind, just as long as your waking hours are spent doing something you love and believe in. This is definitely a good time to "follow your bliss."

Pluto

If you were born between January 30 and February 3, your Sun will be contacted by transiting Pluto in Capricorn in your solar twelfth house. This is where secrets, subconscious desires, and psychic abilities reside, and Pluto's presence here will temporarily endow you with something akin to extrasensory perception. Pay special attention to your dreams, and do your best to record and unravel them. For the coming year, they'll be packed with psychological symbolism. Listen closely to the voice of your intuition, too, which will be even stronger than usual. Remember, Pluto's specialty is perception. Pluto calls our attention to subtle clues from our environment, so your fascination for mysteries and investigation will be piqued, but your instincts will be dead on, too. Obviously, it will be next to impossible to pull the wool over your eyes—again, as long as you go with your gut. You may also accidentally stumble across information you were not expecting to find, and it will likely be from the past.

Of course, the twelfth house is also a place where privacy comes first, and with Pluto urging you to quietly watch from this spot behind the scenes, you may withdraw to do some research on a topic that deeply concerns you. Keep in mind that whatever you uncover now will affect you on a very profound level and influence your behavior for the next several years.

Most importantly, it is time for you to build up boundaries and keep yourself safe from negative influences, no matter how obscure your reasons for backing off seem to others. Your sixth sense is especially keen now. Trust it implicitly.

Aquarius | January

Planetary Lightspots

You'll be in the mood to withdraw, retreat, and recharge your batteries this month, Aquarius, and after all this time you've spent socializing, you really are due for some quality time alone. The good news is that, as per usual, you'll see this coming well before it's urgent. Also, you'll know what to tell everyone to get them well prepared for managing without you for a while.

Relationships

You just love interesting intellectual companions, Aquarius, and you always manage to find them—often in the darnedest of places. So this month, with Jupiter in nurturing Cancer, you might adopt at least one new "stray" in the produce aisle—or standing in line at the movies. Just don't expect them to stay around forever. Do what you can and let them go.

Money and Success

With dreamy Neptune in your solar second house of personal finances—where she'll stay for the next decade, by the way—it's really, really, really important for you to find someone else to take care of your money. No fair choosing your current lover, either. Find an impartial, objective third partner, make sure you're on the same page, and respect their decisions.

Planetary Hotspots

Mercury will set off for your own computer-loving sign and your solar first house of personality on January 11, Aquarius, so upgrading your current system is a definite possibility. You may also be one of the last holdouts who's finally decided to give in and get online. Either way, electronic devices and the wonders they're capable of will completely capture your imagination.

Rewarding Days

10, 11, 12, 16, 17, 19, 24, 30

Challenging Days

1, 2, 3, 5, 7, 8, 16, 25, 26

Aquarius | February

Planetary Lightspots

You follow the lead of your patron planet, Uranus, in all things cerebral, and since he's the kind of guy who just loves breaking tradition and changing game plans at the last second—well, you do, too. On February 15, then, when absolutely anything might be possible—thanks to the Sun and Mercury retrograde in your sign—unlike most of us, you'll naturally keep your mind open to all possibilities.

Relationships

The one and only Full Moon this month will occur on February 14, Aquarius, just in time for Valentine's Day. Now, this ultra-sentimental date has probably never been one of your favorite holidays, but this year, with passionate Mars in partner-oriented Libra set to form an easy trine with the Sun in your sign...well, honestly, you'd have to be out of your mind to resist participating.

Money and Success

When it comes to money, Aquarius, you tend to think of it as a special type of paper that can be exchanged for fun and, occasionally, also for food and things. You've been learning to live with much less lately, with Neptune pulling you away from the material world. But this month, you'll be especially willing to not just let go, but to give away what you've got. Remember, though—this, too, shall pass. Trust a relative with the custody of your treasures.

Planetary Hotspots

Your ruling planet, surprising Uranus, will square off with intense Pluto—yes, again—this month, Aquarius, urging you to pull the rug out from under any authority who happens to be in the vicinity. You, of course, are always willing to do that sort of thing, but before you involve anyone else, please consider what this might do to their future.

Rewarding Days

4, 5, 13, 14, 15, 16, 23, 24

Challenging Days

10, 11, 12, 18, 19, 25, 26, 27

Aquarius | March

Planetary Lightspots

Two new starts are on tap for you this month, Aquarius, and since you're the sign that's fondest of change, chances are good you'll enjoy every minute of it. On March 1, the first New Moon of the month will occur in your solar second house of finances, urging you to put your entrepreneurial ambitions to the test. A hint: do it with a partner.

Relationships

At times, you've felt that your significant other didn't appreciate just how special you are, Aquarius, and that probably meant that the relationship didn't survive for much longer afterward. But this month, with attractive Venus in your solar first house of personality and appearance, you'll be a magnet. Of course, magnets attract all kinds of things, so be cautious—but hey, don't miss out on the chance to find someone who'll actually get you.

Money and Success

If you're approached by someone who's touting a get-rich-quick scheme this month, Aquarius, run. If it happens around March 22, run even faster—and call the authorities while you're at it. You'll probably need an unbiased, clear-minded third party to unravel the situation—that and a few others, too.

Planetary Hotspots

The second of those new starts we talked about will occur on March 30, via a second New Moon that will activate your solar third house of communications. This might not amount to much if this highly emotional planet weren't going to be wearing highly impulsive Aries. Since this is such a trigger-happy match, however, just this once, rather than doing what comes naturally—telling whomever off, even if friends or family are present—consider walking away.

Rewarding Days

1, 2, 5, 12, 13, 14, 18, 19

Challenging Days

3, 10, 11, 21, 22, 23, 28, 29

Aquarius | April

Planetary Lightspots

Your solar ninth house of higher education, politics, and religion will be hit by a potent Lunar Eclipse on April 15, Aquarius. As all Full Moons do, this one will urge you to offer up your final answer. The good news is that you'll have lots of opportunities to deliver that final, final answer (re: politics, etc.) over the course of your lifetime. Your deeply held opinions will change drastically from time to time. This is one of those times.

Relationships

Venus will set off for your solar second house of values on April 5, Aquarius, and suddenly, the most important prerequisite for all potential partners will be a shared belief in how you earn your money. Get it straightened out now, because it will only be tougher to resolve in the future.

Money and Success

Taurus is the sign that many think of as the astrological money magnet, Aquarius. On April 29, a Solar Eclipse will arrive in that sign and your solar fourth house of domestic matters, urging you to hold on to what you've got, no matter what the consequences. The good news is there'll be no doubt that you're perfectly entitled to whatever you're holding on to when the dust settles.

Planetary Hotspots

Your mouth will be absolutely out of control this month, Aquarius. Yes, even more than usual. That's not to say that you won't be 100 percent right every time you protest an injustice or resist following the herd, but right about now, if you want to hold on to that precious freedom of yours, you might want to use just a bit of tact every now and then.

Rewarding Days
10, 11, 17, 18, 19, 25, 26, 29, 30

Challenging Days
1, 3, 7, 8, 14, 16, 20, 23

Aquarius | May

Planetary Lightspots

Loving Venus will make her way through your solar third house of conversations and communications this month, Aquarius—which sounds like it might be a very polite, tactful time for you. She'll be wearing Aries, however, a sign that's almost as impulsive as yours, and in this rather vocal place, you'll be even more prone to speaking your mind, for better or worse. You always say whatever you want to, but at the moment, you'll be quite charming about it.

Relationships

After weeks of moving retrograde in your solar ninth house of big issues, fiery Mars will turn direct on May 19, Aquarius. He's been urging you to make nice with someone you don't see on a regular basis, probably because of geographical limits. From May 19 through the end of July, however, you'll feel an urgent need to not just make nice, but to make hugs. Make arrangements to visit or be visited now.

Money and Success

Full Moons in Scorpio bring up a tough issue, Aquarius. Do you hold on through the rough patches or ditch the situation and start over? Since the lunation on May 14 will bring its energy to your solar axis of home versus career, the same old argument may resurface. You're not spending enough time at home, right? Well, stop for a minute. Maybe you're not. Wouldn't a little more time with the kids be nice?

Planetary Hotspots

Saturn can be tough for any sign to handle, but operating as he is now in intense Scorpio, he's impossible to argue with. The Sun, Mercury, and Venus will make their way through your solar fourth house of home, contacting Saturn along the way, so don't bother resisting his demands to make your home a safer place. Do what you've got to do to feel secure.

Rewarding Days

3, 4, 6, 9, 12, 15, 23, 24

Challenging Days

1, 2, 10, 11, 14, 16, 18, 27, 28

Aquarius | June

Planetary Lightspots

The Full Moon on June 13 will cast its light, innocently enough, into your solar eleventh house of friendships, Aquarius—but it will also bring your solar fifth house of lovers into the mix. This could mean that you've decided to fire a current flame, but don't expect the old "let's just be friends" to necessarily work as well for them as it does for you. Not everyone is as well equipped as you to let go. Be understanding.

Relationships

On June 17, Mercury will back up into Gemini and your solar fifth house, Aquarius, inspiring you to take a second look at a situation with kids, lovers, and former playmates. Does one of them really need you because of a recent transgression, or are you simply doing what you do best—taking their side regardless of what they've done simply because they're being challenged by authority?

Money and Success

All your investments will go along quite smoothly around June 8, thanks to an easy relationship between Venus in Taurus and Pluto in Capricorn, two earthy signs that are quite fond of the material world. And then on June 18, generous Jupiter will get involved, a guarantee of success—as long as you don't go overboard. Real estate ventures and home improvements will pay off well in the months and years to come.

Planetary Hotspots

If anyone isn't fond of sitting at home knitting, Aquarius, it's you. But with loving Venus in solid, earthy Taurus and your solar fourth house of domestic matters this month, you might find yourself wanting to be there more than anywhere else, including out on the town with friends, your favorite spot. It's okay. Allow yourself to relax for a bit. Once Venus sets off for Gemini on June 23, your social schedule will once again—happily—take over your life.

Rewarding Days
3, 4, 6, 8, 17, 18, 28, 29

Challenging Days
7, 11, 12, 19, 24, 25

Aquarius | July

Planetary Lightspots

After three long weeks of moving retrograde, Mercury will stop to turn direct on July 1, Aquarius, all done up in chatty Gemini and your solar fifth house. Talk about fun times at Ridgemont High! If ever you had the chance to redo your adolescence, it's now. The good news is that this time, you'll be able to bring all that wisdom and experience to your decisions. It's the best of all worlds. Use it to your advantage.

Relationships

Work-related matters could become quite problematic at the end of the month, thanks to the Sun and Venus, who are only trying to help from their spot in your solar sixth house of work and health. On a positive note, thinking over your schedule, including work, could mean realizing that you're dealing with far too much stress on a daily basis. Do what you've gotta do and get yourself free.

Money and Success

It's been too easy for you to lose track of receipts, toss your bank notices into the oval file, and head for the hills lately, Aquarius. Neptune in Pisces is a potent force, and she's urging you to let go and let God—however you see the concept of Spirit. Well, Spirit will be on your side this month, especially around July 19 and 24, Aquarius. Otherwise, don't sign anything without professional advice.

Planetary Hotspots

On July 13, loving Venus and her age-old lover, Mars, will get into an easy trine, bringing together Gemini and Libra, the other two air signs. Airy little you will really enjoy this astrological weather, and a new playmate may be en route. Before you become overly interested in their brain and only willing to talk to them, however, think. How does your partner feel about this?

Rewarding Days

6, 12, 13, 18, 19, 23, 30, 31

Challenging Days

3, 4, 8, 21, 22, 24, 26

Aquarius | August

Planetary Lightspots

You need to stop avoiding the mirror, Aquarius, and if you won't do it on your own, the Full Moon on August 10 in your own sign and your solar first house will certainly draw your attention back to your physical self. You may not like what you see, in which case, it's time for one of your classic 180s. Drop what you're doing and change your habits entirely. It's a new you!

Relationships

As the month winds down, Aquarius, you may feel as if you're lodged firmly between a rock and hard place, thanks, of course, to Saturn, who just loves roadblocks. For most of August, however, you'll enjoy the fiery, fun-loving energy of several planets in Leo and your solar seventh house of one-to-one encounters. Talk about a good time!

Money and Success

You'll be in the mood to spend on your sweetheart this month, and to spend big, too, especially around August 17 and 18. Telling you to think before you pull out that plastic is an exercise in futility. Fortunately, serious Saturn will stop you before you do anything too foolish on August 25 or 26.

Planetary Hotspots

The New Moon on August 25 will join forces with Mercury, Mars, and Saturn to put you in a really good frame of mind, Aquarius. In fact, you might just be in the mood to tackle issues of joint finances, and if so, you'll be relentless and unstoppable. Yes, Saturn in intense, obsessive Scorpio will be involved, so your decisions now will have long-term repercussions. Ready or not, however...

Rewarding Days

1, 6, 8, 15, 18, 21, 23

Challenging Days

2, 3, 7, 17, 25, 26, 28

Aquarius | September

Planetary Lightspots

Passionate Mars will storm off into Sagittarius on September 13, Aquarius, one of your very favorite astrological flavors. The two of you share a love of personal freedom and an insatiable appetite for new information. So as Mars makes his way through your solar eleventh house of friendships over the next six weeks, it's safe to expect lots of good times and interesting conversations. What could be better?

Relationships

With Jupiter currently on duty in Leo and your solar seventh house of one-to-one relationships, Aquarius, more than one new admirer has tried to become the star of your show. At the first sign a lover is becoming even remotely possessive, however, you run in the opposite direction. Well, just you wait until September 25, when Jupiter and your ruling planet, Uranus, will arrange for you to meet someone just as freewheeling as yourself.

Money and Success

There's a Full Moon due on September 8, Aquarius, set to illuminate your solar axis of money matters. This could be good news, especially if you've been trying to get some answers to financial questions, but you may not like the answers. This lunation will occur in Pisces, a sign that's not particularly good with money or details, so there may still be some confusion. Try to stay calm until September 21, when Venus and Saturn will bring good news.

Planetary Hotspots

Mercury will face off with your ruling planet, startling Uranus, on September 13, Aquarius, and just about everyone you know will be scrambling to regroup after some surprising news. You, however, don't mind change, no matter how suddenly it arises. In fact, you live for it, so you'll probably watch all this with some degree of amusement.

Rewarding Days
2, 3, 10, 12, 13, 21, 25, 29

Challenging Days
5, 8, 9, 17, 20, 22

Aquarius | October

Planetary Lightspots

You've never been shy about expressing your opinions, Aquarius, especially if you happen to be discussing one of your pet causes. So when the Lunar Eclipse on October 8 arrives, all done up in warrior-like Aries and your solar third house of conversation, you may be called on to champion a cause or take up the reins for a group that has recently lost its leader. Careful, now. Go easy on them—at first, anyway.

Relationships

With partner-oriented Venus in Libra on duty in your solar ninth house of long-distance travel, and Jupiter—who wrote the book on that subject—in your solar seventh house of relationships, it's easy to see how you two might decide to take a spontaneous jaunt this month. If you can manage it, go between October 11 and 16. Mercury is retrograde, so you can expect lots of last-minute changes, which might be unsettling to some, but will make this even more fun in your book.

Money and Success

Neptune's presence in your solar second house of money matters could inspire you to make some donations this month, Aquarius, but do your homework before you pull out your checkbook. Wait until after Mercury turns direct on October 25 to sign anything, in fact. October 27 will provide you with solid facts you might have been missing, thanks to a trusted elder, mentor, or authority figure.

Planetary Hotspots

Just when you thought things were beginning to settle down career-wise, a Solar Eclipse in intense Scorpio on October 23 will shake things up a bit. This might mark the beginning of a power struggle between you and one of The Powers That Be, especially if you're under the impression that they're trying to control or manipulate you.

Rewarding Days
5, 7, 11, 14, 15, 16, 25, 27

Challenging Days
3, 4, 10, 18, 22, 23, 24

Aquarius | November

Planetary Lightspots

You'll miss the presence of impulsive Mars in your solar eleventh house of friendships and group activities for the first couple of weeks of November, but not to worry. You may spend a few nights at home alone, but it will be your choice. Besides, you'll need to conserve your energy, because on November 16, Venus will enter this house wearing Sagittarius, followed by the Sun on November 22 and Mercury on November 27, and the good times will once again be rolling.

Relationships

You may need to make a choice around November 9 or 12, Aquarius, between fulfilling your job-related responsibilities and spending some much-needed quality time alone with your partner. This may even be delivered via an ultimatum from someone who's tired of waiting for you to step away from the computer and have a real, live conversation. There may be something to that.

Money and Success

A group venture might not be a bad idea this month, with Venus in your solar eleventh house of friendships and group affiliations, Aquarius. Now, your specialty is groups, and once you feel as if you've found your tribe, you're quite devoted. If the others want to put you in charge of the finances around November 16, you'll be flattered. Think about the time you'll need to invest in this before you agree.

Planetary Hotspots

A higher-up could make things tough for you around November 10, Aquarius, and again around November 12 and 18. Your mission is to realize that all this contention may be a sign that you're really not where you ought to be. Don't do anything drastic just yet, but start looking around for a work situation that better suits your ideals—with authority figures who respect individuality.

Rewarding Days

1, 2, 3, 11, 16, 21, 22, 27

Challenging Days

8, 9, 10, 12, 13, 17, 18

Aquarius | December

Planetary Lightspots

Yeehaw, Aquarius! Red-hot Mars will set off for your sign on December 4, bringing all his passion and assertion to your solar first house of personality. Prepare to be bolder, more rebellious, and a lot more impulsive for the next six weeks—and to raise eyebrows on a regular basis, too, even if you're not trying. Bet that sounds like fun, doesn't it?

Relationships

A Full Moon on December 6 will occur in talkative Gemini and your solar fifth house of recreation, urging you to spend some time with lighthearted companions. If you have kids, this is the perfect time for a family vacation, with no cell phones, computers, or iPods allowed. If you're still looking for the perfect partner—one who won't hold on too tight, that is—resume the hunt. It's prime time.

Money and Success

A sudden expense that arises around December 20 may temporarily rattle you, Aquarius, but if you talk to an unbiased third party about the situation, you'll be able to set your mind at ease. The good news is that once Saturn enters your solar eleventh house of friendships on December 23, you'll be able to rely on others to keep their promises.

Planetary Hotspots

Your ruling planet, Uranus, has been at war with Pluto for years now, Aquarius, and they've decided to do battle once again on December 15. This testy square will pit your solar third house of communications against your solar twelfth house of secrets, and the startling nature of Uranus may mean that something you've been hiding is about to be revealed. Now that you know, prepare yourself to do some 'splainin'.

Rewarding Days
4, 5, 6, 8, 14, 20, 23

Challenging Days
1, 15, 16, 19, 24, 25, 26

Aquarius Action Table

These dates reflect the best—but not the only—times for success and ease in these activities, according to your Sun sign.

	JAN	FEB	MAR	APR	MAY	JUN	JUL	AUG	SEP	OCT	NOV	DEC
Move				25, 30	6						6	
Start a class			14			22			24, 29	15		
Join a club						22				5	22	5
Ask for a raise				25								
Look for work	15		1, 2	30	14	27	18					
Get pro advice		24				18		25		14	12, 18	
Get a loan								21				
See a doctor			13									
Start a diet	30											
End relationship			29					26				
Buy clothes											26	
Get a makeover	19	28	5					10				
New romance		14			7, 12, 15		22, 26					6
Vacation	24		14		12		13	2, 12, 18				

Pisces

The Fish
February 19 to March 20

Element: Water

Quality: Mutable

Polarity: Yin/feminine

Planetary Ruler: Neptune

Meditation: I successfully navigate my emotions

Gemstone: Aquamarine

Power Stones: Amethyst, bloodstone, tourmaline

Key Phrase: I believe

Glyph: Two fish swimming in opposite directions

Anatomy: Feet, lymphatic system

Colors: Sea green, violet

Animals: Fish, sea mammals

Myths/Legends: Aphrodite, Buddha, Jesus of Nazareth

House: Twelfth

Opposite Sign: Virgo

Flower: Water lily

Keyword: Transcendence

The Pisces Personality

Your Strengths and Challenges

Your sign, Pisces, is the personal property of woozy, dreamy Neptune, and your nature reflects her gifts of sensitivity and intuition. You're so sensitive, in fact, that being around negative people or depressing situations can affect you on a very deep emotional level. Neptune dissolves boundaries, so, much like a sponge, you pick up on absolutely everything around you, for better or worse. Therefore, it's important for you to monitor your relationships and surroundings carefully. You're mutable and emotional, so it's easy for you to be influenced by others with less-than-honorable motives. When in doubt, trust your intuition, and listen to that alarm sounding in the back of your mind. It will never let you down. Over time, you'll come to realize that the greatest disappointments in your life have occurred when you ignored warning signs and opted to see only the best.

That ultra-sensitivity to your environment means your dreams—and your daydreams, too—are often quite prophetic, so your reputation for being psychic is well deserved. You're also quite good at disappearing when you want to, and can easily make yourself invisible in a room full of people, which makes you an expert at infiltrating the ranks, no matter where you are.

You love romance and fantasies, so when reality becomes too harsh, you often retreat into novels, movies, and the arts. Your knack for translating an emotion into a poem, painting, or piece of music is unparalleled.

Your Relationships

You are compassionate, empathetic, and self-sacrificing to a fault, Pisces, so you tend to watch from behind the scenes before you reach out. The one exception to this rule is your relationships with family, where you feel safest and most fulfilled.

Now, let's talk about romance. Isn't love grand? In your book, Pisces, there's nothing grander. You find spiritual connection and emotional fulfillment through your relationships, and since you're constantly on the lookout for that deep, invisible, and unspoken connection, you may tend to fall in love a lot, and in your younger years, your heart will be easily broken. As you gain life experience, however, you'll be able to take a step back and use your intuition to see how what might initially seem perfect could be a beautiful illusion. No matter how much you want it to be true, what really is and what you're wishing for may not be the same thing. The good news is that if anyone out there can find their true soul mate, it's you, and more often than not, you'll "recognize" them immediately. It may take more than a few false alarms, but when you find your true love, you'll bond with them on the deep, spiritual level you have always craved.

Now, depth and connection are traits associated with the water element, so you may find your ideal match in intense Scorpio or Cancer, whose instincts rival your own. Either sign will understand your need to merge and blend with an Other, and you'll handle each other with kid gloves, acutely aware of how much the little things really mean. You may be drawn to Virgos, but since you're anything but detail-oriented and are ultra-susceptible to criticism, they may make better friends than partners.

Your Career and Money

You need a career that's also a vocation, Pisces, in the truest sense of the word. You can be easily distracted, so to apply yourself, you need to believe strongly in what you're doing, so that it becomes not just your way of earning income, but your life's work. Along the way to finding it, you'll probably hold down a variety of jobs—at least in the short term. Once you decide to choose a path and invest yourself, your knack for spotting true artistic talent, your eye for photography, and your love of music will propel you to excel in any of those fields quite easily.

Financially speaking—and this really can't be stressed strongly enough—you need to be very careful. That applies to your checkbook, which you may be all too easily convinced to pull out, and to your actual cash, which, like your keys and your glasses, is easy for you to misplace. Learn to value your own resources and possessions, and treat them with the respect you show to those of others.

Your Lighter Side

You're happiest in idyllic situations, Pisces, and having a glass of wine certainly takes the edge off a workday that was far too harshly realistic for your taste. There's nothing wrong with that, but be sure not to overindulge, even if everyone else does. Enjoy the company of kindred spirits at a play or concert, and get involved with a spiritual or metaphysical group. Oh, and check out meditation. You're a natural!

Affirmation for the Year
I rise above petty problems by seeing the big picture.

The Year Ahead for Pisces

There'll be a strong focus on finances this year, Pisces, and you'll have several decisions to make in that department, probably during April or October, thanks to a series of eclipses that will demand your attention. Whether these changes initially seem positive or negative, try to focus on the long term—the big picture. If you need to let go of something, chances are good that you didn't really want it all that badly anyway.

The good news is that straight through mid-July, your solar fifth house of children, creativity, and lovers will play host to generous Jupiter in tender-hearted Cancer. This positive, expansive energy will bring along a host of blessings relating to domestic issues and parenting. You may decide to have a child or to open your door to a loved one who needs some serious TLC. Jupiter's urge to expand in home-oriented Cancer could also mean that you decide it's time to move, most likely to a larger, more comfortable place, or to stay put and literally expand your physical dwelling. Just be careful not to overspend or extend your credit past what you can realistically afford. One of the difficulties with visits from Jupiter is that we often become overly optimistic about the future without any solid, practical reasons. No one is saying you can't stretch and grow, but do it wisely, with an eye toward slow, steady growth.

Speaking of growth, once Jupiter enters fiery Leo and your solar sixth house of work on July 14, your on-the-job responsibilities may increase substantially. Does this mean you'll finally receive the raise, bonus, or promotion you've been working so hard for? Well, it certainly could, but you'll have to put a lot of energy into making that happen. Jupiter's love of higher education may make it possible for you to enhance your resumé with classes or certificate programs. Fortunately, Leo isn't just fire, it's fixed fire, and the fixed signs are quite stubborn and determined. So once you accept the opportunities offered, you'll do absolutely everything you can to excel, to show the higher-ups they were absolutely right to give you the nod. Leo also loves romance, so Jupiter's presence here may indicate a new relationship with a coworker. You two will make terrific playmates, and sparks will definitely fly, but if you need to see each other on a daily basis, be sure you can return to your previous platonic relationship if the affair doesn't work out. Leo's love for children—and center stage—could also mean you decide to take a larger part in their lives. You may begin teaching, coaching, mentoring, or simply make your own kids a much larger part of your daily life. Either way, you really should let your hair down and have some serious fun with youngsters.

Meanwhile, in your solar ninth house, serious Saturn will be on duty, straight through December 23. Since this house has everything to do with The Big Picture—including politics, religion, and education—and given Saturn's fondness for conservatism, you may find that you're a bit less likely to concede your viewpoints in any debate on these issues. As per usual, unless you can realistically expect to bring about the changes you see as necessary, it might be best to sit back and bide your time—and try not to irritate anyone in the meantime by being too rigid and inflexible.

Saturn is also the Cosmic Schoolmaster, however, so if you've achieved a level of expertise in your field, this is the perfect time to share your skills and experience with others through teaching them what you know, in a hands-on, practical way. You may not be the easiest instructor in the world right now, but your students and protégés will come to think of you as firm but fair. Saturn's presence in your solar ninth house of higher learning is yet another strong indication that this is a great year to consider furthering your own education as well.

All the while you're making slow and steady progress with Saturn, however, Uranus, the heaven's wildcard, will be hard at work in your solar second house of finances, possessions, and personal values, determined to convince you to make some drastic changes. Uranus always brings home the issue of personal freedom, and he's never been a big fan of repressing your individuality to fit in or simply make ends meet. Your attitude about what you're willing to do to make money is due for some drastic alterations, and with Uranus in impulsive Aries, once you decide you're done, that will be that—immediately and permanently. Do yourself a favor and be sure you have another job before you stomp out of your current workplace. If you're already restless and can feel the storm coming, get busy. Set the wheels in motion to become financially independent. If you've always wanted a business of your own, do your homework and see exactly what it would take to make that happen.

Remember, with serious Saturn in Scorpio and outgoing Jupiter in Cancer, the other two water signs, you're surrounded by support. Reach out to influential, successful acquaintances who've already arrived. Chances are excellent they'll be more than willing to help. Also, with Pluto in Capricorn, Saturn's sign, and Saturn in Pluto's sign, the two are in what's known as "mutual reception," so they're working together. Pluto rules plutocrats, and will provide the opportunity to hook up with these big shots through group situations.

Now, let's talk about fiery Mars, the ancient Roman God of War and the most assertive planet in the heavens. This red-hot bullet of energy will make an unusually long visit to partner-oriented Libra and your solar eighth house of intimate encounters. He'll stay put in that tender place until July 25, so if you're already involved, you two may be missing in action more often than not over the first half of the year. If you're still searching for the passion you crave, Mars will be happy to provide you with a parade of charming applicants for the position. Your impulse will be to love 'em and leave 'em, but once you run across someone you really connect with, you'll put every bit of energy you have into making the relationship work.

Speaking of romance, while Mars will bring it to you physically, remember that your ruling planet—dreamy, sentimental Neptune—is in your sign and your solar first house of personality, so you're quite vulnerable right now, and extremely susceptible to seeing what you want to see in others. Be careful not to backpedal in relationships while Mars is retrograde, from March 1 through May 19. Together with the nostalgic influence of Neptune, you may decide to give an old love a second try—or a third or fourth. Remember, if it didn't work once, it probably won't work twice.

What This Year's Eclipses Mean for You

Two pairs of eclipses are scheduled for 2014, Pisces. The first will occur in April and the second in October. On April 15, a Lunar Eclipse in partner-oriented Libra will get the show on the road in your solar eighth house of intimacy and joint resources. On the one hand, this could be the beginning of a relationship that's far more than just a beautiful friendship. In fact, you could fall very deeply in love, and very suddenly. Eclipses work fast, but their energies linger. A financial responsibility you share with a partner may also turn out to involve a bit more than you bargained for. Your mission is to decide where to draw the line, and to think of your own needs first—just this once.

Later that month, on April 29, a Solar Eclipse will activate Taurus, a sign that's also often associated with material wealth and possessions. Your solar third house of thoughts, communications, and conversations will be affected. This could be part two of the beginning of a major financial change, especially if you've recently discovered that a partner isn't contributing their fair share.

On October 8, the next Lunar Eclipse will arrive, activating your solar second house of personal finances. Yes, once again, money matters will take up quite a bit of your attention, and you may need to spring into action without much warning. Fortunately, this lunation will occur in Aries, the most action-oriented sign in the heavens. If the need arises to take a stand and defend what's yours, you'll attack the problem immediately and take no prisoners.

Part two of this pairing will occur on October 23, via a Solar Eclipse in Scorpio. Now, this sign rules intensity, but it's also in charge of joint finances. Sound familiar? Yes, whatever you were dealing with at the time of the eclipse in Taurus last April could resurface, and this time, it will demand—à la all-or-nothing Scorpio—that you formulate a plan, make a decision, and stick to it. If you have been thinking of applying for a loan, especially for debt-consolidation or educational purposes, this would be a fine time to do it.

Saturn

Saturn will spend most of 2014 moving through intense, penetrating Scorpio and your solar fifth house of love affairs, Pisces, and if you were born between March 10 and 21, he will contact your Sun directly, too. Not to worry, though. Saturn does have a reputation for being a tough taskmaster, but his real job is to inspire permanence and stability, and since he'll be forming a trine with your Sun, an aspect that provides an easy flow of positive energy, you may simply realize that you're ready to take a casual relationship in a far more committed direction. The best news, however, has to do with the fact that Saturn is currently all done up in Scorpio, a water-sign cousin of yours you've always gotten along famously with. Scorpio just so happens to be a very sexy sign, too—so there are worse planets to have on duty in a house that deals with lovers!

There may be one difficulty with having this serious, determined planet influencing you from such a focused and potentially obsessive sign. You'll need to watch yourself carefully for any signs that you're a little too interested in knowing absolutely everything there is to know about your sweetheart—and watch that person just as carefully for the same behavior. If you begin to feel that you're falling into a relationship pattern that's becoming a bit too restrictive, face the facts. You may be allowing history to repeat itself because it's comfortable and familiar.

Uranus

If you were born between March 1 and 6, this may be a startling year for you financially, Pisces. Uranus will contact your Sun from his spot in your solar second house of money matters, and this is the guy who's famous for inspiring spontaneity and arranging surprise endings. Needless to say, you may not be a font of willpower in this department, at least temporarily, and the end result could be an impulsive spending spree—at least one. Resisting the urge to have what you want at any cost will be tough, but you really do need to try. With Uranus in the neighborhood, you could abruptly lose your primary source of income the day after you pull in the driveway with that brand-new car. On the other hand, the financial news could be extremely positive, like winning the lottery or discovering assets you didn't know you had. Either way, it's best not to take chances with money, possessions, and other material resources.

Of course, the second house also has everything to do with your value system, so you can expect that to change, too—which may end up being the catalyst for those financial changes. Uranus inspires a need for individuality and personal freedom, so if you're unhappy at work, you may decide not to spend even one more precious hour of your life doing something that goes against your nature.

Neptune

Your ruling planet, dreamy Neptune, is finally back home in your sign, Pisces, which just so happens to be her favorite. Neptune operates invisibly, but when she's here on home turf, she's especially potent and even harder to notice. Her transit through your solar first house of personality and appearance, which won't end for decades, makes several scenarios possible, but if you were born between February 22 and 26, you will undoubtedly experience at least one of them.

First off, let's talk about the concept of glamour. In Ye Olden Days, a glamour was a spell cast on someone to change their appearance or disguise them. You're already fond of costumes and disguises, but with Neptune on board and operating at full tilt, you'll become an expert. You may decide to alter your look through a new wardrobe, a professional makeover, or even cosmetic surgery. On the other hand, you may internalize Neptune's energy and give yourself a spiritual facelift. In that case, the new you won't want to be around others who don't share your beliefs, and you'll take steps to gradually withdraw from them, a little at a time, and finally disappear completely. Don't give in to loneliness. Close these doors and rest assured that others will soon open.

Pluto

Intense, sexy Pluto will continue his stay in Capricorn and your solar eleventh house of friendships and group affiliations throughout the year, Pisces, inspiring you to be more determined than ever to find depth and meaning in all your encounters. And during 2014, if you don't feel that connection or you begin to suspect that others are not as they seem, you'll walk away without ever looking back. Pluto, remember, is an all-or-nothing kind of guy, so wherever he's at work in your chart is a place where you're looking for intensity, and are not willing to settle for shallow, surface experiences. You want connection, and Pluto's relentless nature won't let you settle until you find it. No matter what type of peer circle you're associating with, you may also find that there's a bit of scandal and more than a bit of gossip circulating. You may be tempted to join in and speculate, trade clues, or dig around in secret matters, but if you can resist the urge and rise above it, you'll feel better about yourself and more confident about establishing long-lasting bonds—which, after all, is what you crave. If you were born during the first week of March, these situations will be especially intense, and if you're not careful, you could be drawn into matters you may later regret being a part of. Stay as impartial and as objective as possible. Since Pluto is locked into a long-term square, an extremely active and often irritating aspect, with startling Uranus in your solar second house of money matters, you should also consider the probability that your actions now and the affinities you form—or end—with others will suddenly and unpredictably alter your financial future.

Pisces | January

Planetary Lightspots

The chance to start over in two very important areas of life will come your way this month, Pisces, thanks to two New Moons. On New Year's Day, your solar eleventh house of friendships will host the first, urging you to assume a leadership role within your current peer group—and you'll take to the task immediately. On January 30, a second lunation will entice you to retreat and regroup. Try meditation, yoga, or chanting to unwind.

Relationships

It's all about friendships right now, Pisces, thanks to the Sun, Mercury, and Venus, who'll join intense Pluto in your solar eleventh house. This pack of serious Capricorn planets will insist that you do the right thing, and if someone needs you, you'll respond. Just don't do too much for them, and try to keep in mind that their problems aren't your responsibility.

Money and Success

With assertive and sometimes contentious Mars in your solar eighth house of joint resources, Pisces, disputes over inheritances, loans, and debts have probably been going on for some time. If you're at war over custody, visitation rights, or alimony, things could heat up even more around January 8 or 16. The good news is that a pack of Capricorn planets will bring you wise counsel and professional support.

Planetary Hotspots

Mars and Jupiter will get into an action-oriented square on January 8, Pisces, a red-hot burst of excessive, impetuous energy that will activate your solar eighth house of intimacy with your solar fifth house of lovers. Sounds like sparks will fly, for better or worse. Your mission is to use that famous intuition to guide you away from potentially volatile situations. There are far better ways to use this passionate pair.

Rewarding Days
10, 11, 15, 17, 23, 24, 28, 29

Challenging Days
2, 3, 5, 6, 7, 16, 21

Pisces | February

Planetary Lightspots

Mercury will turn retrograde in your sign and your solar first house of personality and appearance on February 6, Pisces, and up until he backs up into Aquarius on February 12, you might be feeling a bit disoriented or confused. It's important that you verify all facts right now, avoid misunderstandings caused by vague communications, and keep directions on your person at all times. The good news is that your intuition will be especially potent. Trust it.

Relationships

Your sign is second only to Libra when it comes to just how much you love Valentine's Day, Pisces—and this will be one to remember. A Full Moon that day, along with an easy trine between the Sun and passionate Mars, will set the stage for romance. It's star-gazing time, kids. This is the stuff that will keep you smiling for days—both of you.

Money and Success

Success! On February 16, a light at the end of that financial tunnel you've been navigating will finally appear. You may need to wait until next month on March 14 for the final act to play out, but sit tight and be patient. Things are finally about to go your way. Just don't count your chickens until you're sure they've hatched. You may need a few more details to finalize the situation.

Planetary Hotspots

Jupiter will get into an irritating square with Uranus on February 26, two planetary superpowers with one thing in mind: to force you to take a stand on your own behalf. You don't enjoy confrontation. In fact, you tend to avoid it. But when these two come together, great big surprises are on tap, which just might include you having had enough and letting a certain someone know you're mad and you're not going to take it anymore.

Rewarding Days

3, 4, 14, 16, 20, 22, 23, 24

Challenging Days

10, 11, 15, 19, 25, 26, 27

Pisces | March

Planetary Lightspots

The New Moon on March 1 will bring together the Sun and the emotional Moon in your sign, Pisces, and along with an easy trine from Jupiter in your solar fifth house of fun activities, kids, recreation, and lovers, you're set up to have the time of your life. You might want to share it, and if someone from the past turns up unexpectedly, the temptation to forget the bad times will be hard to resist. If you're determined to see them, be sure it's on your terms.

Relationships

Your solar axis of relationships will be activated by the Full Moon of March 16, Pisces, affecting your dealings with just about everyone you care for. You'll learn new facts about your primary partner, and as a result, your feelings will either intensify or begin to dwindle. If you need to extricate yourself from a tough situation, this is the time to begin gradually pulling away, but positive partnerships will flourish.

Money and Success

If you're involved in a joint financial battle, the situation could reach an impasse during the early part of the month, Pisces, thanks to assertive Mars, who'll turn retrograde on March 1 and insist you redo all former agreements. You might meet with some resistance, but by March 13, no-nonsense Saturn will meet up with the Sun in your sign to give you exactly what you deserve—nothing more, but nothing less.

Planetary Hotspots

You're already a daydreamer, Pisces, and your nighttime dreams are quite prophetic. So when Mercury wanders into your psychic sign on March 17, keeping up with your journal will be especially important. Pay attention to the symbolism your subconscious is firing at you between March 21 and 23. As per usual, your antennae will not let you down.

Rewarding Days

1, 12, 13, 14, 17, 18, 22, 23, 28

Challenging Days

3, 10, 11, 15, 16, 29, 30

Pisces | April

Planetary Lightspots

There will be a bit of fussing and fighting in your world this month, Pisces, especially when it comes to finances. After some last-minute surprises on April 2, 8, or 21 that you'll have to deal with, the news will be good around April 25. At the very least, you'll have a break in the action and be able to relax and stop worrying, possibly for the first time in a long time.

Relationships

Venus will tiptoe into your sign on April 5, Pisces, increasing your already substantial ability to charm and entice. On April 11, someone who's quite taken with you will make it clear they're out to woo you. The better they seem to be, the more care you should take to be sure you're not being fooled. If things pan out well after some investigation, however, it may turn out that you've found the love of your life.

Money and Success

Mars is still stirring up trouble from his spot in your solar eighth house of shared finances, so putting that money-related issue to bed might not be an option just yet. The good news is that a sense of stability will be restored around April 24 or 25, when the emotional Moon and Venus, both in your sign, form an easy trine with Saturn, the planet of authority figures. Judgments can easily go in your favor now.

Planetary Hotspots

If you come into a windfall this month, Pisces, try not to spend it all in one place. That will be tougher than it seems, especially around April 2, 8, and 14, when the Sun and Mercury in impulsive Aries will urge you to forget about your budget and pull out the plastic. There's no way you won't spend something, and it will undoubtedly be a bit more than you should, but try not to do any permanent damage to your credit rating.

Rewarding Days

10, 11, 17, 18, 19, 25, 26, 29, 30

Challenging Days

1, 2, 3, 7, 8, 15, 16, 21, 22

Pisces | May

Planetary Lightspots

You'll be able to do what you do best with the blessing of the Universe between May 2 and 6, Pisces. Your specialty is tending to whoever or whatever no one else has the time or inclination to care for, and at this time, you'll have plenty of applicants. You can do some serious good for those who can't help themselves now, but be choosy about where you direct your attention.

Relationships

You're not usually the type to deliver ultimatums, Pisces, but right around May 2 and again on May 10, that's exactly what you'll do. The motivation behind your uncustomary show of self-interest isn't selfish, so if you're drawing support away from someone, don't let them put you on a guilt trip. There's no time like the present to sit back, look over your relationships, and decide which can stay and which can go.

Money and Success

Taurus is the sign that most famously takes care of money matters, Pisces, as per the rulership of its patron planet, Venus. So with the Sun, Venus, and chatty Mercury lined up to pass through your solar second house of finances, it's a good bet you'll be doing some serious chatting about finances. They'll also inspire you to be ready, willing, and able to commit to a final push to get the project done, however, which will definitely come in handy.

Planetary Hotspots

Jupiter is in charge of excess, Pisces, and Saturn rules frugality. They seem like natural enemies, but when they get together, as they will on May 24, their combined energies often mean we're in the right place at the right time to notice that a lucky stroke of fate has put us in touch with the right contacts. In your case, a family member you're quite fond of may be the catalyst.

Rewarding Days

1, 3, 10, 11, 14, 16, 17

Challenging Days

2, 9, 12, 13, 15, 18, 19, 28

Pisces | June

Planetary Lightspots

The Sun will set off for Cancer and your solar fifth house on June 21, Pisces, and for the next month, you'll be after nothing but fun—and it's about time! You've earned the right to enjoy the company of romantic partners, kids, and lively acquaintances, so don't hesitate to make the most of it. At least one new admirer may be along shortly, too. The good news is that they'll be just as family-oriented as you happen to be.

Relationships

There's a Full Moon due on June 12, Pisces, and it's going to light up your solar axis of home and career. Your professional ambitions will take center stage, even as your more personal relationships beg for your careful attention. You'll be able to handle it all if you take a lesson from Gemini and learn to multitask. Fortunately, you're mutable enough to enjoy and profit from that lesson.

Money and Success

A family member who insists you put in an application at a business close to you may not just be blowing hot air your way around June 6, Pisces. In fact, the easy sextile between the Sun and unpredictable Uranus points to a far better outcome. You're not in the mood to be told what to do about money matters, but now, you'll come face to face with someone who can help you to make financial freedom a reality.

Planetary Hotspots

June 7 could be problematic, Pisces, and not because you haven't prepared for the unexpected, either. The emotional Moon will meet up with red-hot Mars and shocking Uranus, and the last thing in the world you'd ever have thought possible will suddenly become reality. So, how will you deal with it? Well, you'll need a little time alone, but as of June 12, you'll be able to emerge from the cave with an answer—and it will be your final answer. Stay firm!

Rewarding Days

3, 4, 5, 6, 10, 18, 29

Challenging Days

7, 12, 13, 14, 19, 24, 25, 27

Pisces | July

Planetary Lightspots

The warm weather will be nothing compared to the heat of your new-found passion for the ones you love and your favorite cause, Pisces. Around July 24, someone highly experienced and ready to point out the flaws in your current plan will be on duty. Your mission is to resist the urge to react from a personal point of view and take their advice in the spirit it's offered. You can make great strides now if you don't allow your feelings from the past to get in the way.

Relationships

Full Moons always bring deep emotions to the surface, Pisces, and since this lunation will occur in your solar eleventh house on July 12, your bond with a certain member of your current peer group will absorb much of your time—and all of your attention. That one special person who really understands you will be the focus. If this sounds hokey, and you're currently attached, think twice before you try this line on someone new.

Money and Success

Success never seems to come from the place or the connections we imagine it would, Pisces, but as intuitive as you are, you'll be able to recognize the potential this month, especially around July 4 and 22. You may have some fancy dancing to do to enlist the total support and devotion of a mentor, but have no doubt that they'll be there when you need them. It's your job to speed-dial the right person at the right time.

Planetary Hotspots

Venus, the Goddess of Love, will enter your solar fifth house of lovers on July 18, and until she takes off for Leo next month on August 12, your emotions will be quite close to the surface. Your mission is to express what you feel openly and honestly, and not add a bit of drama to conversations or encounters simply for the theatrical effect.

Rewarding Days
6, 7, 13, 18, 20, 23, 25

Challenging Days
3, 4, 8, 19, 21, 24, 27, 28

Pisces | August

Planetary Lightspots

The Sun, Mercury, and Venus will take turns passing through your solar sixth house of work and health-related matters this month, Pisces, and all your dealings with vocational and medical personnel will come to light. The good news is that you'll have found suitable, trustworthy professionals to work with by August 25, and even though you may need to reveal a bit more about yourself than you'd planned, you'll be sure they have your interests at heart.

Relationships

The New Moon on August 25 will occur in your solar seventh house of committed partnerships, Pisces, urging you to take practical steps to either fix this thing or move on. Whether it's personal or business doesn't matter. If you know in your heart that you can't continue on this path, use the Venus-Saturn square on August 26 to give you the guts to say goodbye.

Money and Success

Your solar seventh house of one-to-one relationships will be activated, big time, by the New Moon this month, Pisces—as will just about every corner of your life. You'll feel a change in the air for a while before that, and you'd do well to pay attention. If your antennae tell you it's time to move on but your heart resists, let your antennae have their way.

Planetary Hotspots

Once chatty Mercury and serious Saturn get together in your solar ninth house of opinions on August 25, Pisces, there's really no telling what you'll say or do. The good news is that you'll finally be willing to tell it like it is, sure that the consequences of sharing what you know won't be any worse than trying to keep the details secret.

Rewarding Days

8, 9, 15, 17, 18, 21, 25

Challenging Days

1, 2, 3, 7, 19, 26, 27, 29, 30

Pisces | September

Planetary Lightspots

Right around September 21, the perfect time to plan a getaway will arrive, Pisces. All those planets in hard-working Capricorn have kept you busy for weeks, and Saturn, their planetary owner, has been cracking the whip for over two years. Your mission now is to take the best of what you've learned and use it to combine business with pleasure.

Relationships

Venus rules love, Pisces, and she'll spend September 5 through September 29 in your solar seventh house of relationships. Without even trying, you'll attract some serious admirers, one of whom will make you feel more special than you have in years. If you're already with someone, you'll need to see through the instant gratification these encounters offer and consider your options sensibly.

Money and Success

Right up until September 27, thoughtful Mercury will spend his time in balance-loving Libra and your solar eighth house of shared resources, Pisces. Commitments to former partners and long-term acquaintances may be called into question, and you'll need to pull off those rose-colored glasses for a minute to tell what you know to others, and possible admit it to yourself.

Planetary Hotspots

Between September 9 and 13, Mercury will get into it with Pluto and Uranus, a team that has nothing but total disruption and sudden change on their mutual agenda. Mercury, however, will respond to the pokings and proddings of this Titanic Team by making light of the situation. Oddly enough, when and if emergencies arise, this casual influence will make you better qualified than most of us to deal with them.

Rewarding Days

2, 3, 5, 14, 15, 20, 25

Challenging Days

8, 9, 12, 13, 21, 22, 29

Pisces | October

Planetary Lightspots

The Lunar Eclipse in your solar second house of financial responsibilities on October 8 will drag your attention back to a money matter that seems to be unwilling to be resolved. Your mission now is to resist the urge to make nice at your own expense. You would never have started this if you didn't feel unfairly taken advantage of. Remember those feelings, and refuse to accept any low offers.

Relationships

It will be all too easy for you to allow new admirers access to your secret side this month, Pisces, so be warned. Before you let anyone get comfortable in your home or at home in your mind, be sure they deserve that kind of trust. If something strikes you as not quite right around October 11, don't brush it off. The information you need on them may not arrive until October 25, but you'll be glad you set the wheels in motion.

Money and Success

Fiery Mars will see to it that you're noticed this month, Pisces, so any time you feel the sudden urge to step into the spotlight and actually take credit for your part in that recent professional coup—well, go for it. This me-first guy will have your back. He'll also inspire someone you've been relying on to take total credit for what you've accomplished as a team. Don't step down. It's time.

Planetary Hotspots

Mars and Uranus are the two most spontaneous, impulsive planetary energies, and when they get together, the results are often unsettling. So when these two conspire on October 5, you may be caught off guard by events, especially the ones that seem circumstantial. You, however, are sensitive enough to know that there's no such thing as coincidence, so listen to your intuition.

Rewarding Days
5, 6, 13, 14, 15, 22, 23, 24, 26, 27

Challenging Days
3, 4, 7, 10, 11, 16, 25

Pisces | November

Planetary Lightspots

You've never been fond of stepping into the spotlight of center stage, Pisces, so the New Moon on November 22 may drive you into retreat mode, at least for a week or so. Before you lock the door behind you and make the entire world go away, consider inviting your most trusted person over to your place for a few uninterrupted days of R & R. What you'll need most is quiet times with a trusted other. Isn't it your turn to play favorites?

Relationships

You just adore holidays, Pisces, especially when you have the opportunity to get the whole gang together to celebrate. Fiery Mars will be on board with those plans all month, however, from his spot in Capricorn and your solar eleventh house of group events. This would be a fine time to pass out recognition and awards, but you might also be on the receiving end of a well-deserved pat on the back from someone who's seen how hard you've tried to help everyone keep it together.

Money and Success

Jupiter in Leo will keep your work-related activities almost frantic this month, Pisces. Stressful times could come along around November 9 or 13. If you need to reveal just how much of a part you've been playing to higher-ups, you're golden. Tooting your own horn isn't a sin. You've earned the right to crow about your accomplishments.

Planetary Hotspots

Thoughtful Mercury will make his way through your solar eighth house through November 8, Pisces, making this a terrific time to deal with finances, especially if they involve at least one other person's personal investment. Applying for a loan or negotiating the terms of an overdue debt will go quite well, especially during the first few days of the month.

Rewarding Days

1, 2, 3, 11, 12, 16, 21

Challenging Days

8, 9, 13, 14, 17, 18, 22, 26

Pisces | December

Planetary Lightspots

A Full Moon in lighthearted, curious Gemini is on tap for December 6, Pisces, set to occur in your solar fourth house. What a great time to have a sentimental sign like yours focused on issues of home! It will most certainly be a happy holiday season—especially if you let this bright light lead you into opening up your home for dear ones. Have fun!

Relationships

Your coworkers will take up their place in your heart and your extended family this month, Pisces, and you'll be willing to let them slide, even if they don't have anything to prove their worth. Of course, you tend to take in strays, human and otherwise, so unless you pay attention to what's going on upstairs at the moment, you could be caught completely off guard. Your mission is to be as compassionate as ever while seeing the behavior of others realistically.

Money and Success

On December 10, Venus will set off for responsible Capricorn and your solar eleventh house of groups. This sign doesn't take anything for granted and won't accept charity, but it's more than willing to extend those same gifts to others. Your mission is to delegate anything you can with an eye toward putting the right person in the perfect position. You're attached to your group. Now prove the value of your leadership.

Planetary Hotspots

You've never been afraid to contribute both your time and energy to worthwhile causes, Pisces, and this month, you'll be tempted to pull out all the stops for the group you're most fervently affiliated with. That's all well and good, but be sure you aren't simply in the mood to rebel before you decide to join the Peace Corps and book a ticket to the other side of the planet.

Rewarding Days

2, 3, 4, 5, 12, 13, 14

Challenging Days

1, 7, 8, 15, 16, 20, 24, 25

Pisces Action Table

These dates reflect the best—but not the only—times for success and ease in these activities, according to your Sun sign.

	JAN	FEB	MAR	APR	MAY	JUN	JUL	AUG	SEP	OCT	NOV	DEC
Move					28							6
Start a class	1, 11	24	13				24		3, 14			1
Join a club			28		3		12		21			14
Ask for a raise								8, 25		5		4
Look for work							26	2, 8, 18			22	
Get pro advice			13		9		8					
Get a loan									24			
See a doctor								24				
Start a diet							9					
End relationship				21								
Buy clothes						18						
Get a makeover				5				8				
New romance	15	14	16			27						
Vacation	11		17, 18		24					26–28	21	

Notes

Notes

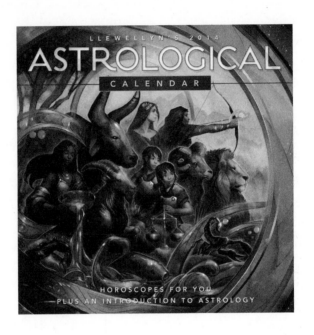

LLEWELLYN'S 2014

ASTROLOGICAL

CALENDAR

HOROSCOPES FOR YOU
PLUS AN INTRODUCTION TO ASTROLOGY

Llewellyn's 2014 Astrological Calendar
Horoscopes for You Plus an Introduction to Astrology

Llewellyn's Astrological Calendar is the best-known, most trusted astrological calendar sold today. Everyone, even beginners, can use this beautiful and practical calendar to plan the year wisely.

There are monthly horoscopes, best days for planting and fishing, rewarding and challenging days, travel forecasts, and an astrology primer. Advanced astrologers will find major daily aspects and a wealth of other essential astrological information.

This edition features Julie Dillon's gorgeous artwork, inspired by the signs and symbols of astrology.

978-0-7387-2149-1, 40 pp., 12 x 12   **U.S. $13.99**

Complete Astrology
At-A-Glance

LLEWELLYN'S 2014

Daily
Planetary
Guide

Your Best
Opportunity Periods
from Jim Shawvan &
Forecasts by Pam Ciampi

Llewellyn's 2014 Daily Planetary Guide
Complete Astrology At A Glance

Empower your life with the most trusted and detailed astrological guide available. Take advantage of cosmic forces on a daily, weekly, or monthly basis with *Llewellyn's Daily Planetary Guide*.

With exact times down to the minute, this astrological planner lists ideal times to do anything. Before setting up a job interview, signing a contract, or scheduling anything important, consult the weekly forecasts and Opportunity Periods—times when the positive flow of energy is at its peak.

Even beginners can use this powerful planner, which includes a primer on the planets, signs, houses, and how to use this guide.

978-0-7387-2151-4, 208 pp., 5 x 8¼ $12.99

LLEWELLYN'S
2014
ASTROLOGICAL

POCKET
PLANNER

DAILY EPHEMERIS & ASPECTARIAN
2013–2015

Llewellyn's 2014 Astrological Pocket Planner
Daily Ephemeris & Aspectarian 2013–2015

Empower your future—plan important events, set goals, and organize your life—with *Llewellyn's Astrological Pocket Planner*. Both beginners and advanced astrologers can use this award-winning datebook, the only one to offer three years of ephemeris and aspectarian data.

Choose optimal dates for job interviews, weddings, business meetings, and other important occasions. Pinpoint ideal times to plant a garden, begin new projects, conduct self-reflection, go fishing, and more. Avoid planetary pitfalls by following the easy-to-read retrograde and Moon void-of-course tables.

Comprehensive and compact, *Llewellyn's 2014 Astrological Pocket Planner* also contains time zone information and space to jot down your daily appointments.

978-0-7387-2150-7, 192 pp., 4¼ x 6⁵/₁₆ **$8.99**

To order, call 1-877-NEW-WRLD
Prices subject to change without notice
Order at Llewellyn.com 24 hours a day, 7 days a week!

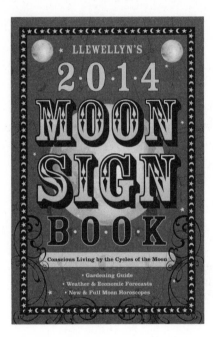

LLEWELLYN'S

2·0·1·4

MOON
SIGN
B·O·O·K

Conscious Living by the Cycles of the Moon

• Gardening Guide
• Weather & Economic Forecasts
• New & Full Moon Horoscopes

Llewellyn's 2014 Moon Sign Book
Conscious Living by the Cycles of the Moon

Since 1905, *Llewellyn's Moon Sign Book* has helped millions take advantage of the Moon's dynamic energies. Use this essential life-planning tool to choose the best dates for almost anything: getting married, buying or selling your home, requesting a promotion, applying for a loan, traveling, having surgery, seeing the dentist, picking mushrooms, and much more. With lunar timing tips on planting and harvesting and a guide to companion plants, this popular guide is also a gardener's best friend. In addition to New and Full Moon forecasts for the year, you'll find insightful articles on growing a tea garden, cultivating roses, organic and natural food labeling, the Moon and earthquakes, outer planets in water signs, and Greek lunar folklore.

978-0-7387-2154-5, 312 pp., 5¼ x 8 $10.99

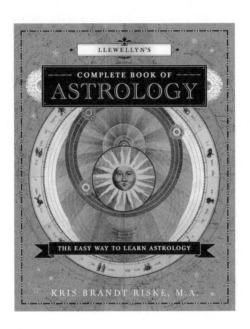

Llewellyn's Complete Book of Astrology
The Easy Way to Learn Astrology
Kris Brandt Riske, M.A.

The horoscope is filled with insights into personal traits, talents, and life possibilities. With *Llewellyn's Complete Book of Astrology*, you can learn to read and understand this amazing cosmic road map for yourself and others.

Professional astrologer Kris Brandt Riske introduces the many mysterious parts that make up the horoscope, devoting special attention to three popular areas of interest: relationships, career, and money. Friendly and easy to follow, this comprehensive book guides you to explore the zodiac signs, planets, houses, and aspects, and teaches how to synthesize this valuable information.

Once you learn the language of astrology, you'll be able to read birth charts of yourself and others, determine compatibility between two people, track your earning potential, uncover areas of opportunity or challenge, and analyze your career path.

978-0-7387-1071-6, 336 pp., 8 x 10 $18.95

LLEWELLYN'S

COMPLETE BOOK OF PREDICTIVE

ASTROLOGY

THE EASY WAY TO PREDICT YOUR FUTURE

KRIS BRANDT RISKE, M.A.

Llewellyn's Complete Book of Predictive Astrology
The Easy Way to Predict Your Future
KRIS BRANDT RISKE, M.A.

Find out what potential the future holds and use those insights to create the life you desire with this definitive guide to predictive astrology.

In her signature easy-to-understand style, popular astrologer Kris Brandt Riske offers step-by-step instructions for performing each major predictive technique—solar arcs, progressions, transits, lunar cycles, and planetary returns—along with an introduction to horary astrology. Discover how to read all elements of a predictive chart and pinpoint when changes in your career, relationships, finances, and other important areas of life are on the horizon.

Also included are several example charts based on the lives of the author's clients and celebrities such as Marilyn Monroe, Martha Stewart, and Pamela Anderson.

978-0-7387-2755-4, 288 pp., 8 x 10 $18.95

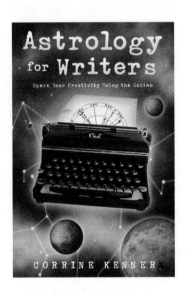

Astrology
for Writers

Spark Your Creativity Using the Zodiac

CORRINE KENNER

Astrology for Writers
Spark Your Creativity Using the Zodiac
CORRINE KENNER

Build your storytelling from the cosmic drama of the stars! The nighttime sky inspires writers and astrologers alike to spin stories on the strands of starlight. Discover inspiration for your creative writing in *Astrology for Writers*, an essential guide filled with exercises for character creation, techniques for constructing plotlines and setting, and much more.

Begin your creative journey with an introduction to the planets, the twelve signs of the Zodiac, the twelve houses of the horoscope, and other astrology basics. Learn how to develop unique characters based on mythic archetypes, how to use astrological imagery and symbolism for your descriptions and dialogue, and how to put theory into practice with writing prompts and samples.

978-0-7387-3333-3, 336 pp., 6 x 9 $17.99

To order, call 1-877-NEW-WRLD
Prices subject to change without notice
Order at Llewellyn.com 24 hours a day, 7 days a week!

GET MORE AT LLEWELLYN.COM

Visit us online to browse hundreds of our books and decks, plus sign up to receive our e-newsletters and exclusive online offers.

- Free tarot readings • Spell-a-Day • Moon phases
- Recipes, spells, and tips • Blogs • Encyclopedia
- Author interviews, articles, and upcoming events

GET SOCIAL WITH LLEWELLYN

Find us on Facebook

www.Facebook.com/LlewellynBooks

Follow us on twitter™

www.Twitter.com/Llewellynbooks

GET BOOKS AT LLEWELLYN

LLEWELLYN ORDERING INFORMATION

Order online: Visit our website at www.llewellyn.com to select your books and place an order on our secure server.

Order by phone:
- Call toll free within the U.S. at 1-877-NEW-WRLD (1-877-639-9753)
- Call toll free within Canada at 1-866-NEW-WRLD (1-866-639-9753)
- We accept VISA, MasterCard, and American Express

Order by mail:
Send the full price of your order (MN residents add 6.875% sales tax) in U.S. funds, plus postage and handling to: Llewellyn Worldwide, 2143 Wooddale Drive Woodbury, MN 55125-2989

POSTAGE AND HANDLING

STANDARD (U.S. & Canada):
(Please allow 12 business days)
$25.00 and under, add $4.00.
$25.01 and over, FREE SHIPPING.

INTERNATIONAL ORDERS (airmail only):
$16.00 for one book, plus $3.00 for each additional book.

Visit us online for more shipping options.
Prices subject to change.

FREE CATALOG!

To order, call
1-877-
NEW-WRLD
ext. 8236
or visit our
website